AURORA

AURORA

The Psychiatrist Who Treated the
Movie Theater Killer Tells Her Story

Lynne Fenton, MD,
and Kerrie Droban

BERKLEY

New York

BERKLEY
An imprint of Penguin Random House LLC
penguinrandomhouse.com

Copyright © 2022 by Lynne Fenton, MD, and Kerrie Droban
Penguin Random House supports copyright. Copyright fuels creativity,
encourages diverse voices, promotes free speech, and creates
a vibrant culture. Thank you for buying an authorized edition
of this book and for complying with copyright laws by not reproducing,
scanning, or distributing any part of it in any form without permission.
You are supporting writers and allowing Penguin Random House
to continue to publish books for every reader.

BERKLEY and the BERKLEY & B colophon
are registered trademarks of Penguin Random House LLC.

Library of Congress Cataloging-in-Publication Data

Names: Fenton, Lynne, author. | Droban, Kerrie, author.
Title: Aurora: the psychiatrist who treated the movie theater killer tells
her story / Lynne Fenton, MD and Kerrie Droban.
Description: First edition. | New York : Berkley, [2022]
Identifiers: LCCN 2021057347 (print) | LCCN 2021057348 (ebook) |
ISBN 9780593101292 (hardcover) | ISBN 9780593101308 (ebook)
Subjects: LCSH: Holmes, James, 1987- | Fenton, Lynne. |
Mass murder—Colorado—Aurora. | Mass murderers—Colorado—Aurora--Psychology. |
Mental health personnel and patient—Colorado—Aurora. |
Colorado Shooting, Aurora Colo., 2012.
Classification: LCC HV6536.55.A97 F46 2022 (print) | LCC HV6536.55.A97 (ebook) |
DDC 364.152/34097888—dc23/eng/20220131
LC record available at https://lccn.loc.gov/2021057347
LC ebook record available at https://lccn.loc.gov/2021057348

Printed in the United States of America
1st Printing

Book design by Ashley Tucker

[These] are the images that America needs . . .
If you can verbally paint that picture for them to see
and imagine, then perhaps we can change hearts and minds.

—Mother of slain victim Jessica Ghawi

Dedicated to the victims and survivors
of James Holmes' unspeakable atrocities,
for their courage and, most especially, their *voice*

C O N T E N T S

This is the story of Lynne Fenton, MD, the treating psychiatrist of mass murderer James Holmes, whose horrific crimes have left us all reeling and asking, *Why?* He was unique among mass shooters for deliberately surviving his massacre, to be publicly prosecuted and condemned to serve an eternity as a case study in evil. Dr. Fenton's legacy is equally extraordinary, as the only psychiatrist in the history of the United States to have been publicly outed, vilified by the press and media, her life threatened, and subjected to an internal investigation by her own university. For nearly three years, she was under court order to remain silent for the integrity of the prosecution. Now, for the first time, the trial judge having lifted the gag order and unsealed all confidential records, Dr. Fenton shares her harrowing experiences as the target of public wrath and reveals her chilling sessions with Holmes, a patient who she believed personified evil.

Wherever possible, names have been changed to protect identities and privacy. In addition to hundreds of hours of interviews with Dr. Fenton and her colleagues, this book relies on more than seventy-five thousand pages of discovery, which include police reports, Holmes' infamous notebook, hundreds of audio and video recordings, countless expert evaluations, transcripts, trial testimony, witness interviews, emails, texts and G-Chats between Holmes and others, and Holmes' nine video-recorded pretrial interviews (nearly twenty-three hours in length) with his court-appointed psychiatrist, Dr. William Reid, offering what Dr. Reid described as an unprecedented "look behind the curtain" into his "memories, thoughts, explanations and impressions as expressed in his own words."

The many quotes and excerpts from transcripts you will read, while sometimes graphic and disturbing, are intended to "verbally paint the picture" that twelve innocent people lost their lives and countless others (including Dr. Fenton's) were forever changed, forever scarred, by a highly intelligent, ruthless killer whose chosen field of study was his own mind. Even more chilling was the fact that Holmes, surrounded by the brightest university academicians, selected for one of the most strenuous and prestigious neuroscience programs in the country and treated by nationally renowned and highly respected psychiatrists, eluded them *all*.

As a former prosecutor and capital defense attorney, I am well versed in death penalty litigation and the many challenges of bringing justice to the victims of horrific crimes. But after spending more than a year writing about one of the most monstrous minds of this century, it will take me many more years to recover. And though the lives of all those tragically impacted by Holmes' senseless massacre will never be made whole again, and the twelve who died at his hands are lost forever, it is our hope that Dr. Fenton's story may bring some answers and encourage us all to continue to share our determination, strength, and experiences to effect lasting change.

—Kerrie Droban

PART I

CHAPTER 1

HERE WE GO

March 15, 2012
(127 days before the massacre)

*They laugh at me because I'm different. I laugh at them because
they're all the same . . . And . . . here . . . we . . . go . . .*
—The Joker, *The Dark Knight* (2008)

FENTON

"He's coming," a young girl sobbed to dispatch, her frantic whisper barely audible over the bullet blasts and piercing screams. *"It's a boy with a gun . . ."* Male voices in the background, loud and calm, ordered, *"Everybody get up, this is your day to die!"*

As a psychiatrist on the faculty of the University of Colorado's School of Medicine and director of the Student Mental Health Center on the Anschutz campus, I lectured yearly on mass shootings and school violence, the last in a six-session course on student mental health. The Columbine massacre seemed a fitting topic since many in my audience of fourth-year psychiatry residents had lived in the Denver area at the time of the shooting and, like the murdered victims, would have been in high school then. The 911 screams reminded them what it must have felt like for the Columbine students and faculty in those moments before two psychopaths blew apart their worlds, instilling in them fear, panic, and an often-noted perception of weightlessness. Their ears were assaulted by pops, blasts, and booms, followed by what some survivors later described as a weird silence lasting only seconds. Victims scrambled for cover in classrooms and libraries, ducking behind bookshelves and cubicles made of flimsy particleboard, crouching beneath metal chairs, hiding under computer desks, maybe foolishly hoping that *if they just closed their eyes, the shooters wouldn't see them.*

My goal with the lecture was to relay statistics on school shootings and explore the roles played by mental illness and the accessibility of guns. Most mass shooters had narcissistic or antisocial personality disorders (both of which were psychiatric diagnoses) and attacked as a way to resolve their own distress and hatred of people who were different. When Eric Harris and Dylan Klebold walked into the Columbine school on April 20, 1999, in celebration of Adolf Hitler's 110th birthday, they intended to detonate ninety-nine homemade bombs and kick-start a revolution against those they referred to as niggers, spics, Jews, gays, fucking whites, and all of humanity.

Eric listed a dozen reasons for killing, only one of which included being bullied:

1. I am the law, if you don't like it, you die.

2. [It's] the only way to solve arguments with all you fuckheads out there, I just kill!

3. If I don't like you . . . you die.

4. [If] I don't like what you want me to do, you die.

5. I live in denver [*sic*], and god damnit I would love to kill almost all of its residents. Fucking people with their rich snobby attitude.

6. I would get rid of all the fat, retarded, crippled, stupid, dumb, ignorant, worthless people of this world.

7. ALL gays, should be killed.

8. The human race isn't worth fighting for, only worth killing. I say "KILL MANKIND" no one should survive.

9. I have a goal to destroy as much as possible . . . I want to burn the world.

10. If I could nuke the world I would, because so far, I hate you all.

11. I want to tear a throat out with my own teeth like a pop can. I want to gut someone with my hand, to tear a head off and rip out the heart and lungs from the neck, to stab someone in the gut, shove it up to their heart, and yank the fucking blade out of their rib cage! I want to grab some weak little freshman and just tear them apart like a wolf, show them who is god [*sic*]. Strangle them, squish their head, bite their temples in the skull, rip off their jaw, rip off their colar [*sic*] bones, break their arms in half and twist them around, the lovely sounds of bones cracking and flesh ripping, ahhh . . . so much to do and so little chances [*sic*].

12. Everyone is always making fun of me because of how I look, how fucking weak I am and shit, well I will get you all back, ultimate fucking revenge here.

The teens, dressed in full combat gear, unleashed their rage and opened fire with shotguns and semiautomatic weapons, killing twelve teenagers, one teacher, and themselves in what was then the worst mass shooting in American history.

I played for the class a clip from the video Harris made in his bedroom a month before the tragedy, in which he thanked his mom and dad for being the best "fucking parents" he'd ever known, for teaching him self-awareness and self-reliance. Psychiatrist Frank Ochberg later described him as "the 'Mozart' of psychopaths, the kind of person who came along only every two or three hundred years."

"Psychopaths are master manipulators," I said. And though they rarely became our patients, the few who did seek therapy usually did so under court order and with negative results, such as higher recidivism rates than those convicts who did not participate in therapy. In at least one prison study, psychopathic inmates participating in therapy described it like "finishing school," where they learned from their *therapists* how to "put the squeeze" on people. It's the level of deception that's most disturbing. The *ease* of it, the *coolness*.

"They either tell us what we want to hear, or they reveal by omission," I added. "We'd never know the difference because what we know about them is limited by how much they *tell* us. We can't climb inside their heads and know what they're thinking. And though male students, more than any other demographic, were the most likely perpetrators of mass school killings, according to a 2002 Secret Service report, 'no accurate or useful profile of these individuals' exists. It's not as if we can 'spot them' in the student population."

We can only spot the emotional scars they inflict on their surviving victims.

Dylan Klebold's mother, for instance, worried she might be accosted by the press, angry citizens, or families of her son's murder victims. She had been afraid to turn on the news, afraid to hear how others demonized her as a terrible parent, a "monster who had raised a monster." She had panic attacks in the office, in the hardware store, even while reading a book in bed, her mind locked into a spinning cycle of terror, which she described as though "her brain was trying to kill her." Eventually, her mental suffering turned physical as she battled breast cancer.

Hard to imagine that kind of public hatred or identity crisis. I could see on my students' anguished faces the toll just hearing about the tragedies had had. As my slides highlighted the alarming rise in school violence since the worst incident—a 1927 bombing by a disgruntled employee in Bath Township, Michigan, that left thirty-eight schoolchildren dead—to the most recent massacre, in 2007 at Virginia Polytechnic Institute in Blacksburg, my focus turned toward action. What could we, as psychiatrists, as educators, as students, do to prevent another mass murder? What did these tragedies teach us? How could we stop these monsters, especially since most had never directly threatened anyone and instead compiled secret "shit lists" and "girls' lists" and had histories of unchecked or unreported violence like invisible rap sheets?

Maybe, I told my students, by first knowing who they were and who they were not. And by talking about what we knew.

Which brought us to twenty-three-year-old Seung-Hui Cho, an English major at Virginia Tech. I described his attacks: how, armed with a 9-millimeter handgun, a .22-caliber handgun, and hundreds of rounds of ammunition, he first opened fire in a dorm (fatally shooting two students), then two hours later entered a classroom building, where he chained and locked several main exits to prevent escape. Going from room to room, he murdered twenty-five students and five professors before killing himself. He left behind writings, recordings, and many clues to who he was and why he killed.

Two days after the massacre, NBC News received a package that was mailed sometime between Cho's first and second shootings. Inside were photos of Cho posing with his guns, as well as a video diatribe in which he ranted about wealthy brats. Though Cho, like the other shooters I'd highlighted, didn't name any specific individual as a target, police later learned he'd stalked certain classmates and had an imaginary girlfriend, a "supermodel" named "Jelly" who called him "Spanky."

In an interview with *Good Morning America*, the chairman of the English Department described Cho as "so distant and lonely it was almost like talking to a hole, as though he really wasn't there most of the time." What she didn't (couldn't) know was that Cho was also writing "manifestos" about all the people he hated and who had wronged him. And he'd purchased a Glock and a Walther and created an alter ego named "Ax Ishmael, the Anti-Terrorist of America."

Classmates described Cho as a loner, nondescript, barely memorable, someone who didn't talk much. His social awkwardness and brooding silence, even as a young child, so disturbed his family that his relatives feared he might actually be mute. And though his mother prayed regularly her son would "snap out of it," his silence only worsened and soon she lost him altogether to the world of video games, where he could be a silent spectator or a violent avatar.

Cho's creative writing instructor, famed poet Nikki Giovanni, knew only what she could observe: that he was "extraordinarily lonely" and mean, an "evil presence," a bully who wore sunglasses, headphones, and a ball cap during class, signed his name on attendance logs with a question mark, and inappropriately photographed the knees and legs of her female students.

Classmates found Cho's violent and sexually aggressive writings "morbid" and "worrisome," with a quality so "dark and graphic" they asked to be exempt from critiquing him in class.

For one poetry assignment he wrote:

What Barbarians you people are . . . I thought this was a poetry class—yet everybody—everybody but me that is—spent the whole hour and a half talking about eating . . . and soon an animal massacre butcher shop. Somebody began talking about chopping off turtles' heads, dipping them into eel sauce . . . cooking lions' balls deep fried and thin sliced . . . eating them with Ketchup. . . . chewing on a . . . fat, bird's head with a nice bottle of wine . . . the animals that she ate are now her friends . . . she once deliciously, joyfully gobbled them up like one jolly clown . . . as long as she's sorry! *As if! You disgust me. In fact, you all disgust me!*

I'm talking to you, you, you, you all of you. You low-life barbarians make me sick . . . if you despicable human beings who are all disgraces to the human race keep this up before you know it you'll turn into cannibals . . . uncivilized monsters!

His plays were similarly nightmarish, twisted and macabre. In one, titled after the Guns N' Roses song "Mr. Brownstone," teenagers discussed killing their teacher, "an old fart" who "made their lives miserable." They wanted to "watch him bleed the way he made them bleed." In Cho's one-act play *Richard McBeef,* the protagonist accused his stepfather of pedophilia, plotted to kill him, and repeatedly chanted, "must kill Dick . . . Dick must die . . . I can kill you Dick." His stage directions were equally disturbing: "John sticks half eaten banana cereal bar down his stepfather's mouth and attempts to shove it down his throat."

Cho's playwriting professor, hoping to alleviate his students' guilt at not doing or saying something about Cho, wrote in an email: "There was violence in Cho's writing—but there is a huge difference between writing about violence and *behaving* violently . . . We could not have known what he would do."

Giovanni agreed. "I've taught crazy students, and I've taught weird students," she said. "I've got to say, Cho's alone in being evil . . . but you can't go to people and say, 'I have this feeling.' You know, you're not allowed to say, 'I got this feeling that maybe we should, you know, have this kid shot and save a lot of people.'" "We're America," she later recited in her convocation poem following Cho's massacre. "And America shoots people."

Before Giovanni removed him from her class, she encouraged

him to seek counseling, but she couldn't force him; "everyone's hands were tied." Giovanni was prepared to resign if Cho was not removed from her class. Her department head, Lucinda Roy, accommodated, tutoring him individually, implementing safeguards like "code words" (the name of a dead professor) in case Cho became too scary and it was time for her assistant to call security. Roy also alerted the student affairs office, the dean's office, and the campus police, all of whom said they could do nothing. Cho's threats were "beneath the surface, not explicit."

He wasn't *actually* saying he was going to kill anyone.

Cho's roommates, too, found him to be "strange" and "kind of weird," but not especially "menacing." And though they noticed a marked change in Cho's routine in the few weeks before the massacre— he'd chopped his hair into a short military style, woken early to train at the gym, and listened incessantly to "Shine" by the rock band Collective Soul—they did not leap to the conclusion that Cho's uncharacteristic behavior was necessarily a precursor to murder.

Even as disturbing as Cho's writings were, "sometimes in creative writing, people reveal things and you never know if it's creative or if they're describing things, if they're imagining things or just how real it might be, but we're all alert to not ignore things like this," Professor Carolyn Rude, chairwoman of the English Department, remarked.

Several professors, trying to balance the freedom needed to be creative against the warning signs of possible psychosis, formed a task force to discuss how best to handle Cho, but they only met twice in the eighteen months before the shooting, and though they reached out to university officials, no action was taken by school administrators, including the dean at the College of Liberal Arts and Human Sciences, who had no information about Cho's prior hospitalization at a mental health facility in 2005. Federal and state disability laws prohibited the disclosure and sharing of mental health records between institutions, academic professionals, even departments. Student privacy trumped safety.

But protecting Cho's right to privacy unwittingly violated *everyone's* right to safety.

In the case of Virginia Tech, Cho's emotional disability was not disclosed on his admissions application. (Unlike most schools, at that time, Virginia Tech did not require letters of recommendation or personal essays on their applications and did not conduct personal interviews.) In 1999, following the Columbine massacre, Cho wrote an essay for his English class expressing his desire "to repeat Columbine." It so alarmed school officials, they encouraged his parents to seek a psychiatric evaluation, which led to his diagnosis of mutism and depression, *information that was never relayed to Virginia Tech.*

"His mental health records might have been sealed, but his behavior was overt. There's not a law in the United States that says if a student engages in strange behaviors that the university can't respond to those behaviors," said Dr. William S. Pollack, one of several panelists appointed by Virginia's governor to evaluate the massacre.

In more than three out of four school shootings, the attacker made no *direct* threat against the teachers or students. But they still posed a threat. Most had engaged in some violent or aggressive behavior prior to the shooting. Virginia Tech taught us to take more care, to share information, to be vocal about our concerns and engage, engage, engage.

"Report what you see—and *don't* see," I told my students. "Pay attention to that gut sense that something is off about this person. Don't hesitate to share information, be vocal about your concerns, and think 'safety first,' always."

HOLMES

Across campus in another lecture hall, James Eagan Holmes, a "weirdly awkward" twenty-four-year-old doctoral student in neuroscience, howled something nonsensical in response to his professor's invitation to present his research project on the auditory system of Mongolian gerbils to an audience of students, scientists, and faculty. Wearing dirty black jeans and a faded *Star Wars* T-shirt, Holmes moved spiderlike toward the podium, his lanky legs folding beneath him.

One of a handful of academically gifted students accepted from hundreds of hopeful applicants into the college's prestigious neuroscience program, Holmes appeared robotic onstage, as mechanical as if he had suddenly shed all human qualities and become a kind of "system" to be studied. He stood at the podium sweating and, according to one professor, "largely disengaged, never fully present as if off in another world."

This wasn't the first time "Jimmy" (as he was called in his undergraduate years) struggled with public speaking. Years before, at the age of eighteen, he had served as a research intern at the Salk Institute at the University of California, San Diego in La Jolla.[1]

Holmes, under the tutelage of John Jacobson, studied "subjective experiences that took place inside the mind, illusions that al-

---

1   The center, regarded as one of the world's top biomedical research facilities, was once partnered with the Defense Advanced Research Projects Agency (DARPA) and the Mars company (manufacturers of Milky Way and Snickers candy bars). The institute's research, according to freelance journalist Jerry Mazza in his August 2, 2012, article, "James Holmes Had Links to DARPA, the Salk Institute and the DoD [Department of Defense]," "was part of a larger DARPA program known as the 'Peak Soldier Performance Program,' which involved creating brain-machine interfaces for battlefield use, including bionics for legs, arms, and eyes," and addressing combat fatigue "through the enhanced use of epicatechina (an antioxidant flavanol found in cocoa and, particularly, in dark chocolate)."

   According to Mazza, Holmes' father also worked for DARPA, as well as a software company (HNC Software, Inc.) focused "on developing 'cortronic neural networks,' which would allow machines to interpret aural

lowed us to change the past." He suggested the practical application of his research might be to video gamers "who might feel euphoric, like they have super-powers." And though Holmes smiled shyly at the podium, fellow interns later described his delivery as being "as if a fuse had been lit on a small grenade." His discomfort with public speaking was revealed through poor eye contact and odd humor. ("His dream," a fellow intern said as he introduced him before his final presentation, "is to own a Slurpee machine.") Jacobson would later disclose that it took him an entire day to prepare Holmes for his "undistinguished" ten-minute presentation.

At first, Holmes' "quirky behavior was not particularly alarming" among other, equally eccentric scientists in the neuroscience program, but soon his "one-word" responses, "flat affect," and stiff slide presentations peppered with bizarre and often "inappropriate" cartoons began to be more than just "off putting."

One of his graduate presentations began with a picture of a chicken saying to an egg, *"Jimmy, answer me please!"*

"It's not that I'm against humor"—there was a little catch in the professor's voice—"I'm against bad humor and humor without con-

---

and visual stimuli to think like humans. James Holmes was the grandson of Lieutenant Colonel Robert Holmes, one of the first Turkish-language graduates of the Army Language School, later called the Defense Language Institute, in Monterey, California."

Mazza wrote:

> The links between the younger and elder Holmes and U.S. government research on creating super-soldiers, human brain-machine interfaces, and human-like robots brings forth the question: Was James Holmes engaged in a real-life Jason Bourne TREADSTONE project that broke down and resulted in deadly consequences in Aurora, Colorado?

> [Are] the Batman movies now serving as a newer version of J.D. Salinger's "Catcher in the Rye," i.e., subliminal messaging triggering mechanism. Salinger's novel was of interest to a number of American political assassins.

text. What, for instance, does a chicken, egg, cooking, or food have anything at all to do with *rodents*, the subject of his presentation?"

"That's a good question, let me *mullet* over." Holmes' next slide, a photo of a man with a mullet hairstyle, seemed to anticipate his professor's confusion.

"I have some concerns about your performance," the professor emailed Holmes afterward. "When are you available to meet and discuss?"

But Holmes had no interest in hearing what his professor had to say and replied, "Aww, that's too bad. I'll be joining another lab. Cheers."

March 19, 2012
(123 days before the massacre)

FENTON

Building 500, a towering Art Deco structure on the university's campus, had a gray facade and marble interior reminiscent of the cold, sterile environment found in sanatoriums.

I attended Chicago Medical School on an Air Force scholarship and served several years as chief of physical medicine at Wilford Hall[2] at the Lackland Air Force Base in San Antonio. Since arriving at the University of Colorado in 2005, I was determined after graduation to make my office an oasis for my patients.

I knew firsthand that plants were the perfect antidote to people. After hours with patients and colleagues saturated in *talk*, it was calming to be surrounded by colors and fragrances and to help

---

2   Now it is the Defense Department's "largest outpatient ambulatory surgical center."

something grow. Even in my cramped apartments during medical school, I brought the outdoors in, beautifying drab white corners with vibrant, living art. Eventually, when I owned a home, my hobby became a passion and I designed elaborate gardens full of color, soft topiary creatures, and native plants. And though I considered gardening a delightful pastime, the results had more far-reaching effects of making *others* happy.

In my office sunlight streamed through large-paned windows. Several philodendrons filled large ceramic pots. Orchids dotted my bookshelves and vines draped my desk. Snake plants formed a natural partition with their dark green leaves jutting toward the vaulted ceiling. Water trickled over stones from a Zen desk fountain. A hummingbird often hovered outside near a spike of scarlet firecracker petals on the windowsill.

Exhausted after a full day of seeing patients, I dropped into my swivel chair, kicked off my clogs, and listened to a voicemail from my battle-weary colleague, social worker Margaret Roath. Her Southern drawl held a tinge of urgency: "I know you have a long waiting list, but I think you should make an exception for this one. He's a bit . . . unusual. It might be best to keep him in the system." That was code for not referring him to an outside colleague for care. She wanted him monitored closely.

"He is the most anxious guy I've seen," she followed up in an email, "and has symptoms of OCD . . . hard to interview . . . stares, takes a long time answering . . . most concerning is that he has thoughts of killing people, though I do not think he is dangerous . . . has never done anything to harm others . . . recently broke up with his girlfriend . . . Gargi Datta."

I remembered her—a feisty graduate student from the Computational Bioscience program. She had breezed into my office several months earlier for a brief intake session before I determined my schedule was too full and referred her to a colleague. I recalled that she'd said I resembled the actress Holly Hunter and had come in carrying a worn copy of Bret Easton Ellis' book *American Psycho*. She said she enjoyed books about serial killers even though they gave her nightmares.

Before I could respond to Roath's email or contact her patient to schedule an immediate appointment, my close friend and colleague Toby rapped loudly on my office door, poked her head inside, and then, catching the hem of her floral blouse on a protruding nail and ripping a small tear, said, "I'm freaking out!" She looked pale and visibly shaken as she paced, her shock of curly blond bangs falling across her glasses. "I'm worried my face is going to be on the front page of the *Denver Post* with the headline 'Psychiatrist Failed to Realize Her Patient Was a Homicidal Maniac.'"

"What's happened?"

"I think I'm having a panic attack," she half joked, dropping onto my claw-footed couch and clutching her chest. "How are you always so *calm*?"

I preferred "resilient." All of us psychiatrists, Toby included, were trained to handle crises. I liked to think that my stint in the Air Force, cramped in a two-seater T-38 fighter jet, dressed in a G-suit and a fogged-up oxygen mask, trying not to vomit up my Life Savers and coffee, only added to my resolve. But none of us ever fell apart; instead, we processed experiences in our own ways. We were, after all, human; sometimes we just needed permission to be human. That and a safe space to vent. On this day, I gave that to Toby.

For several weeks she'd been treating a patient I'll call the Butcher. "I sensed him before he entered the room," she said, shaking. "Like an evil compression, like I knew he was rotten, but I had no reason to know, understand?"

I'd experienced that same kind of "knowing," that sixth sense that defied logic, an overall shift in energy that resounded like an internal alarm.

"He had never mentioned his violent proclivities, but last night he chopped up his girlfriend into little flesh bits and dumped her remains in a blender." Toby giggled, her misplaced laughter a kind of shelter, a natural stress release in cases of extreme shock. She bunched a tissue in her hands and described how "fine" the Butcher had seemed during their appointments, how quiet, reserved, and guarded, betraying nothing of the animal inside him. (Only later, as she prepared for the Butcher's trial, would she learn that "for kicks" he'd regularly choked, raped, and shot halos of bullets around his girlfriend's face while she drifted in and out of consciousness.)

"Still, he made the hair on the back of my neck prick. When he spoke, it was as if he were searching for answers in some kind of mental Rolodex. I *hated* him, Lynne, hated treating him. When he left my office, I wanted to light candles, play classical music, wipe the walls with sage. He just exuded evil."

Toby blew her nose loudly and shook her head as if gathering her wits so that she could more calmly lay out her worst fear: being outed as the Butcher's therapist and seeing her career and reputation ruined. What if she had to testify at the Butcher's trial? She'd have to relive her sessions with him, maybe for *years*, as she was grilled by attorneys about her treatment, asked over and over how she had missed his monstrous intent. I let her talk, knowing there was great relief in self-expression, in just being heard. Her fear wasn't especially rational. After all, she *had* to know the names of treating psychiatrists were never made public by the press or ever deliberately leaked. The consequences would be too dire. The threat that their professional judgment might one day become public fodder could potentially compromise a psychiatrist's treatment of a patient. It would be like exposing a confidential informant who often risked his life to obtain critical crime-solving information.

What psychiatrist, or patient for that matter, would risk having his or her life being publicly scrutinized?

CHAPTER 2

THE AMERICAN PSYCHO

October 2011—March 2012
(294–115 days before the massacre)

I'm not a monster. I'm just ahead of the curve.
—The Joker, *The Dark Knight* (2008)

HOLMES

Holmes first met Gargi Datta at the university's orientation. She was fresh-faced with dark eyes that crawled over his bright blue mirrored sunglasses and chapped lips.

"You look like someone who appreciates horror," she said, introducing herself, all chunky Doc Martens and brown paisley dress. "Yes? No?" A clear little drop of snot dangled from her nose when she bobbed her head up and down and side to side.

Holmes shrugged.

"Great!" She made a small fist with her right hand and pumped it into the air. "The film festival starts at seven."

"If you text me, I'll tell you an amazing, world's greatest, best-ever knock-knock joke!" Holmes replied.

"She was the Alpha," their mutual friend, Ben Garcia, later told police about why their relationship worked. "They hung out a lot, mostly in his apartment," on Paris Street in a cramped one-bedroom on the third floor. The old brick building bordered clusters of small ethnic eateries and overlooked an elementary school in a fringe neighborhood one block from the Department of Psychology and Neuroscience. Holmes frequently rode his "petty cash BMX" bike to classes and to the nearby dilapidated strip mall, where he frequently sipped Coronas alone in a Spanish-speaking bar. Only the front half of his apartment was tidy. Often after class Gargi went over and they held hands, sipped Slurpees, and snuggled on his dingy gray sofa, watching reruns of *Saturday Night Live* and *Arrested Development* beneath a giant poster of a screaming zombie head titled BRAINS. For snacks, he offered her hunks of cheddar cheese. On his refrigerator door he'd taped a poster of a half-naked woman, bent over with her bare ass in the air, and a flirty caption: SHY GUYS ALWAYS KEEP THEIR BEER ON THE BOTTOM SHELF.

Gargi watered "Planty," his potted succulent, but it didn't help. The leaves dried up. And a fan blew the dead parts around the room. When she asked him why he kept it if it was "dying," he replied, "It senses it's alive."

"Like the patients in Oliver Sacks' book *The Man Who Mistook His Wife for a Hat!*" Her face lit up as she explained how his patients' bizarre neurological disorders caused them to "sense their missing parts." Some had lost all sense of their bodies and lived "disembodied," relying only on their vision to "keep track of their hands, legs and other parts." And others, like the man who tried to "put on" his wife, viewed the world in entirely abstract terms, like a musical composition; they were unable to see faces or scenes with any clarity, but somehow they understood how the various components fit together.

"Exactly."

After a while Holmes invited Gargi to lie with him on his red satin sheets, beneath posters of *Pulp Fiction* (where John Travolta and Samuel L. Jackson pointed revolvers at her head) and *Soldiers of Misfortune*, and one depicting a whiskey cocktail and a slice of lime with the caption WHEN LIFE PRESENTS A CHALLENGE, TAKE YOURS SLOW. In the shadows, amid empty pizza boxes, Subway sandwich wrappers, and roaches that looked like spent shells, he and Gargi had "relations," as he later acknowledged in interviews with his court-appointed psychiatrist. They grunted and moaned and when he pressed his chest into her breasts, he felt and heard her heart, her breathing, her life sounds. She felt different from the strays he'd brought home and paid in cash with the hundred-dollar bills he'd stashed in his nightstand.

Holmes frequently invited Gargi over to play *Limbo*, a strategy video game in which players had to guide a nameless boy from a forest on the "edge of hell" through dangerous environments as he searched for his sister. He especially liked the game because it reminded him of his own relationship with his sibling. With dark grayscale graphics and minimalist ambient sounds, the game had a haunting atmosphere similar to film noir. Some of the boy's deaths included dismemberment or beheading; always, he was prevented from reaching his sister. When the boy got too close, he was thrown through a glass window back into the dark forest, where he resumed wandering in limbo.

"I like this game. Not too violent, more of a psychological mind fuck," Gargi said.

Holmes shuffled a deck of cards and said, "Want to try *Dominance*? The goal is survival of the fittest. The player who gets the most victory points wins."

They ended each "playdate" with sex and Netflix. Holmes initiated their next rendezvous with "You can't get enough of my sexy Neo body."

"I can't sleep," Gargi wrote in a G-Chat one night. "If I come over, what do you got?"

He paused the latest version of *Grand Theft Auto*. He had just blown apart the enemy's face. The whole point was to kill as many people as possible and he had already earned quite a few "stars" for his wild, destructive rampages. Under his breath he repeated his avatar's rant: *"Niggers, beaners, fags, Arabs, and sand niggers. Die. Die. Die."*

"I can't hear you."

"Vicodin," he responded.

"What else?"

"Ambien. Maybe you should stop reading books about serial killers?"

"I don't want to take anything that will make me lose awareness. Hopefully therapy will help."

"When are you going to see the rapist?" Holmes cradled the phone between his cheek and shoulder and sent her a link to "googles-broken-promise-the-end-of-don't-be-evil."

He saw *his* first when he was eight after he punched his three-year-old sister in the face and she bruised like an eggplant. According to his mom he was "very Nintendo-oriented" and hurled around his stuffed animals. But after three sessions with the Rapist No. 1 and a diagnosis of "oppositional defiant disorder," "all seemed normal" and the counseling stopped. Meanwhile, to his teachers at Castroville Elementary, he was "intelligent," and "helpful," a "renaissance kid" with a "wonderful smile." He played soccer; his dad coached his team. And he participated in other sports too: basketball, kickball, martial arts, track (even winning a medal at his first meet).

Later, in middle school, when his family relocated from rural Salinas, "the salad bowl of the world," to a subdivision in San Diego, Holmes sat in the back of his family's van and tried to saw open his wrists with a stiff edge of cardboard.

Soon after, in his "downtime," recurring visions of nuclear bombs clouded his vision. These images filled his "blank spaces," exploding in the dull moments before sleep when nothing really happened. He told no one. These he kept private, just as he did his fantasies of killing an "abstract humankind." The random thoughts just "popped into his head." He hated people the way he hated broccoli. Still, his mom insisted he see "Mel," a social worker at PsyCare and the Rapist No. 2.

"He spends a lot of time reading and playing video games alone in his bedroom closet. He's not adjusting well to the move." His mom hugged the edge of the plaid sofa in the Rapist No. 2's office. Water gurgled from a corner fish tank. Several baby koi swam into the glass. Fish were not agonized by wild mood swings. Plastic seaweed swirled in the sandy bottom. Reflected in the dirty pane, Holmes' boneless little arms looked thin and yellowish, like they'd been dipped in wax.

"Do you have a favorite book?"

"That's easy, *Of Mice and Men*." Holmes liked Lennie best, the mentally slow "gentle giant" whom George, the wiry, smart migrant worker, protected from a world that didn't understand him. That's probably what made it hard for George to kill Lennie. He was his closest friend.

"How about a favorite video game?"

Massive multiplayer online role-playing games (MMORPGs), where he could "escape from reality," "control the hero . . . live out the hero's life," and communicate with other players online. He wasn't into the violent ones, the "first-person shooters."

The Rapist No. 2 looked at his clipboard and reached for the folded pair of black-framed glasses sticking out of his chest pocket.

"He doesn't talk much. He's scientific, nonemotional." His mom's voice sounded like waves advancing, retreating, advancing, retreating, retreating, retreat, retreat. "I can't even get him to use a telephone. He clams up. He just won't do it."

She was referring to his "frozen episodes," when floating saws popped into his head and "chopped off limbs or heads."

The Rapist No. 2 clicked and unclicked his ballpoint pen and Holmes imagined what he scribbled furiously in his notes. *Not the*

*sharing type . . . typical happy suburban family. Mom takes him to the zoo
and cooks him spaghetti. Once, to test if it was al dente, she threw a noodle
onto the cabinet and when she pulled it off, it stripped the paint.*

"My husband's aunt didn't talk much either. She liked to go to
bed every night at seven." His mom's hand massaged her throat as
if she had swallowed a wad of tuna fish.

"How are things at home?"

Thoughts of strawberries and artichokes and "family time" filled
his head.

His mother volunteered, "Our neighbor is a prison artist. Some
of our relatives have been institutionalized a few times and one suffered paranoid delusions."

The Rapist No. 2 just stared at his mom.

"It's not like that; we're a fairly normal family, a good family. We
have our share of alcoholics and minor emotional issues, bouts
of depression and psychosis, but nothing alarming." Her laughter
sounded tinny. "I'm a nurse at Scripps Memorial. His father, Bob—
we call him 'Bobbo'—studied mathematics at Stanford, then got
his master's at UCLA. His grandfather is a West Point alum and
graduated from Annapolis. He had distinguished military and ci-
vilian careers that included service in the Pacific during World War
II." *Blah, blah, blah . . .*

Her words crushed together. "Bobbo's mother once served as
governor of the exclusive Monterey Bay Colony of Mayflower De-
scendants. His twin sister had some mental health problems, but
she's always been kind and loving to Jimmy. Isn't that right, Jimmy?"

Holmes said nothing, but he wondered if he, too, had a "broken
brain."

"Tell me about school." The Rapist No. 2 leaned forward, seemingly studying Holmes as if he were a rare and dangerous spider.

"I played a dead soldier once in my English class's reenactment
of a scene from *All Quiet on the Western Front*. My character had been
shot in the head."

Gargi planned their outings: Saturday hikes to Dinosaur Ridge, dinners at ethnic eateries, road trips to the New Belgium Brewery in Fort Collins to sample Fat Tire beer and once to see Infected Mushroom, the Israeli psychedelic trance electronica band. They even went to showings of *The Hunger Games* and *Sherlock Holmes* at the Century 16 in Aurora.

Holmes confessed the film had inspired his email name, dsherlockb@gmail.com, a combination of "Sherlock *Holmes*" and *b* for "*James* Bond" (though he had no explanation for the *d*). Gargi thought it was "cute" and invited him out for Ethiopian cuisine. Holmes would later write in his notebook about preparing for his dates, which typically involved hours of looking in the mirror, sometimes as often as ten times a day, to study his appearance and style his hair, combing and uncombing it with his fingers. He jumped to Tiësto's techno drumbeats, repetitive blasts that mimicked a machine gun.

In the near-empty restaurant, they sat on floor mats with a view of the parking lot and garish neon storefront lights. When the food arrived in mushy colorful clumps, Holmes said he now understood why the Ethiopians were starving.

"It's called *gursha*," Gargi said, ripping off a piece of teff and dipping the flatbread into chunks of sautéed meat. With her right hand, she fed him bites of *tibs*. "It's tradition to do this with close friends and family."

Holmes opened wide and wrapped his mouth around her fist.

When Gargi asked about his classes, Holmes insisted graduate school beat working in a factory operating a pill-coating machine, where he'd monitored fluctuating temperatures and unclogged nozzles so he could load "bullets" into a drum. And at least he could live alone, not like in college at Riverdale, when his entomologist roommate let his tarantulas loose.

Gargi crinkled her nose, wiped small clumps of yellow legume stew on a napkin, and sat back on her knees. "I'm suddenly not very hungry."

When they returned from Christmas break, Holmes complained of "excessive fatigue," said his head was full of "boogers," and the "usual remedies" for congestion and postnasal drip—Claritin-D, Benadryl—hadn't helped. "What's wrong with you?" Gargi asked.

"They diagnosed me with mononucleosis."

> dattabase@gmail.com: that sucks that you're sick. I heard you had the magic touch for healing.
> dsherlockb@gmail.com: I'm more like delusional psychotic . . . Didn't you know Ben was paranoid?
> dattabase@gmail.com: How do you think we connected? We met at a paranoia support group!
> dsherlockb@gmail.com: and all this time I thought u met through alcohol . . . did you know too much acetaminophen will fuck the liver . . . many people who don't read the Tylenol directions wind up in the hospital . . . if you die there won't really be a tomorrow.

Holmes, deeply bothered by his body's betrayal, wrote about it later in his notebook:

Concern with nose, often drippy, a leaky faucet requiring continuing wiping. Nose interferes with quality of living . . . pores are squished to the point of skin feeling queer. Concern with ears . . . cannot hear well . . . Concern with eyes, [suffer from] imperfect biology, had to wear glasses. This problem with biology leaves me with an odd sense of self . . . the biological me is driven by biological needs . . . like hunger, thirst . . . programmed things . . . the other me does things because I choose to . . . I'm losing this battle, I have succumbed to falling in love.

He shared his "psychotic delusions" with his friend Ben Garcia but insisted his didn't involve hearing voices, though that "might actually have been fun," and said the subject of his delusions was a secret. Instead, he saw "flickers," "fleeting movements in his peripheral vision" that sometimes appeared light and other times dark and splotchy "like crows or beatles [sic]." And though he considered Ben a friend, he found relationships exhausting and would have preferred to "avoid social interactions" altogether, but, as he later acknowledged in his notebook, sometimes "discourse was unavoidable."

Best to keep my socially unacceptable responses . . . short or turn them into question form so other people are the ones talking. I have an inability to communicate what I want to say although I can understand it, typically with an image in my mind but can't say the images or draw them, would be nice if there was some form of telepathy to transfer the images . . . best not to reveal too much.

"We were the 'California Boys,'" says mutual friend Tim Tapscott. "James and I were both from California. But honestly, he never talked about his family or his life there. I'm not really sure he was actually from California at all. In fact, I'm not really sure *where* he was from."

"He described himself as a 'lone wolf.'" Ben ran a hand through his red-dyed hair and recalled with a smile how Holmes had once given him a cell phone cover that resembled a tape cassette so they could stay in touch. "Mine was white, his was black." He said they "woofed" at each other—

"Woof. Woof."

"Woof, back atcha," Holmes said, adding, "How about those San Diego Chargers."

"How about those Denver Broncos? We're in Arapahoe [County] now."

In the end, Holmes found it too exhausting to be friends with anyone for a significant period of time. Still, he tried. Once, in response to Ben's depression, Holmes suggested his friend use his feelings "to be destructive" to the world around him.

"We discussed 'killing' each other," Ben said. Their exchanges were meant to be "playful" references to the *Highlander* video game series in which so-called Immortals were executed by decapitation and avatars "killed" one another in less than sixty seconds. Holmes thought about other things that lasted sixty seconds: *a person could inhale twelve to twenty breaths, have seventy-two heartbeats, fire eight hundred rifle blasts, buy forty guns . . . and commit mass murder.*

"He seemed outwardly hostile toward people," a college friend remarked. But Holmes' friends admitted they had not quite grasped the gravity (or reality) of what he would later reveal to them was his "long-standing hatred of mankind or that he wanted to kill *people.*"

Tim Tapscott, a recreational shooter, once invited Holmes to go shopping with him for a Glock 26 9-millimeter pistol, a gun Gargi insisted "James showed no interest in and had trouble racking the slide." Eventually Holmes joined her in the fishing section, where he stared at rows and rows of colorful rubber bait.

Probably a hold-over from childhood, Holmes later journaled in his notebook, *when I began to scan my environment with no object or target in mind especially in boring situations . . . like presentations or when people rambled on about frivolous information.*

He prepared for his next oral presentation on the nervous system of lobsters, hoping to show how the crustacean's neurons created behavior in the creature's stomach.

"*We* should make an artificial brain," he challenged Gargi, adding that "even if scientists had a computational understanding of the brain there was still a huge amalgam of wiring and hardwire . . ."

And the potential for "a million abnormalities."

dsherlockb@gmail.com: I doubt we will see a brain that will match
the epicness of the esteemed Gargi brain.

dattabase@gmail.com: hahaha I'm pretty sure there are brains much better than mine.

dsherlockb@gmail.com: Well, that's a given. Just take that James guy's brain for example, Superior X 100.

dattabase@gmail.com: Oh, James Dean you mean?

dsherlockb@gmail.com: Nope, the James that has a dead brain.

On Valentine's Day, Holmes prepared a special dinner for Gargi, including home-cooked French onion chicken soup and vanilla ice cream for dessert. He lit candles, "the good smelling" kind, and used cloth napkins and real spoons. Steam swirled above the stainless-steel bowls bobbing with cubes of slippery meat. The room smelled of boiled carrots. Wind whistled through the tiny cracks in the window. They ate in silence, and between slurps Gargi ended their relationship: "I'm feeling disconnected. I don't see a future with this. Let's just be friends with benefits."

Soon after, Holmes began seeing things that weren't there. These were different from the "nail ghosts," the monsters that hammered nails through his bedroom wall when he was a kid. At first, there was flickering in his peripheral vision when he was alone in the lab; "then there'd be like shadows moving with nothing causing them." And when he turned toward them, they "kind of danced . . . usually in the shape of a person . . . juggling or doing something." Sometimes he saw these "juggling heads" when he was in bed in the dark, and often they had guns. They didn't frighten him; they were just shadows.

He emailed his mother, whom he called Goober, with an update on the "Gargi situation":

Goober,

It's gotten complex, I did my usual complete dissociation but then she wanted to get back together, and we did last week but not as

in a boyfriend/girlfriend relationship capacity or as just friends. A
"noncommittal relationship."

~Jimmy

She asked him whether he had Kaiser health insurance and sent
him photos of their trip to Canada. Bobbo was traveling again, this
time to Istanbul, Houston, then Frankfurt, Germany. Next, Carmel,
where Bobbo was catching up on his golf. Holmes sent her photos
of cells and lists of supplies he needed, among them Mongolian gerbils, "7 ready to rip apart," "one Poodle, male and not too good condition," "one pillow" and "100 pee pee pads."

She informed him the family poodle, "the Rockster," had passed
away.

"Hey Goober, that's too bad," Holmes wrote.

"Hope you're taking care of yourself, Jimmy! Love, Momma."

He *was*. He had just invented a game featuring a maze with a
serial killer.

CHAPTER 3

THE PROBLEM WITH BIOLOGY

March 23, 2012

(119 days before the massacre)

Smile, because it confuses people. Smile, because it's easier
than explaining what is killing you inside.
—The Joker, *The Dark Knight* (2008)

FENTON

The sky threatened rain. James Holmes was my last patient of the afternoon.

I expected to see a socially awkward, anxious student pacing my otherwise empty lobby, fidgety, sweaty, with overbright shifty eyes. Instead, my new patient sat ramrod straight in the vinyl cushioned office chair, legs splayed wide, wiry arms stiff on the wooden armrests, like a strange effigy.

As I approached, he jerked toward me, his large bug eyes empty and seemingly devoid of emotion.

"You must be James." I extended my hand, and when he didn't

shake it, or even move, the hair on my forearms prickled against my sleeves. "Shall we go inside?"

Holmes sprang up as if propelled by a slingshot, suddenly too close, too much in my space.

I was trained to observe gait, the way a person moved, the subtle body distress signals, having practiced physiatry before transitioning into psychiatry, and having developed an expertise in all manner of physical disabilities including spinal cord injuries, degenerative conditions, and amputations. In the Air Force, I'd worked in a prosthetic clinic, replacing missing body parts with fake but functional limbs, helping to restore the lives of amputees, and lecturing orthopedic surgeons on sexual function after paralysis. In fact, my skills at fixing the physically injured were so valuable, I was among a minority of doctors at Wilford Hall Medical Center whom the Air Force did not deploy overseas for combat duty in Desert Storm.

Surprisingly, Holmes exhibited none of the symptoms I expected to see given Roath's email describing him as the most anxious person she'd ever seen. No skittish movements or facial tics, no bald patches or plucked eyebrows that would have been consistent with someone suffering from trichotillomania, which Holmes claimed he had.

Rain spit against the glass. Outside, gray buildings blurred into wet, dirty streaks. Inside, I sat across from Holmes surrounded by lush plants, soft lights, and boxes of white noise. I found it difficult to look at him, the black gloss of his stare so intense, it was as if I were being sucked into a black hole. Typically, the patient set the pace, the flow, the dance, until slowly, slowly, he found his beat. His past would rush at him in clips and pulses as he dipped and bent, drew close, pulled away, spun, led, and followed, until the music finally stopped. But Holmes refused to dance. Instead, he fixated on my black boots, his eyelashes straight, short, dry.

Several minutes passed as I struggled for an opening, a way to draw him out, to learn his reasons for being here.

"The end of relationships can be so hard," I began, "it's easy to get depressed, even derailed." I thought of my own divorce, when, after seven years of having a witness to my life, I'd suddenly faced a glaring void. And in the days and weeks that followed The End, I'd lived in the past, mired in memories, unsure how to move forward or stay connected to a man I would always love but didn't want as a life partner. After a few beats of uncomfortable silence, Holmes shrugged and, still averting his gaze, replied slowly, "I don't have relationships with people. They have relationships with me." His voice had a slight metallic rasp as if from disuse.

"Tell me more about that?"

"They usually last four months and then I just stop talking to them."

"Why do you think that is?"

Holmes remained silent for a few minutes, his expression suddenly blank, as if curtains on his face had been drawn. "I wanted to overcome biology." He overenunciated his words, each syllable sticking to the roof of his mouth. Haltingly, he explained his "problem with biology," how at ten he had needed glasses, how his deteriorating eyesight caused his "OCD symptoms to worsen" and now he needed a solution.

"What kind of solution?"

"Killing people." He said it matter-of-factly, as if he'd just plucked lint off his pants.

"You have *thoughts* of killing people?"

"Yes."

Destructive or even violent thoughts, in and of themselves, were not necessarily abnormal. I'd treated postpartum patients haunted by intrusive thoughts of flushing their infants down the toilet. The mothers had grown depressed, their lives defined by endless nursing, pumping, diaper changing, and scrubbing bottles. They'd described a kind of soulful emptiness punctuated by scary murderous thoughts that left them feeling strangely disconnected from others, as if there was an invisible wall between them and the rest of the world. They'd relayed fantasies of just ending the misery—driving off the road, swallowing too many pills. I wondered, *Did Holmes, too, hope for relief from his thoughts of killing?* I'd had anxious patients like him who'd described similar horrifying visions of chain saws buzzing off heads, swimming pools filling with blood, bits of flesh floating on the surface.

"Some people who have thoughts like yours," I suggested, "will try to distract themselves." Or distract *others.* I'd known of patients who'd described their partners' disarming humor as both a draw and an attempted distraction from insidious fantasies of violence. One woman described being drowned in "verbal vomit" and love bombs from a boyfriend who'd pledged to "always be with her," and, so dazzled by his pretty words, she'd missed his more ominous implications—that he'd *never* let her go.

Holmes shrugged, his unblinking gaze staring over my shoulder at my silk wall hangings. "I don't mind it." In fact, he admitted, he thought about killing "three or four times a day."

My stomach clenched. There was something so cold and predatory about the way he said it that I wrote in my notes, *his violent ruminations not entirely ego-dystonic . . . seems unfazed by his homicidal thoughts.* Sufferers with ego-*dys*tonic thoughts found these thoughts distressing, as opposed to ego-*syn*tonic, which meant in sync with their self-concept. Holmes wasn't repulsed at all by thoughts of killing people.

The *DSM* (*Diagnostic and Statistical Manual of Mental Disorders*), the virtual bible of psychological conditions, listed ten types of personality disorders categorized into three "clusters"—A, B, and C (or, as I'd learned in residency, Mad [madmen], Bad [badly behaved], and Sad [socially awkward, anxious/avoidant]. The A's (largely odd, bizarre, and eccentric) were the paranoid, schizoid, and schitzotypal personality disorders; B's (dramatic, erratic) were the antisocial, borderline, histrionic, and narcissistic personality disorders; and C's (anxious, fearful) were avoidant, dependent, and obsessive-compulsive personality disorders.

Though A's rarely sought help unless they were appointed by the court to do so, I suspected Holmes was an A.

"But you can't kill everyone, so that's not an effective solution." His flat monosyllabic tone made me uneasy. His words fell out of his mouth like Scrabble tiles he then painstakingly rearranged to form a whole sentence. His speech was so slow, at times I wasn't sure he had actually finished formulating his thoughts. It was as if he spoke without punctuation—no periods, exclamation points, or question marks, just unending ellipses. His delivery sounded rehearsed, forced, as if he were reading from a script or learning a new language, unsure of pronunciation or meaning.

"Is there anyone in *particular* you've thought about hurting?" If he posed a "serious threat of imminent physical violence against a specific person or persons," I would have a "duty to warn." This Colorado law closely tracked the language of the famous Tarasoff case, the 1976 murder of a graduate student whose stalker confided in his psychologist his intent to kill her. Though the psychologist alerted police to the possible threat, he failed to also warn the victim, whom the stalker eventually murdered.

"No."

"If you *were* to kill people, any thoughts about how you would do it?"

Roath had been concerned that Holmes had withheld information for fear she might report him or lock him up. Omission was sometimes just as revealing. Once, as a second-year resident, I was part of a team of doctors who met with a suicidal and distraught ex–military recruit. His wife had filed for divorce. The soft-spoken, polite patient knew what to say and how to behave, almost as if he'd memorized a laundry list of appropriate responses to ordinary events. He'd convinced us all he was "fine" and so we released him; hours later he fatally shot his wife's boyfriend and barricaded his children in the basement. It reminded me of a case Dr. Robert Hare discussed in his book *Without Conscience: The Disturbing World of the Psychopaths Among Us*, about a psychopathic lawyer named Norman Russell Sjonborg who, after fooling everyone (including his third wife) with his soft-spoken charm, brutally murdered one of his clients.

The lawyer was masterful at deception, careful to project only a "socially acceptable persona." According to Sjonborg's probation officer, "he was the kind of man who could contemplate killing his own children with the detachment of someone considering various auto-insurance policies." In fact, Sjonborg had once written a list of options for "handling the problem with his wife"—"do nothing," "file for paternity/conciliation court," "take girls w/o killing," "take girls Killing 4," or just kill.

"Ever think of harming yourself?" I hedged.

Holmes smirked, took his time responding. "I wouldn't hurt *myself.*"

No specific target. No specific plan. Does not appear to be currently dangerous but warrants further understanding and following. OCD and possible schizoid personality disorder, a chronic and pervasive pattern of detachment from social relationships and restrictive emotional expression. So far, Holmes did not meet the criteria for a mental health hold. He was not "gravely disabled" and there was "no evidence of suicidal or homicidal ideation." The rules for involuntary hospitalization for homicidal ideation required "imminent danger" and a "specific plan to hurt someone and/or an identifiable victim." But Holmes had disclosed none, so I focused on treating some of his more debilitating symptoms.

"Would you be open to medication?"

"I guess."

After I suggested several options and reviewed with him possible side effects, he agreed to a trial of 50 mg of sertraline to help curb his obsessive thoughts and small doses (0.5 mg) of Klonopin for immediate relief of his anxiety.

"Let's meet next week to see how you're doing."

"I can't get him out of my head." Toby sounded frantic over the phone as she described the lingering "icky" feeling the Butcher evoked, his eyes, empty, like the edge of an abyss. *Very much like Holmes' eyes.*

As she spoke, I retreated outside into my Colorado version of an English garden, needing respite from the ugliness. I inhaled crisp morning air full of sage and oregano as I headed down rose-scented pathways through the shrubbery gate. A slight breeze loosened my ponytail and stirred the soft purple clematis-covered trellis that climbed the walls. A robin pecked at clods of dirt near my muck boot; in the shade of my honey locust tree, I put the phone on speaker and clipped errant bamboo shoots near the edge of my pond. This was not the first call I'd received from Toby about the Butcher that week. Our friendship had morphed temporarily into informal emergency therapy. My therapy was plants. Gardening was a kind of meditation; learning about the individual plants—what they liked, what they needed to grow—took me out of the present and into a natural world of color and sound, a quiet order where things just made sense.

Toby rehashed all the reasons to worry if her name became public knowledge; anyone could get her phone number and address from the university's website. How was she supposed to protect her kids? She was processing; the more she talked about her feelings, the more grounded she became.

"If something bad happens to me," she said, "I'm going to open up a coffee shop and try not to eat all the baked goods."

"I may join you," I said, laughing, as a small snake slithered through the spout of an antique watering can. Woolly thyme blew along the curved pathways and dead-ended into my boxed topiary as I removed my rubber garden gloves, knelt by the Japanese irises, and listened to the gentle lap of the pond water.

"I'm serious." Toby's voice hitched as she recounted her recurring nightmares, the replaying of the Butcher's murder over and over. She had recently dreamed of stabbing her own baby with a paring knife, cutting her so deeply, she split her apart at "the seam." "I'm a horrible person," my friend choked out. "I don't even know why I did it, but I did it. I'm revolted." She had dreamed of harming her child in a way she could never take back, and now she was just shuffling through under an oppressive sense of darkness. She couldn't even wait in line for coffee at Starbucks because the grind of the blender made her shake.

My friend was having an acute stress response to the Butcher's crime and to the prospect of being publicly vilified for failing to stop him. Words, in this instance, seemed somehow inadequate, so I just listened to the subtext, the question she really wanted answered: *Did I do enough? Did I do enough to stop him?* It reminded me in a small way of some of my distraught patients who, following a painful breakup, wanted to be reassured that they'd *mattered*, that they'd left scar tissue, that the hours and hours of time they'd invested in the relationship had actually meant something. It was the not knowing that left us so raw. Not knowing why something happened, why a boyfriend left, why we missed the red flags. At some point we had to reconcile the unknown and the unknowable and accept that sometimes we'd just never know why.

A dragonfly skimmed the water's surface, drawing my attention to the pond. Algae covered the decorative rocks on the bottom. Raccoons had chewed through the black plastic lining around the edges and eaten several of my koi. The water was too shallow. I'd have to dig deeper.

"Don't open that coffee shop just yet. I'd miss you."

I stood, wiped the mud from my jeans, apologized to Toby for having to go. And as I left my shady backyard retreat and entered a portal draped in blowsy roses, I thought about what I'd have done in Toby's circumstance, how stressful it would have been to have all eyes on me, questioning my patient relationship, my diagnosis, my treatment. So much of what we all did happened in private, in session. What would it feel like to be exposed the way Toby feared?

"Shakespeare would have loved your garden," Toby said wistfully. "You captured his *Midsummer Night's Dream*."

"Minus the fairies," I said, adding, "Call me anytime."

CHAPTER 4

HUMAN CAPITAL

March 25, 2012
(117 days before the massacre)

Forgive my laughter, I have a condition.
—The Joker, *The Dark Knight* (2008)

HOLMES

Holmes found the whole "friends with benefits" arrangement and on-again, off-again partnership with Gargi somewhat confusing. When he felt conflicted about how best to spend his time—sleep, play *Skyrim*, or read—Gargi suggested he "do what he felt like doing and fuck the future for once." That was all well and good except that what he felt like doing was evil.

What do you mean by "evil?" Gargi wrote in a G-Chat that police would later seize.

Kill people of course.
You'll end up locked up. Most people are not worth it even if you go postal, what do you gain?

That's why you kill many people . . . Experience and memories all
vanish, poof. Dead.

How would that help you? Gargi wrote. What would taking a life
give you?

Human capital. He elaborated, Some people may make 1 million dollars, others 100,000. But life is priceless. You take away life and your human
capital is limitless.

I don't understand what you mean.

The value of a human being. The importance of a life makes my life
more meaningful, increasing my human capital by taking theirs.

Gargi persisted, I don't understand the concept of human capital . . .
how is it useful . . . it's not being incorporated into you . . . you are just taking away a life. That seems to be like destruction.

I don't believe there's absolute good and evil, Holmes wrote.

If you want to kill people, why don't you kill me and Ben and other
people who are around you and have wronged you?

I would be caught and could not kill more people. I would also lose
the rest of my life. That's why I won't kill until my life is nearly over.
Your meaning of life doesn't address the meaning of death. Life
came into being and ever since has been a cancer upon death.

I don't think the way you do, Gargi wrote.

Were we not dead before we were alive?

We didn't exist.

Holmes insisted life and death were the "same thing," and that
preexistence *was* still a kind of death. In what he called his probabi-
listic universe, "some outcomes were more likely than others," but
all shared "the absence of life."

When Gargi didn't respond immediately, Holmes added, I am not inherently evil. My outlook on destroying life is plan B. I also found a purpose for 'good'.

I know you are not inherently evil. But what is your purpose for good?
You sure you want to know? Not something you want to find out on your own?

I'm worried about you, Gargi told him later. Maybe you should see someone?
I am. But he would never share his thoughts about human capital with his psychiatrist.

March 27, 2012
(115 days before the massacre)

FENTON

Holmes sat stiffly, his chair angled sideways, away from the wall, as if someone had placed a dead body in my waiting area. That Holmes showed up at all was a good sign. That he showed up early was a plus and signaled his grasp of, and willingness to accept, a basic social rule of engagement. His attendance was a form of communication and satisfied one of the items on my mental checklists. Canceled appointments or late arrivals or no-shows were all information. *Was the action deliberate? Did it signal hostility? Was it meant to punish? Or was the patient's ambivalence a symptom of something else? Maybe a part of them wanted treatment, while another part of them didn't.* Holmes pushed to his feet, clean-shaven and casually dressed in his jeans and black T-shirt. *Good hygiene meant he cared not only about himself but also about others' perceptions of him.* He moved as if propelled by hydraulics, increasing and decreasing body pressure to power his legs.

"I like to depart at an orderly time," he said, "top of the hour or bottom of the hour. And I like to walk after eating."

I held the door open for him, not sure at first how to respond to this seemingly random comment. "It's good to be prompt."

As he dropped onto my plush couch draped in rich woven blankets, he reported that the medications made him "less anxious," "extremely sleepy," but "still him." I wasn't entirely sure *who* Holmes was yet—the snapshot he presented was out of focus. I needed the whole album, access to negatives and lost photos that revealed his whole story, the underlying themes, who he was before he was born. Without this backstory, I was left to interpret and fill in the blanks. Holmes seemed to suffer from a kind of emotional poverty. When I asked him how he *felt* about certain situations, his brief responses lacked any references to bodily sensation. It was as if he'd borrowed phrases from psychology textbooks and used them when it was appropriate to cry, to laugh, to fear. His face was a mask; his words, diversions. Still, he'd said the medications had *helped*; they just hadn't helped *enough*.

"Let's substitute propranolol for the Klonopin," I said, and scheduled a follow-up visit.

My next patient, Mellie, penciled stick figures on a sheet of butcher paper in the waiting area. She looked visibly agitated as Holmes bumped her elbow with the edge of his backpack.

"Watch yourself!" she said, her hooded eyes following him down the hall. She licked the tip of her index finger, smudged the sharp black line that cut through the drawing of her father's head, and rolled her eyes. "He's not like us." She folded her drawing into four tiny triangles, tucked the paper into her textbook, and pushed out of the chair. "You *get* me. You *know* I'm just a little misunderstood. You could be my BFF if I wasn't schizophrenic and you weren't my psychiatrist." Her laughter sounded like glass clinking as she skipped into my office. Mellie didn't need to give me an album. Her story was all about present sense impression. Her breezy banter, so strikingly different from Holmes' truncated speech, held a different kind of inaccessibility. Mellie could *feel* things; she just had mental blocks and distortions.

As she settled onto the couch, in her mismatched socks and half-tucked shirt, she paused, seemingly struggling to quiet the chatter in her head.

"You need to be careful, especially since you've already met *him*."

I played along. "Met who?"

Mellie scanned the room, cupped a silk-gloved hand to her mouth, and whispered, "The devil."

Did she mean Holmes? Had Mellie sensed his darkness too?

April 3, 2012
(108 days before the massacre)

I saw Holmes again a week later. "How are you feeling on the medications?"

"Fine." The word, so nondescript, typically masked unrealized pain. I thought of how many of us were "fine" and in the quiet dark reached for a bottle, or a pill, or a credit card. *Or a gun.*

"More relaxed?"

"I have memory issues."

"Sometimes that can be a good thing?" My attempt at humor actually made him crack a smile. But his face quickly snapped back into place as if it were elastic, as if he'd unwittingly slipped out of character and revealed something he wished he hadn't.

"How has your sleep been?"

"Fine." *That word again.*

"How many hours are you getting?"

"A lot."

"How much is a lot?"

He waited several seconds before answering. "Nine hours or more a day." *That was a lot.*

"How are your classes going?"

"Good." The tip of his tongue darted out, skimmed his upper lip in the exact center, and went back in. Our whole exchange was exhausting, like trying to engage a robot.

"Are you passing?"

"Yes."

"As and Bs?"

"Yes."

"Both?"

"I got a perfect score on my final." Holmes sounded strangely unimpressed by his achievement, as if he were reporting a rain shower.

"That's great." I made a mental note that he was at least attending class and still engaged. Depressed or suicidal individuals wouldn't care, might slack off, let their grades drop. "What about your labs?"

"Got an A in my systems neuroscience course." His bug-eyed gaze scanned my framed diplomas on the wall, stopping briefly on the one from Chicago Medical School, before absorbing my collection of miniature Egyptian vases and terra-cotta figurines, similar to objects Freud had had in his office. Like most psychiatrists, I refrained from displaying anything too personal. Patients understandably want to feel they are a priority; too many family photos or mementos could inadvertently cause some patients to mistrust, to feel less than, to worry their psychiatrist is too distracted. It was important for my patients to feel safe enough to have circular conversations, perseverate, *feel* whatever it was they felt but still be able to talk about it or, as in Holmes' case, say almost *nothing* for the entire session. His nonverbal cues were like the long pauses between gun blasts as I waited for him to reload.

And when he didn't say anything, I asked, "Are you still having thoughts of hurting people?"

"Yes." His eyes held every shadow in the room.

I was having trouble forming an alliance with him, the trust needed before any real work could begin. "That must be . . . frightening," I said, hoping he might find it easier to talk to me if I didn't look at him.

"Not really."

Maybe I made him self-conscious? Maybe he felt ignored? I'd never had a patient who talked so little.

His awkwardness was making *me* uncomfortable. Without context I had no way of knowing *why* he was so reluctant to have a conversation. Was it that he couldn't or wouldn't? He'd just had a romantic relationship, so he must have been able to communicate to some extent. If that was the case, what made him so silent now? It felt like deliberate withholding, maybe more to do with his lack of trust than any underlying psychological issue, but if that were the case, there would at least be more nonverbal cues, such as certain eye movements indicative of dishonesty, a bowed head or fidgety hands displaying boredom or unease, crossed arms, usually a sign of anger or being closed off, a strong handshake, a sign of confidence (or dominance), or touching the face or mouth, betraying insecurity or fear.

Holmes exhibited none of these. And my efforts to engage, redirect, and prompt him all led nowhere. I was no closer to understanding the underlying cause of who he was or what made him that way.

CHAPTER 5

AN INCONVENIENCE

April 17, 2012
(94 days before the massacre)

I'm an agent of Chaos.
—The Joker, *The Dark Knight* (2008)

FENTON

"I still want to kill people," Holmes reported two weeks later, his eyes reminding me of black holes.

"Anyone specific?" He still had no plan or targets, but the three categories of obsessive thoughts he shared, "women, men and everyone," sounded a lot like a hit list.

When he didn't elaborate, I continued. "What about suicidal thoughts?"

"*No.*" He appeared agitated, as if my question had flipped an internal switch. Then, out of nowhere, perhaps in an attempt to change the subject, he demanded, "What's *your* philosophy on the meaning of life? I've told you mine."

When had he told me his? His non sequiturs led me to suggest a change in dosage, or medication.

"What are you, just a pill pusher?"

Though this was only our third session, I'd formed some initial impressions, jotting in my notes, *psychotic level thinking, possible schizotypal personality disorder,* extremely *guarded, paranoid, hostile thoughts he won't elaborate on.* And though ours was a *very tentative therapeutic relationship,* it wasn't "unsafe"; there was *no imminent threat* even if he *didn't reveal much.*

"He hates being human." I cut into my perfectly seared rib eye as I brought up Holmes and his "problem with biology," his disdain for drippy noses and poor eyesight, and his chilling, murderous solution. Bloody juice circled my plate and soaked into my vegetables.

A group of my friends and I, all psychiatrists, met regularly for dinner at the elegant Capital Grille, in downtown Denver. At a round table under sophisticated orange lights, we all looked a little like flowers at various stages of bloom. Kat, whose husband managed the restaurant, sipped her soup quietly, the steam fogging her glasses. These get-togethers were like informal group therapy, a chance to unwind, consult with one another, recenter ourselves. So much of our work happened behind closed doors. Like priests taking confession, we were keepers of secrets; sometimes we needed validation, perspective, another opinion, and, at least until dessert arrived, assurances that we'd either handled a situation well or needed improvement.

Gayle squeezed a lime into her water glass. "Do you think he's dangerous?"

"He makes me uneasy."

Toby waved her fork in the air. "My last uneasy left my office and butchered his girlfriend."

It wasn't like that. We'd all had challenging patients, ones we dreaded so much we scheduled them as our last appointment of the day. But Holmes was different; he filled me with an unshakable dislike that bordered on hatred. I wondered about my response to him;

even my most frustrating patients with psychotic disorders had always at least evoked my sympathy. Their bizarre delusions—that aliens had hatched from eggs or impostors had replaced their family members—didn't alarm me the way Holmes' intrusive thoughts did. But even more than *what* he said was *how* he said it; there was a negative energy about him, an undercurrent of darkness that *felt* evil. And though such a notion sounded illogical, even implausible (especially for a psychiatrist, like me, grounded in science), the sensation was *there*. *Exactly as Toby had described the Butcher.* He caused the hair on my neck to prick and my skin to pebble; it was as if his very presence sucked all the air out of a room.

Even so, I was determined to find a way in, gain his trust, help him.

My friends, trying to be supportive, offered up options. *Could I transfer him? Did he need a higher level of care, an intensive outpatient program, residential treatment?* We all agreed Holmes didn't qualify for a mental health hold—he wasn't an evident danger to himself or others, gravely disabled, or suicidal. And although he had homicidal thoughts, he had yet to identify any specific target or plan. Interestingly, he didn't seem angry and, so far, hadn't revealed any history of bullying, simmering resentment, or buried hatred.

In fact, he seemed indifferent to violence, disengaged, even bored.

"Maybe Steve would take him?" Gayle said with a snort and an eye roll, knowing full well my supervisor never would. He regarded challenging patients as "teachable moments" and opportunities for growth, though I was pretty sure my colleagues who'd gone to him for help when a hostile patient knocked over a bookshelf, screamed obscenities, threatened suicide, or fiddled with a Buck knife during session found Steve's tough-love approach frustrating.

Still, his methods made us better psychiatrists and taught us never to give up, especially not when our patients seemed the most ill, most confused, most in despair. He cared so much he'd formed a Psychotherapy Scholars Program (I was one of the instructors) precisely to mentor residents who wanted to become better therapists. Only one or two residents were chosen each year to participate in the apprenticeship. Through coursework, hands-on evaluation, and role play, they learned techniques for positively engaging difficult patients and calmly averting crises.

When I served as chief resident of the outpatient clinic, I often mitigated out-of-control patients by talking to them reasonably and calmly and devising an action plan or course of treatment they could understand and embrace. After watching me cut through their patients' rage, some incredulous residents who were at their wits' end joked that I was the Mary Poppins of psychiatry.

"You had the patient talking and laughing as if the two of you were discussing what fruit to buy at the grocery store," a resident said, laughing and shaking her head in disbelief after she'd endured hours of abusive name-calling and tantrums by her patient. His erratic mood swings and delusions had derailed her and she'd dreaded continuing their sessions, fearing their fractured relationship was beyond repair.

She'd lamented that she didn't know how to talk to him, didn't know the right words, tone, speech. "I'm not like *you*. He doesn't respond to me the same way."

"If anyone can handle 'tough,' it's you." Gayle saluted me now with her glass. Then she cleared her throat and did her best impersonation of Steve: "But is it possible you dislike your patient because he reminds you of someone from your past?"

The very suggestion unnerved me, though Gayle had a point; we always considered the sources of our reactions to our patients. But Holmes reminded me of no one and was seemingly missing something vital—the "human" part of being human.

"Maybe it's the death instinct?" Gayle said, referencing a drive Freud proposed in his essay "Beyond the Pleasure Principle" to account for self-destructive behavior (such as Holmes' homicidal ideations)—an idea we'd recently discussed in our weekly intensive review of Freud's complete writings.

Kat swallowed the last of her wine and halfheartedly suggested Holmes might be a bad seed, like the murderous eight-year-old in that novel and film, whose eerie intensity repelled most children, though to adults she seemed, in every way, a model girl.

Just then, the chocolate mousse arrived and we each grabbed a spoon and dug in.

That night, I paced my bedroom fully dressed in jeans and a sleeveless pullover. My cat, George, purred on the windowsill surrounded by loose rose petals. His eyes looked like slivers of glass. Moonlight spilled through my sheer curtains. It was three o'clock in the morning and I hadn't slept yet. My head was pounding as I padded to my open window. In the milky darkness, my topiary resembled armed guards. Wind hit my cheeks, reminding me of the time I participated in a night combat drill in the Air Force, when I was stationed in the desert near San Antonio. As I crouched low behind "enemy lines," my goal was always safety, and outsmarting the "evil" Special Forces group that tracked my movements in the dark. Because they were creeping on hands and feet, their silhouettes over the ridge looked like giant spiders.

The maneuvers helped me learn to shift focus quickly, to respond suddenly to unforeseen circumstances. "Battles," my leader would bark, "are like exclamation points," and war consisted of long stretches of boredom punctuated by moments of terror. In the military, we lived by "one for all, all for one." We relied on recognizable signals, prescribed codes of conduct, and an ability to do a job regardless of whatever interpersonal differences might exist. Being effective in combat required individuals to have nothing in common beyond a shared mission and the camaraderie of belonging to a group that adhered to a set of rules and constructs. As one of the women who made up only 20 percent of the Air Force, I knew all too well what it felt like to be on the periphery of a social group. In that limited sense, I understood Holmes' disturbing retreat from the world. But unlike with individuals who returned from deployment and struggled to fit into their old life again, Holmes' codes and signals were in a language all his own.

A sudden slap of water from the pond startled me. I pulled on my rubber work boots and headed outside, down the winding dirt path toward the water's edge. Gold eyes glowed in the dark. Damn raccoons. In the half-light, I marched to my garden shed, grabbed a rope, a spade, a shovel, a measuring tape, a rake, and a level. I dumped everything into a wheelbarrow and steered it toward the pond, which I had realized I'd made too shallow; my fish were easy prey, too exposed to critters like raccoons. It was time to build a new one, deeper, with sides that extended straight down at least three feet. Dragging the rope behind me, I framed the perimeter of the pond, plunged my shovel into the sod, and dug until dawn bruised the sky, my hands stung from fatigue, and my thumb blistered.

"Most people at this point would hire a crew." My neighbor sipped coffee on his back porch, still dressed in his bathrobe.

"I prefer to work alone."

"I can see that." He saluted me with his mug. "Looks like you've been digging a mass grave."

"I promise it will look amazing in a few weeks." I leaned against the shovel and surveilled my dismal progress, already making plans to construct rafters and rig a pulley system using bungee cords, when my phone buzzed in my pocket.

A pharmacist was checking on a prescription I'd written for a James *Hughes*. James *Holmes* had picked it up.

The mistake unnerved me, chipped away at my resolve. I was usually so meticulous, but he was getting to me, getting under my skin like a slow-acting poison.

Later Holmes let me know how he felt about the slight; though the symbols in the subject line were incomprehensible, they felt like expletives.

<(o.X)>Q(o.O)Q

An inconvenience Fenton.

—Holmes

April 19, 2012

(92 days before the massacre)

HOLMES

Having decided he wanted a more "committed" relationship, he finally broke it off with Gargi in favor of Hillary. "It's Jimmy James
from neuro, want to hang out?" He found her "sexy shorts distracting" and invited her on a hike. He picked a trail in Golden Gate Canyon State Park, a steep path that led to panoramic views of Mount
Evans. Not that he was interested in that kind of scenery. He brought
snacks—cubes of cheddar cheese, pepperoni medallions, black pep-
per water crackers, and blue Gatorade.

Hillary towered over Holmes with her long model-like legs, soft,
puffy cheeks, and eyes like coal dust. Wildflowers skimmed the cuffs
of her high-top hiking boots. They trekked mostly in silence along
the steep rocky path. Wisps of clouds streaked the sky. The air was
hot and sticky. Hillary's face glistened with sweat. "It's warm out
here." She gathered her glossy red hair into a ponytail. And though
they walked side by side, Holmes texted her, "Pfft, as if you could
get any hotter." His eyes traveled the curve of her body, her neck, her
back, her ass. He noticed tiny blemishes, a spray of freckles on her
cheek, an old scar on her bare left shoulder, her heavy breathing.
When she caught him staring at her, she cracked a half smile and
said, "Last week, I had an attempted break-in. I thought at first the
thugs might have slashed a screen door, but then I found broken
glass underneath a window."

Holmes envisioned faceless shadowy creatures wielding shiny

machetes and his heart rate quickened. This felt different from his childhood "frozen situations" where pairs of saws glinted in the murky dark, waiting to cut him up. What if the thugs came after him next? He lived only blocks away from Hillary.

"I worry they might try again." She crunched on salted apple chips.

He should protect himself . . . before they robbed him, beat him up.

After the hike, he walked home to his Paris Street apartment, all the while seeing "the thugs" lurking beneath every bald streetlamp swallowed by plumes of cigarette smoke. Once home, he dead-bolted his front door, latched the windows, checked the screens for holes in the mesh. A cockroach darted onto the sill, flicking its antennae. He pinched it between his fingers and flushed it down the toilet.

"We should study for prelims together," Hillary texted.

"Sure." But he had more pressing goals, and passing his exams wasn't one of them.

Late into the night, he went on Amazon and researched Tasers, mini stun guns with rechargeable LED flashlights, heavy-duty aluminum Viperteks, micro stun guns disguised as flashlights, mini jogger sting rings, and Reax ten-million-volt micro USB key chain stun guns, and settled on a Taser disguised as a cell phone. Next, he purchased a large combat-style Smith & Wesson folding knife. Just in case "the thugs" overpowered him. He came across the website Rationalinsanity.com, which warned of the perils of "Mad Logic"— Khrushchev, Kennedy, and Castro had all been "rational" leaders, and yet all had nearly decimated their followers, who had lived so dangerously unaware.

Fleetingly he thought of Hillary, how he should protect *her*, keep *her* safe . . . from *him*. So, when she invited him to go on another hike, he thought it best to end their relationship; he didn't want her "to be the girlfriend of a murderer."

In anticipation of being single again, he created a profile on Match.com and reinvented himself as "Classic Jim." He uploaded stock photos of porn stars licking a shoulder and added the teaser: "Will you visit me in prison?"

In his "Self-Summary" he wrote,

Look Down. Look Up. Learning is really great knowledge is power as the famous Sir Bacon said. Prefer listening to yuh, talking not so much. So, if you need an ear, I am here. The first things people usually notice about me are my soul penetrating eyes. I'm looking to meet people outside my social circle.

At "five-eleven, with hazel eyes, and dark brown hair," he lied that he "enjoyed basketball, bowling, cycling, football, running, skiing soccer, tennis and racquet sports, walking and hiking and weightlifting." Under "social interests" he checked camping, dining out, hobbies and crafts, movies/videos, museums and art, music and concerts, exploring new areas, playing cards, video games, and watching sports.

At two o'clock in the morning, he stepped out of the shower, his hands and feet pruned and pink, with the sheen of soap still clinging to his elbows and knees. He wrapped a towel around his waist and padded barefoot to the glowing computer screen to check his prospects. Nothing. He pulled on his boxers and checked again. Nothing. Twenty minutes passed. Still nothing.

Focus. Focus. Focus.

April 20, 2012
[91 days before the massacre]

FENTON

I needed a way in. Holmes challenged me to think about the reasons I'd pursued psychiatry at all, it being my *second* residency, when most doctors were relieved to have completed just *one*. I didn't go into the field as a way to understand myself (though that was probably a perk) but because I realized that, as clichéd as it may sound, mental health was in many ways more important than physical health to our quality of life and ability to function. Psychotherapy had certainly helped *me*. Most patients came to me somewhere in the middle of their epic story; their beginning was foggy, their end undetermined. My job was to understand where they were in that moment, not to endorse their perceptions, not to change them, but to help them help themselves feel better. Yes, sometimes their symptoms needed to be treated before we could do the work, but after that most had enough mental clarity (and courage) to look in the mirror I held up for them and *see* their true selves staring back.

But with Holmes it seemed he looked in the mirror and the mirror was blank.

"Does he play video games?" a young resident asked me one morning over coffee. "Maybe that's a way for you to relate to him in a language he can understand."

He tried to bring me up to speed on the complicated *World of Warcraft* role-playing game, which invited players to customize their own avatars.

"Players go on quests. Their objective is to kill," the resident said. He described how players could choose from ten "race characters" and nine "character classes," each empowered with certain assigned bonuses and value points. Each creature had "racial abilities" that set them apart in their magical universe. Monsters, though considered "savage species," were desirable because each "kill" increased an avatar's value.

A patient's avatar could reveal something important about him. If he identified with a "Demon Hunter," he might be looking to have what he lacked in the real world, an "uncanny sense of awareness." If he related to the "Monk," he might want to be expert at something—for example, "bare-handed combat." If a patient had been bullied, he might choose to *be* the bully in the virtual world and select as his avatar a "Death Knight," who wielded icy rune blades and infected his foes with crippling diseases. A Necromancer killed indiscriminately; there were no "saves," no "resurrections," no second chances. A shy, reserved patient who chose a dangerous nonconformist like the Warlock might be masking deep-rooted aggression beneath his impenetrable mental armor.

The resident shared how his patient, a socially awkward, mercilessly bullied biophysics graduate student, had aligned with a "Hunter," from a Prestige class of "Assassins, Bone Crushers, Dead Shots and Death Knights." He'd identified most with "Gunman," a character who he said did "cool stuff with firearms." The patient explained how, the more he progressed in the game, the more "aggressive" his characters became, and with that newfound hostility, the patient said he felt compelled to "say the vilest things" as he "killed," like "racist comments, religious insults." In the patient's fantasy video game world, he could reveal aspects of himself without getting too personal. He could be the person he *wanted* to be: superior, fearless, valid, with "God-like" control in a world with definite rules and logical simplicity. With a simple click, he could change weapons, speed, strength, monsters. And if he wanted, he could turn shooting competitions into massacres, "me against them," and win.

"Do *you* have a favorite avatar?" I tried this out on Holmes during our next session.

"*World of Warcraft* isn't my thing." He shrugged. "I prefer *Diablo III*. There are no avatars."

"What do you like about that game?"

"Killing people."

I looked it up later. *Diablo III* had a feature that allowed participants to choose a first-person shooter.

Whether simulated carnage led to actual violence had been the topic of heated debate as early as 1976, with the release of a coin-operated arcade game called *Death Race*, which gave points to players for running down pedestrians. So-called video nasties were also front-row center in the James Bulger case of 1993, at the dawn of VHS; the toddler's ten-year-old killers watched slasher films like *Child's Play 3* in the comfort of a living room, which, prosecutors argued, inspired the boys to kidnap Bulger from a shopping mall, torture him near a railway line (because the toddler loved trains), blind him with modeling paint, and beat him more than forty-two times with an iron bar just to see what would happen. The question of whether the film's fake violence instilled a desire to commit real violence was never resolved. In any event the boys were convicted of premeditated first-degree murder.

But one thing was certain; many video games *rewarded* violence, with players earning extra points for brutality. Most players surveyed apparently found it "thrilling" to be able to commit unspeakable crimes without any real-life consequences. Just as Holmes had, the Columbine killers immersed themselves in first-person-shooter games like *Postal* (coined for "going postal"), where players were invited to "spray protesters, mow down marching bands, charbroil whole towns," and "pick off" police and other "hostiles" while their screaming victims bled out on the sidewalk. *Doom*, their favorite game, featured a "space marine" who battled demonic "undead marines." The pair had invested more than a hundred hours in creating fictional landscapes where they could "play God." They wrote about their creative endeavors in English essays, insisting the game was just an "intellectual" outlet.

But did the games make the kids violent, or were the kids violent already and simply attracted to violent games? In 2011, the American Psychological Association, after conducting an exhaustive review of the subject, concluded that video games *did* increase aggressive behavior, that players were not just spectators but actors in the process of creating violence. Academicians, however, quickly found flaws in the research and said after three hours of *Call of Duty* or *Manhunt* a player might feel "pumped" but certainly not up for murder.

In another study, researchers at the University of York found no evidence that video games made players more violent. In a series of experiments using three thousand adult participants, the research team found no correlation. The experiments tested players' reactions to two combat games—one used "ragdoll physics" to replicate realistic character behavior and movement and the other did not. Players were asked afterward to complete word puzzles, with the expectation being that those who had played the more realistic version would produce more violent word associations to the questions. But there was no marked difference.

In a 2011 Supreme Court decision that sought to ban the sale and rental of violent video games to minors,[3] Justice Samuel Alito described, in obvious disgust, the graphic gore depicted in most:

> *Victims are killed with every imaginable implement, including machine guns, clubs, hammers, and chainsaws, among others. Victims are dismembered, decapitated, disemboweled, set on fire, and chopped into little pieces. They cry out in agony and beg for mercy. Blood gushes, splatters, and pools. Severed body parts and gobs of human remains are graphically shown.*
>
> *. . . There are games in which a player can re-enact the killings at Columbine High School and Virginia Tech. The goal of one game is to rape a mother and her daughter; there is an ethnic cleansing game in which players can choose to gun down African-Americans, Latinos or Jews.*

And yet, the Court concluded there was no hard evidence that such games led to mass murder or grisly killings. The late Justice

---

3   *Brown v. Entertainment Merchants Association* 564 US 786 (2011).

Antonin Scalia, writing for the majority, "scoffed at the notion that violent video games caused real-world violence," criticizing the research studies as relying on "flawed methodology":

> *They show at best some correlation between exposure to violent entertainment and minuscule real-world effects, such as children feeling more aggressive or making louder noises in the few minutes after playing a violent game than after playing a nonviolent game.*

In his article "Do Violent Video Games Lead to Violence?" former deputy editor of the *New York Times* editorial board Phil Boffey stressed that violent video game exposure was only one of many risk factors for aggressive behavior and violence. Others included "racism, ethnic hatred, certain psychiatric disorders, adverse social environments, and easy access to guns and other lethal weapons, which may be the most critical factor of all."

May 1, 2012
(81 days before the massacre)

"You locked me out of your office." Holmes' flat voice held a hint of surprise.

It had been completely inadvertent, though I could see how he might have taken this personally, following my prescription mix-up. Generally, I kept the door to the waiting room closed but not locked when I was expecting patients. "Shall we get started?"

He surveyed the piles of papers on my desk, the worn, coffee-stained textbooks marked up with yellow highlights, and fixated on a large box (containing a pair of UGGs) wedged behind my chair. Later, I would learn that he suspected the package concealed a bomb or a Taser. Eager to focus him, I held up a printout of his email and began to explain my error with the name—James Hughes was an author on a blog I'd read earlier, *blah blah blah*. Tense silence stretched between us, prompting me to finally ask the unsettling question that felt a little like poking a tiger with a stick: "What do these symbols in the subject line mean?"

He clenched his left hand and pumped it in the air. "The *Q*s are fists. I'm punching you in the eye." My head throbbed with fresh awareness—I had never felt in danger from a patient before. My simple mistake with his last name had evoked such a strong reaction in him that his first impulse had been aggression. I felt a little sick inside, the way I had in college when I was held at gunpoint during the robbery of a Capezio dance store. Tied up with silk toe-shoe ribbons, hyperaware of the cool floor tiles against my face and the sounds of muffled sobs nearby, I'd willed myself not to flinch at the shotgun jammed at my temple, or the sour smell of sweat, or the loud voice in my ear: *Scream and I'll blow your fucking head off.*

"Violence, isn't that what you want to hear?" A vein in his throat pulsed, betraying some distress. "It was dumb."

What was dumb? The threat itself, or the confession, which might lead to repercussions?

"Are you going to lock me up now?" He sounded strangely contrite. *Did he think he was dangerous? Was he now a danger to me? Or had he simply defused his threat as an impulsive overreaction to a perceived insult? Poor behavior control, like a baby viper that hadn't yet learned to regulate its venom?*

The fact that he'd loosely recanted, even vaguely apologized, for his outburst, indicated he at least had some awareness of his social impropriety—wanting to punch his psychiatrist in the eye because he'd been inconvenienced *was* "dumb," and this concession, however slight, gave me some hope that he was not without remorse. Still, if I could just learn the *source* of his hostility, I could better determine if he was *truly* dangerous.

"Tell me about Gargi." I pivoted to his girlfriend because losing a loved one could be a profoundly lonely experience, leading to stored grief, even rage. Some patients experienced *flooding*, meaning they couldn't speak, their nervous systems so overwhelmed by hurt or anger that they either lashed out at me or shut down.

"She's going through the five stages of grief." His focus on *her* feelings for *him* revealed a profound lack of emotional depth, a sense that all he knew about feelings was what he'd read. Never mind that there really were no "stages" of grief because everyone's experience was unique; there *were* common responses to loss—such as reduced concentration, numbness, disrupted sleep, and changes in eating habits—that could be helpful in treating grieving patients.

It seemed Holmes had no ability to differentiate emotions—anger had the same response as fear or sadness.

"And what about *you*?" I asked.

"I don't see the glass; I see beyond the glass."

His non sequitur was unsettling, as if he were engaged in an entirely different conversation. His sophomoric pronouncements reminded me of when as a teenager I enrolled in an advanced English literature class and had to write an essay on the concept of carnal knowledge. I'd had no idea what the act entailed emotionally, but I knew the literal meaning of the phrase and pontificated nonetheless, believing my words sounded impressive and philosophical when actually they conveyed the opposite.

Holmes must have had a sense of how different he was, how apart and not part of the human race he was. Surface relationships allowed him to dissociate, be physically present but not present at all. Did that make him angry? If nobody knew who he really was, did that make him feel safe or just increasingly lonely?

"I'm pursuing other options." He shrugged.

"Other relationships?"

"Yes."

I explained that loss could trigger intense feelings of abandonment, causing some people to engage in destructive behavior in order to avoid the devastating pain; others re-created the abandonment because it felt familiar, repeating a cycle of "breakups and make-ups" with the same partner, or replacing them too quickly once the relationship finally ended, ignoring red flags. What would he miss most about Gargi: knowing and being known by her? Having a witness to his life? Who had he been when he was with her, and who had he become as a result? Did he ruminate over their memories, the so-called good times, idealizing the relationship, kicking it into the fantasy realm? Did Gargi represent validation for him as a human being?

He responded with another odd phrase. "The thorn in my side was worth the rose." If he had any grief, it was well disguised, unlike Cho, the Virginia Tech shooter, who, angry at having been rebuffed by women, invented a supermodel girlfriend who was totally different from the women he'd stalked who had "vandalized his heart" and "raped his soul." *But Holmes had been adamant: he didn't have relationships with people; they had relationships with him.* What did that look like? Did he learn the social cues? Was he able to mimic empathy? And how long did it take these women to realize that no matter what they did to engage or *change* him, it was never going to be enough?

I shifted to asking him about school. Coming up were his prelims, exams most students found stressful, because if they failed, the effect on their careers could be life altering.

"My lab experiment isn't work." Again the blank stare. "I have to make up some bullshit."

Suppressing my shock at his irreverence, his seemingly cavalier attitude toward his critical exams, I asked whether he had approached any particular professors who might have been willing to work with him.

Two had already told him he wasn't a good fit. Holmes' features relaxed, his skin loosening like a latex mask that had slightly slipped. Then, unexpectedly, he leaned forward, studying me closely. "You do certain things—crinkle your nose, which means dislike. You have an unconscious and that makes you do things."

No doubt he was referring to my locked office door, suggesting that I had shut him out because subconsciously I disliked him, but I assured him that wasn't the case, that I crinkled my nose because I had an expressive face, nothing more. I tried to refocus him on his reasons for coming to see me, his intrusive thoughts about killing.

"*You* see the problem in a utilitarian way." He sounded defensive. "You'd want to eliminate that. You'd have to see it that way."

"Would you be open to having another psychiatrist consult during our sessions?" I thought he might feel more comfortable with a male; I didn't want to be an obstacle to his ability to communicate.

"Why, so you can lock me up?"

"Not at all." But I wasn't so sure. "I just think it might be good for you to speak to another expert, see if he has any suggestions."

"*You're* in charge of student mental health," Steve said when I approached him, giving me that look that said, *What do you need me for?* Secretly, I hoped Steve would just take Holmes off my hands; it wasn't that I couldn't handle him. It was that I didn't *want* to—and I worried Holmes' hostility toward me might actually impede his treatment.

Ever since Holmes' threatening/nonthreatening email, I'd been uneasy, slept poorly, forgotten my cell phone at home and my credit card at the diner, failed to show up for a dentist appointment. It was so unlike me. I was usually so organized, prompt, meticulous. I remembered things without having to write them down, especially dates and plans. But something alarming was happening to me. My mind traveled back a few months to the black-tie gala my department chair had asked me to attend to commemorate the opening of the new emergency psychiatric unit at the university's hospital. *Gayle could use the support,* he'd said, though at the time I couldn't imagine a scenario in which Gayle would have ever needed help, least of all mine. A former champion powerlifter, she could intimidate colleagues and patients alike just by wearing a dress and flashing her muscular calves.

That night, she met me at the entrance to the party, her flowing black midi fluttering in the wind like a flag, like a distress signal, as we hooked elbows with each other. "You look stunning," I said, "a dead ringer for January Jones," the beautiful actress from *Mad Men*. She smiled, relieved, as we entered the gigantic tent and encountered a mix of strangers and half-remembered faces. Dionne Warwick crooned on the stage, occasionally yelling obscenities into the crowd.

Gayle nudged me toward the stage. "You should dance," she said with a smile, acknowledging my years with a modern ballet company and my offer to tour with a European dance company following graduation from medical school. (I was tempted, but it wasn't practical—I knew it would have been challenging to return to medicine after taking such a break, and besides, I owed the Air Force time.) Interestingly, the rigors of medicine didn't make dance any less important in my life; it actually made it *more* necessary.

Just then, Steve headed our way and introduced us to his girlfriend, Marilyn, a doll-like waif dressed in an ivory sheath with simple pearls wrapped around her throat. The actress/life coach leaned into him, looking a little like cracked porcelain, and said she'd heard so much about me. Steve kissed her on the head, told us what a help she'd been to him, and reminded us again that he was writing a book.

"She's probably helping him by *reading* it," Gayle later joked, rolling her eyes, and reminded me that he'd once called her "histrionic," warning her to "watch for erotic transference" because he was, after all, a "narcissist."

"But *you* he loved."

"Respected," I corrected her.

She shook her head. "It was more than that. You were the only protégé who didn't disappoint."

Whether that was true or not, Steve and I *did* have a special bond; maybe subconsciously I reminded him of the daughter he had never had but always wanted?

CHAPTER 6

TEACHABLE MOMENTS

May 10–28, 2012
(71–53 days before the massacre)

Whatever doesn't kill you simply makes you stranger.
—The Joker, *The Dark Knight* (2008)

HOLMES

While his classmates prepared for their critical preliminary exams, Holmes ordered a Glock 34 9-millimeter handgun from a Wisconsin company that sold firearms through more than one hundred websites. Next, he purchased two grenade-style canisters of Clear Out tear gas and a high-end gas mask with a special air filter. When the pistol failed to arrive, he went to a local sporting goods store and purchased a Glock 22 .40-caliber handgun with hollow-point Saber cartridges. At the checkout counter, he gave his name, credit card, and email address (dsherlockb@gmail.com) so he could "receive future discounts." The cashier smiled, handed him his gun, and snipped off the price tag.

With his weapons safely tucked away in his apartment, he asked

Professor Achim Klug of the Department of Physiology and Biophysics to be his thesis mentor. Klug had serious reservations based on Holmes' past lab performances. Reportedly, Holmes had appeared disinterested or distracted and, according to several peers, had difficulty performing basic requisite steps to do the experiments, sometimes walking out before the lab experiment was completed. More troubling, Holmes had presented data that was twenty years old rather than current results. Overall, his presentations were dismal and awkward and contained ill-timed jokes and cartoons that fell flat. Nonplussed by Klug's rejection, Holmes asked Professor Curt Freed, chairman of the Department of Clinical Pharmacology and Toxicology, to be his mentor. Freed agreed, thinking, "James had made some progress though not the progress he should have." He hoped Dr. Sukumar ("Suke") Vijayaraghavan, who had been assigned to supervise Holmes' labs, had successfully eliminated his "idiosyncrasies."

Freed hoped he'd study hard, but Holmes had other plans. He bought his second firearm, a Remington 870 12-gauge tactical shotgun, at a local Bass Pro Shop. Though the weapon was commonly used to hunt ducks, quail, and other game birds, the version he bought held a few more shells and looked slightly different. With his new guns on either side of him, he played hours and hours of *Diablo III*; his character, Necromancer, excelled at blowing up corpses with the touch of a button. The game allowed him to reset and blow them up again and again, ad infinitum, until there were no more hordes of monsters. There was also loot to accrue—swords, capes, shoes, sundries, pants—which conveyed status. Everything had numbers attached, and the more kills, the higher the number. *Up. Up. Up.* When Freed asked him what he had been doing to prepare during his weeks of "open time," Holmes replied, "Nothing. And everything. And there is nothing to stop me from doing that all the time."

As Holmes battled "The Lord of Terror," he researched effective real-life killing methods. He was fascinated by the Tylenol murders (for which no suspect was ever arrested), particularly the fact that psychologists found the killer "so strange" that their "normal guidelines just didn't work." The capsules, which had been laced with toxic levels of potassium cyanide, came from different production plants and were sold in different drugstores around the Chicago area. The resulting deaths set off a nationwide panic and inspired hundreds of copycat incidents. Pills were tainted with everything from rat poison to hydrochloric acid. Holmes read up on the dead, including a twelve-year-old girl. He particularly liked how the killer never came face-to-face with his victims. Though Holmes appreciated the "randomness" of the Tylenol murders, he wasn't sure how he felt about a child being murdered—or that the name of the killer was never known.

Holmes' growing fascination with bomb making led him to study the Unabomber, Theodore J. Kaczynski, a "shadowy villain" and former math professor with a genius-level IQ who managed to outwit the law for more than a decade in what newspapers described as a "campaign of terror." Beginning in 1978, Kaczynski mailed and hand-delivered sixteen homemade explosives to universities, businesses, homes, and public areas across the United States, killing three people and injuring nearly two dozen more. In 1979, a bomb exploded at Northwestern University and aboard an American Airlines flight; in 1980, another of his bombs badly injured the president of United Airlines. His victims could not anticipate, could not prepare for—could not *imagine*—their own deaths.

Despite Kaczynski's success, Holmes ruled out bombs as too difficult to regulate; there was always a chance they would not detonate. Biological warfare required extensive knowledge of chemicals, something he didn't have time to master. Serial murder was also impractical, too personal, too messy, leaving behind a trail of evidence. The killer, Holmes journaled, was too "easily caught after few kills." He settled on mass murder with firearms because it promised "maximum casualties."

May 29, 2012
(52 days before the massacre)

FENTON

At lunch one day a colleague from Student Mental Health engaged other residents and myself in a provocative debate concerning the link, if any, between mental illness and violence and, more specifically, school shooters. Were there common denominators like rage, bullying, or some other underlying mental health issue that could help us predict (and thereby prevent) future violence? Some residents protested, *But wasn't it true that only 3 percent of the mentally ill ever contributed to violent crime? Weren't they in fact more likely to be victims than perpetrators?* The colleague agreed, adding that statistically mass murderers committed only 1 percent of all killings in the United States and these consisted mostly of fired employees who went on workplace rampages or estranged spouses who shot their partners, divorce lawyers, or psychiatrists. Killers like these typically weren't involved in the mental health care system at all. They'd simply had an explosive reaction to an unbearable humiliation.

Columbia University professor Dr. Michael Stone, a clinical and forensic psychiatrist,[4] was a leading expert on mass murder. Inspired by the structure of Dante's circles of Hell, he created his own "gradations of evil" scale, in which he categorized homicide into twenty-two distinct types. He broke these down even further into three tiers of killers: impulsive (inspired by rage or jealousy), possibly psychopathic (clinically delusional), and profoundly psychopathic (those, like Ted Bundy, who possessed superficial charm, glib speech, and grandiosity and were without remorse).

---

4   An expert who provides testimony on the mental state of accused murderers (when a declaration of insanity can mean the difference between life and death).

According to Stone's research, only 20 percent of murderers (of which school shooters made up 6.6 percent) had ever been diagnosed with a psychiatric illness; the other 80 percent suffered from stress, anger, jealousy, and unhappiness. Still, it *was* striking that though the United States had only 5 percent of the world's population and 30 percent of the world's mass shootings, it did *not* also have 30 percent of the world's mental illnesses.

"Just racism, sexism, hatred, and white supremacy," I whispered under my breath, "none of which were diagnosable mental illnesses."

Dr. Stone categorized mass shooters as a "psychologically strange group" of killers without conscience, plagued with personality abnormalities, like narcissistic or antisocial personality disorder,[5] not symptom disorders like depression or psychotic illnesses like schizophrenia. As a result, these killers rarely if ever sought therapy unless court ordered or forced by family, because they lacked empathy, remorse, or even an awareness that they needed help at all.

Still, they did share certain identifiable characteristics: rage, generalized hatred, bullying, a sense of entitlement, immaturity, and, consistent with those diagnosed with antisocial personality disorder, a history of juvenile delinquency *before* the age of fifteen.

Dylan Klebold's mother, Sue, haunted by her son's involvement, asked psychologist Dr. Peter Langman, author of *Why Kids Kill: Inside the Minds of School Shooters*, what had happened to her son. *Was he psychotic? Was he a psychopath? Was there something else going on? What did she miss?* It was the question on all of our minds, and Dr. Langman's answer was chilling—he didn't know, but he was sure Dylan was dangerous:

> *Considering all the activities Eric and Dylan were involved in with their friends, including soccer, paint-ball, bowling, Dungeons and*

---

5 Sometimes interchanged with the term "psychopath."

Dragons, fantasy baseball, video games, making movies, smoking pot, drinking, raising a ruckus at the pizza shop, and more, it is clear that these were not two isolated boys. They had jobs, they helped out at school, and they had multiple peer groups that included numerous boys and girls. The idea that they were lost and alone simply isn't true. This, however, simply makes the attack harder to comprehend.

Of the many children Dr. Langman had studied, he found most fell into three categories: traumatized, psychopathic, and psychotic.

Eric Houston, for instance, the twenty-year-old who shot fourteen people and killed four, had been traumatized by a family "plagued by incest, alcoholism, and physical abuse." His first victim was a teacher who had molested him. And it seemed killing brought him some relief: "If I die today," he wrote in a note that day, "please bury me somewhere beautiful."

Eric Harris was the quintessential psychopath, writing in his yearbook, "It's been confirmed . . . the human race isn't worth fighting for only worth killing."

Dylan Klebold was psychotic; in fact, Dr. Langman considered him the "saddest shooter," devoting an entire chapter to him in his book. Days before Columbine, Dylan attended prom with a pretty girl, had friends, had a social life, liked to bowl, had plans to go to college. But in his journal, he revealed a darker person, "lost in fantasies, confused, lonely, dependent, self-deprecating and yet elevating himself to Godhood." Dr. Langman believed Dylan suffered from schizotypal personality disorder, where the person "withdraws into a world where reality and fantasy are not always distinguishable." Sue Klebold wrote in her book, *A Mother's Reckoning: Living in the Aftermath of Tragedy,* "these are not full-on delusions, but a fuzziness in the boundary between what is real and what is not."

Dylan made himself in Harris' image, "willing to do anything, even kill people—to win Harris' approval," Dr. Langman wrote, and yet, Sue was convinced Dr. Langman regarded Dylan as a "human being not an evil monster," just a slave to one, and assured her "nothing she did or did not do caused Dylan to do what he did." By the end of his life, Dr. Langman opined, Dylan's psychological functioning had deteriorated to the point that he was not in his right mind.

Bullying was a factor that propelled sixteen-year-old mass shooter Jeffrey Weise to murder nine people (five of them students at Minnesota Red Lake High School) and himself, though inexplicably, it seemed he shot at those students who had offered him friendship. A member of the Ojibwe tribe, raised on the Red Lake Indian Reservation, Weise had styled himself a "Native Nazi," an "Angel of Death," and after watching the film *Elephant*, about a Columbine-style school massacre, he thought it would be "cool" if he, too, shot up his school. Like the Columbine killers, Weise "admired Hitler" and cultivated a dangerous-looking persona, dressing in trench coats and sculpting his hair into devil horns—and generally, according to one survivor, "trying to be evil."

As with each of the mass shooters we discussed, there were warning signs that were either minimized or ignored—weeks before the shooting, Weise created two flash animations called "Target Practice" and "Clown" and posted both on the Internet. The first depicted a character shooting four people and blowing up a police car before committing suicide; the second showed a clown strangling someone. On his profile page, Weise described himself as "16 years of accumulated rage suppressed by nothing more than brief glimpses of hope, which have all but faded to black."

Rage and bullying were also contributing factors in the Thurston High School massacre, which took place one year before Columbine. Fifteen-year-old Kip Kinkel, the son of two doting teachers, parents whom Kinkel acknowledged were "good people," had repeated the first grade because he seemed socially immature, given to tantrums and violent behaviors. His early fascination with firearms and explosives troubled his parents, but they nonetheless indulged him, hoping to connect with him on common ground—they bought him BB guns, which Kip fashioned to resemble rifles.

And on his twelfth birthday, his father gave him the 20-gauge sawed-off shotgun and lever-action rifle he'd owned as a boy and included a new .22-caliber Ruger pistol and thousands of rounds of ammunition. According to the couple's friends, he was trying to be "supportive" and show an interest in his son's "hobbies."

But in addition to amassing an arsenal, Kip also learned to build bombs, even writing about the experience in a school essay (which, sadly, no one reported). Later he confessed to the psychologist his mother forced him to see that he "felt less angry" after detonating bombs. He'd endured relentless bullying by classmates who frequently slammed his head into the school's water fountain. Wanting to learn self-defense, Kip enrolled in martial arts and, encouraged by his father, joined his school's football team, but when he was relegated to the inferior position of "line-man" he journaled, *I sit here all alone. I am always alone. I don't know who I am.* Then: *No one ever makes fun of me, mainly because they think I'm a psycho.*

By the end of his freshman year, there had been at least four school shootings, including one in Jonesboro, Arkansas, where the killers were just eleven and thirteen. Kip studied them as if they were a playbook, analyzing what worked and didn't work, incredulous that the killers had not killed themselves. In his journal he recorded random thoughts: *I plan to live in a big black hole, my firearms will be the only thing to fight my isolation.*

Meanwhile, his father continued to indulge Kip's interest, buying him a .22 rifle and a 9-millimeter Glock pistol for his fifteenth birthday. Kip practiced shooting using squirrels as targets. But when he was nearly expelled for bringing a (stolen) Beretta 90 .32-caliber pistol to school, his distraught father threatened him with military school. In response, Kip executed his parents. The next morning, he played loud opera music (from his favorite film, *Romeo and Juliet*) in the house, taped two bullets to his chest, donned a trench coat, left behind some homemade bombs, and drove to his school; he entered the cafeteria and fired forty-eight shots from a semiautomatic rifle, striking twenty-four students, killing two.

Later, he would tell police he *"had* to kill his parents" because he "loved them" and he had "no choice." As he prepared for trial he claimed "voices" commanded him to kill, voices he'd heard on and off for years but had never disclosed to anyone, not even his psychiatrist. His trial lawyers argued Kip was insane, his "head didn't work right," he "had to kill people," and "he didn't know why." His court-appointed psychiatrists found Kip's delusions "bizarre" and thought he might have schizoaffective disorder or paranoid schizophrenia.

But in September 1999, five months following the Columbine massacre, Kip dropped his insanity defense and pled guilty to four counts of first-degree murder and twenty-six counts of attempted murder and was sentenced to 111 years in prison with no possibility of parole.

As lunch ended, the residents summarized the tenuous, nearly nonexistent link between mass shootings and mental health, highlighting instead the more disturbing apparent factors—Kip's parents *knew* their child was troubled, had anger issues, was bullied. And though his mother had intervened and sought help for Kip from a psychologist who treated him for depression, she could not stop him, could not have known he spent hours in his room studying bomb making or obsessing over other school shootings. She only knew what Kip shared, confiding in a friend her mistaken hope that Kip "had turned a corner."

Would Kip or any of the others have made different choices, I wondered, *had they lacked accessibility to guns?*

May 31, 2012
(50 days before the massacre)

FENTON/STEVE

At Holmes' next session, I introduced Steve as an "expert consultant." Smiling, Steve apologized that he couldn't shake hands; he'd sprained his wrist playing table tennis. We had no idea Steve's injury would evoke all kinds of suspicion in Holmes, including that he'd faked it to test Holmes' empathy and that his sling concealed a knife. Once everyone had settled in, Steve began asking about Gargi, concerned Holmes might have some lingering depression. Unresolved grief could manifest as repressed anger.

"I'm not depressed." Holmes' hard stare reminded me of Alex, the antisocial delinquent from Anthony Burgess' novel *A Clockwork Orange*. "I just hate sheeple and shepherds."

"'Sheeple'?"

"Followers."

"I see." Steve cleared his throat. "Do you want to hurt these sheeple?"

"Not just them."

When Holmes didn't elaborate, Steve asked him if he liked to read, offering that some people who had thoughts of inflicting harm on others borrowed their ideas from books. The strange case of Armin Meiwes came to mind; at the age of twelve he was obsessed with "Hansel and Gretel" (particularly the part where the witch fattened up Hansel so she could eat him); later, the serial killer Vampire of Hanover had actually inspired him to *become* a cannibal.

"Nietzsche." Holmes shrugged.

It was a revealing choice considering the philosopher's nihilistic view of life as "one indistinguishable swirl of becoming" and his notion of *Übermensch*, a superman who would exist above society's rules and norms.

"Is that how *you* feel?" After receiving no response, Steve asked him about his childhood and the family dynamics. Holmes said his mother was "overly altruistic," his father "not a very affectionate statistician," and his sister simply a "rival." With such an unremarkable past, we still had little insight into his intrusive homicidal thoughts. "What about bullying?" Steve asked, knowing that feelings of inferiority or profound humiliation could inspire rage and, ultimately, revenge.

I thought of Barry Loukaitis, the fourteen-year-old whose classmates repeatedly called him "faggot" and spit on him until one day in 1996 he brought a rifle and a semiautomatic pistol to school and killed his algebra teacher and two students. And Charles "Andy" Williams, the fifteen-year-old who, in 2001, opened fire in his school, killing two students and wounding thirteen others after "friends" doused his pants with lighter fluid and set him on fire, and his teacher repeatedly humiliated him in class for being "lazy" and unprepared. One day he made an idle threat to kill his teacher. His friends, believing he was too weak to carry it out, mocked him, calling him a "wannabe." The shooting lasted six minutes; he didn't kill his teacher. Instead, he shot two classmates.

And finally, there was the case of George Hennard, whose transient childhood led to feelings of abandonment and inferiority; he spent his teen years sullen and angry, mostly at women who ridiculed, humiliated, and emasculated him. As an adult he drifted from job to job, growing increasingly lonely, unable to connect with people, especially women, who said he had the "Devil in his eyes." One day in 1991 he drove to a diner, executed twenty-three (mostly women), and injured nearly a dozen more. As he fired, he shouted, "All women are vipers. This is what you've done to me and my family. This is payback day."

Holmes denied ever being bullied, though later I would learn he'd endured relentless name-calling when he worked temporarily at MeriCal, Inc., a dietary supplement factory where he operated a pill-coating machine prior to graduate school. Coworkers described him as "fragile and child-like" and thought he might be autistic; they reported seeing him in a corner, "giggling" at nothing in particular, and started calling him "the Giggler."

After a while, Steve asked if Holmes had any questions for him. Holmes leaned forward with an intense stare so unlike the blank, vacant look he'd typically given me. "Why did you become a psychiatrist?" Was he truly curious, or just appealing to Steve's ego, or was he somehow mocking the patient/doctor relationship with the role reversal? Holmes hadn't seemed at all interested in people, much less his psychiatrists, and what difference did Steve's reasons for choosing his profession make—unless Holmes planned to exploit the information the way a predator homed in on his prey's weakness, as if he, in the words of the psychopathic killer William Bradfield, "could smell insecurity . . . the way a pig smelled truffles." But Steve was too experienced to be fooled by Holmes' flattery, and instead answered coolly that he liked to help people but found "one-sided conversations challenging."

When predictably Holmes didn't comment, Steve pivoted and asked about his pending oral exams. Most students prepared for weeks in order to pass and advance in the neurosciences program. But Holmes shared that he wasn't studying at all; he was playing video games, devoting more than a hundred hours a week to shooting fake people. And though he said it so matter-of-factly, there was something ominous in his tone, as if he had just exposed a row of tiny bombs strapped to his chest and any sudden movement, even sweat, could set them off.

Later, in pretrial interviews, he would say, "Whether I pass or fail is up to fate." But he never told us this, he explained, lest we realize he was psychotic, "focused on his mission"—because, you see, planning to kill people is "time-consuming." By the time Steve came into the picture, Holmes had already begun amassing weapons, and he worried that if we knew about his arsenal we would be "frightened" of him. Perhaps a part of him hoped we'd somehow know his thoughts and plans. He later told his court-appointed psychiatrist, Dr. William Reid, that public speaking (a large part of his graduate work) had "brought an end to his happiness" and he feared it might be "self-centered" to study, because the goal was to learn and improve himself.

He journaled,

Can't tell the mind rapists . . . If plan is disclosed both "normal" life and ideal enactment on hatred foiled. Prevent building false sense of rapport. Speak truthfully and deflect incriminating questions. Oddly, they don't pursue or delve into harmful omissions . . . I was fear incarnate . . .

"Do you have a sense of what *others* think of you?" asked Steve. A person's self-perception, especially if vastly different from reality, could offer valuable insight into his thought process.

"Well, Fenton's clearly afraid of me."

"You think she's afraid of you?"

"Isn't that why *you're* here, to protect her?"

"Does she *need* protection?"

I didn't like the turn in conversation, the veiled threat behind Holmes' declaration.

"She locked me out of her office." *There it was.*

Steve asked him if he thought I'd done it on purpose.

"She hid a large box behind her chair." He spoke in whole sentences, something he'd never done with me. He and Steve were actually conversing.

"Did that scare you?"

Holmes smiled slightly. Then, as if there'd been a satellite delay, he replied to Steve's original question. "Others think I'm normal."

His court-appointed psychiatrist later posed a similar question: "If I had been some kid about your age playing with you—age ten, eleven, twelve—would I have thought you were abnormal?"

"No, just a normal guy."

In fact, Holmes admitted later he had an "odd sense of self," believing he had "a biological self who was driven to eat, drink and sleep," and a "real" self who "frightened the biological self." Though Holmes never shared any of these insights with us, others would later remark that Holmes did appear quite normal; college friends and peers described him as "scary smart," an "introvert" with a self-deprecating sense of humor. He performed "hilarious" snowboarding tricks and achieved the "top five in the world at *World of Warcraft 3*." He had "no interest in weapons or shooting and didn't seem to have any mental issues." Holmes apparently steadfastly believed his graduate school friends would still "care about him" even after the massacre and not be "angry at him unless it interfered with their lives, or the press interfered with their lives. I think they'd be supportive."[6]

"Would you be open to an antipsychotic?" Steve asked. "A low dose might bring you some relief, help reduce those obsessive thoughts." Holmes refused.

After the session Steve and I debriefed in the campus cafeteria. Steve agreed that Holmes was odd but not necessarily dangerous. As usual he'd mentioned no specific targets or plans. Still, what did we really know about Holmes? His history was full of blanks. I stabbed my plastic fork into a hard-boiled egg and snapped a tine. Had he always been so . . . *odd*, or was his presentation new, indicative of some kind of psychotic break? It was a good sign he was at least still enrolled in the program. It signified stability and the possibility that we could still help him.

"I kind of like the guy," said Steve.

---

6   Later, Dr. William Reid noted that Holmes seemed "normal" when speaking with defense expert Dr. Jonathan Woodcock just days after the massacre, and during his postarrest police interrogations Holmes "spoke a little slowly but was completely logical, answered questions without delay, volunteered comments and often explained his answers." In all, his exchanges with the officers were "psychiatrically uneventful."

CHAPTER 7

GRAVITY

June 1, 2012
(49 days before the massacre)

Madness, as you know, is like gravity—
all it takes is a little push!
—The Joker, *The Dark Knight* (2008)

HOLMES

Instead of studying for his prelims, Holmes watched reruns of *Arrested Development*, Louis CK stand-up routines, and episodes of *The Big Bang Theory*, fantasizing he was the "real life" Leonard Hofstadter, the socially challenged, brilliant physicist in lust with Penny/Gargi, the beautiful aspiring actress who lived next door. He especially related when Leonard remarked that losing a friend "would be so much easier if he were a violent sociopath." Most significantly, he watched *TDK* (how Holmes referred to *The Dark Knight*) over and over, fixated on the character of the Joker, a self-professed "psychopathic mass-murdering schizo clown" who appeared in only nine scenes. The Joker's razor-carved grin routinely filled his television screen—"Why so serious? Smile!"

Empty beer bottles littered Holmes' floor as Batman's jailhouse confrontation with the Joker played over and over. By some accounts, he memorized nearly all the dialogue in the film, reciting choice lines as he pranced around his bedroom as the Joker: "The only way to live in this world is without rules." "Does it depress you to know just how alone you really are?" Then, in front of his floor-length mirror, he extended the edges of his mouth with bloodred lipstick, pressed his fingers to the glass, and whispered the Joker's words: "To them you're just a freak like me. . . . They're only as good as the world allows them to be. When the chips are down, these civilized people, they'll eat each other."

He ordered a Batman mask online and wore it around his apartment.

Holmes used his real name when he called "Diggity" Dave Aragon, an actor from the MTV series *Pimp My Ride*, about his low-budget Batman "fan" film, *The Suffocator of Sins*.

"I loved your four-minute trailer," Holmes said, "especially how Batman showed up firing a semiautomatic handgun into a crowd shouting, 'My shield is my vengeance, my armor is my hatred.'"

An uncomfortable Diggity was silent.

Did he use a list? Was he selective with his shots? Holmes asked.

But before Diggity could respond, Holmes pressed him for "the total body count" and suggested Batman could use "a bigger gun."

Sometime in early June, before his prelims, Holmes began recording "Insights into My Mind of Madness" in a black spiral computation book he called simply his "notebook." He titled it "Of Life" and dedicated all thirty pages of writings and illustrations to his parents, "Goober" and "Bobbo," and his sister, "Chrissy."[7] He signed it

---

7 Holmes told Dr. William Reid he intended the notebook to be "his story," a communication to his psychiatrist, Dr. Fenton, "to educate her so something like this wouldn't happen again."

"love yuhs" and added an original logo, representing something he called "Ultraception," a circle enclosing an infinity symbol, bisected with a serif numeral 1. Above it he posed two questions: *What is the meaning of life? What is the meaning of death?*

"The Self-Diagnosis of My Broken Mind" included:

> *Dysphoric mania; generalized anxiety disorder/social anxiety disorder/OCD/PTSD (chronic); Asperger syndrome/autism; ADHD; schizophrenia; body dysmorphic disorder; borderline, narcissistic, anxious, avoidant and obsessive-compulsive personality disorder; chronic insomnia; psychosis; trichotillomania; adjustment disorder; pain disorder, restless leg syndrome.*

"I have trouble communicating very clearly," he later told Dr. Reid, "so I kind of wrote it down as a way to get it out. They might have been surprised that there was all this stuff I didn't mention that I *did* mention in the notebook, the whole human capital kind of explanation of it."

He expounded on his "simple theory" through stick figures and meaningless "equations." Each living person began with a "value" of one. Life equaled "infinity," "ultimate good" or "negative infinity." Notably, murderers had "zero" value. There were rules to acquiring human capital: First, the killing had to be intentional; accidents didn't count. If multiple people did the killing, it still only resulted in one "credit." He'd considered "alternatives" to death: (1) ignoring the problem; (2) delaying the problem; (3) "pawning" the problem; or (4) loving/hating the problem.

"Despite knowing death is false," he told Dr. Reid, "I couldn't find a working alternative. If all of life is dead, then the questions 'Why should life exist?' [and] 'What is the purpose of living?' are irrelevant."

In the end, problem solved if everyone died.

June 7, 2012
(43 days before the massacre)

In a small conference room, a panel of three professors questioned Holmes about auditory systems, cells, and neurobiological development; they asked him to explain how the brain worked and how certain cells communicated with one another. It didn't matter that Holmes answered mostly wrong, or that his shirt clung to him like Saran Wrap or that the lights in the room crawled across their faces. Whether he passed or failed didn't matter. He was going to complete his mission and get locked up or killed.

While his professors decided his fate and sent their recommendations to Dr. Sukumar "Suke" Vijayaraghavan, chair of the Graduate Training Committee, Holmes purchased a Smith & Wesson M&P 15 rifle from his local Gander Mountain sporting goods store.

"We require some paperwork," said a pock-faced clerk, pushing standard forms at Holmes at the register. Calmly, Holmes checked off boxes avowing he wasn't a convicted felon, had never been a psychiatric inpatient, and had no "mental or physical impairments that would preclude safe use" of the weapon. He handed the teenager his driver's license.

"This will just take a few moments." The clerk sounded almost apologetic. "We just have to run a quick background check, which usually takes no longer than a credit check."

While he input Holmes' birth date, Social Security number, and driver's license into an online database, Holmes wandered through the store, stopping to admire gun safes, holsters, earmuffs, tactical gun range bags, scopes, and other accessories.

"All done," the boy said with a smile. "Have a nice day."

He *would*. He spent the afternoon ordering handcuffs, Road Stars, and first aid supplies from an online source in Washington State. Next, he researched "best places to target practice" and found information on "BulletBlockers" (T-shirts fortified with ballistic panels), body armor, and gas masks. He visited multiple websites offering step-by-step instructions on bomb making and watched multiple YouTube videos about potassium permanganate, gasoline, tactical smoke grenades, black powder, and Pyrodex.

Meanwhile "Suke" emailed him: "The prelims committee expressed a number of concerns regarding your performance. . . . You and I need to talk regarding your prelim results and lab choice."

June 11, 2012, 1:00 p.m.
(39 days before the massacre)

"You failed," his professor said, steepling his hands on the conference table. "The university is willing to let you retake the exams in a few weeks."

Holmes stared at him in silence as his professor explained the panel's concerns. It seemed they thought Holmes was "unable to get from A to G in a timely, organized manner." It was possible, he said, that Holmes had only "a superficial knowledge of the material or that he simply knew the words to use without understanding the concepts." His performance on the exam was "uniformly poor," and "no one had failed the preliminary oral exam before." Still, he explained the university was dedicated to retaining its students; it "worked very hard" to select qualified, excellent candidates, and so the panel would allow James "to retake the exam . . . an easier version."

"I am confident you will pass and move on to the second-year labs."

"Thank you, but I quit." Holmes slapped his hands together and moved jerkily toward the door.

Later, he wrote,

Dear Sirs,

I regret to inform you that I will be discontinuing my graduate studies in the neuroscience program effective immediately.

Regards,

James

"Are you being serious?" Hillary texted after he shared the news with her.

"I'm being James. I'm quitting fave red.[8] Best o' luck to yuh."

Later that day, 4:00 p.m.

FENTON

"How did your exams go?" Steve asked brightly as Holmes sat across from us, deadpan, legs splayed in front of him.

"I failed." There was no emotion in his voice. He didn't look at me, and, in fact, since Steve had joined us, he'd consistently acted as if I hadn't been there. Incredulous, Steve suggested Holmes retake the exam: the university would understand; things happened; surely Holmes wasn't the first student to flunk. . . .

"Nah, I'm not interested."

"What will you do, then?"

"Probably get a job."

"Where?"

As the clock on the wall ticked loudly, Holmes spoke haltingly, his words sputtering like a broken machine. He said he'd extended his lease and "probably wouldn't break that." He was sure his parents would support whatever decision he made.

---

8   Favorite redhead.

Steve looked as worried as I was. Without some sort of support or university structure, Holmes might spiral, become increasingly isolated, even depressed. *He* already *had homicidal thoughts, and once out of the program, he'd be withdrawn from the university and no longer eligible for psychiatric help.* With his world crashing in on him and nothing more to lose, what would stop him from taking others with him?

Steve pressed him for more information, knowing that, with his parents' support, Holmes might be less volatile. "Do your parents know you flunked?"

He'd told them "a while ago" he might not stay.

What about work? Money? How would he live? I'd never seen Steve so rattled. Holmes' sudden apathy without any obvious cause (such as a death or a breakup) could signal a more serious condition, even a psychotic break.

Holmes said he'd "get by"; he had $10,000 in the bank.

And he didn't see the point in continued medication or psychotherapy, especially since he was losing his insurance. We pleaded with him to stay.

"We'll help you for free," I said.

"I'm dropping out, so what's the point?"

"What about getting help for your *life*?" Steve tried.

Holmes stood up. "I've got to go."

"Maybe this is what he wants?" Steve focused on the positives: Holmes had a lease, funds in the bank, a plan for employment. And though he was still anxious, he wasn't depressed. *So he said.* But Holmes was like radio static, everything tuned to the same frequency—his breakup with Gargi, flunking his orals, quitting the program, killing people, all said with the same level of dispassion.

"I'm going to call his mother," I said. It was a clear violation of HIPAA[9] (a 1996 federal law that restricted access to individuals' pri-

---

9   Health Insurance Portability and Accountability Act.

vate medical information) to contact a relative without the patient's permission, but this was an emergency and I was willing to risk any penalty (fines, prison, even my license) if it meant preventing possible violence.

Steve was one step ahead of me, already heading out the door to find the mother's phone number. "Better call Legal too, just in case," he added.

Safety first... Like hell was I going to have another Virginia Tech on my watch!

I needed to know whether Holmes had *always* been so strange or if his robotic behavior was new; if so, it could have been indicative of some sort of psychotic break, substance-related psychosis, or medical illness. There were significant gaps in his history; so far, he'd not offered us collateral information, contacts who could speak on his behalf. *What did he not want us to know?* More important: *Who was Holmes* before *he was* this?

I began with his professors, all of whom confirmed who Holmes had become: "extremely anxious," with "awkward and often offputting" lab presentations. They described him as "a fleeting presence, a wisp of a young man who wasn't intimate with anyone—a trace of a person always on the move."

"Quite frankly none of us wanted to work with him despite his stellar credentials," one professor I interviewed said.

On paper, Holmes seemed the perfect candidate for each of the graduate schools to which he applied: the University of Iowa, the University of Illinois at Urbana-Champaign, the University of Alabama at Birmingham, Kansas State University, Texas A&M, and the University of Colorado Denver—having earned a 4.0 GPA; received a dean's fellowship, a regents' scholarship, and Phi Beta Kappa and Golden Key membership; and graduated summa cum laude. In his college admissions essay he'd expounded on his "unquenchable curiosity and strong desire to know and explore the unknown." "Fascinated by the complexities of long-lost thoughts seemingly arising out of nowhere," he'd recounted his summer camp experience counseling schizophrenics. One night, one of his kids, unable to sleep, vacuumed the ceiling. He found that though his kids were heavily medicated, this did not solve their problems: "The medications changed them from being highly energetic creative kids to lax beings who slept through the activities."

Who was this uncharacteristically empathetic Holmes? I wondered. *Had he created a fictitious persona, hoping to mask his true self?*

Clearly, there was a disconnect, because his behavior, according to several professors who interviewed him for admission, was "bizarre, disconnected and aloof" with a "global lack of affect." With his application to the University of Illinois, Holmes included a picture of himself with a llama. And he so unnerved the graduate school admissions committee at the University of Iowa that the director underlined twice "Do NOT offer admission under any circumstances."

But in 2011, after seven faculty members on the admissions committee interviewed him, Holmes was one of six students accepted into the University of Colorado Anschutz Medical Campus; "overall," the panel found him to be "very positive," an "interesting candidate with loads of potential . . . [and] a somewhat quirky character, but what good scientist doesn't!" He was awarded a $21,600 grant from the National Institutes of Health as well as a $5,000 stipend from the University of Colorado Denver. And though Holmes was also accepted to the University of Illinois, where he was also offered a $22,600 stipend and free tuition, he declined "for unspecified reasons."

Having obtained his mother's contact information, I called her, confident that I was doing the right thing, mining the source for information and validation that my uneasiness about Holmes had context and meaning. I had never felt such urgency with any other patient—and in this instance, though I had no evidence other than gut instinct, public safety trumped a patient's right to privacy.

"I've worried about Jimmy every day of his life." Arlene Holmes' voice cracked as she tearfully confessed that my reaching out had evoked in her a "lifetime of guilt," almost as if she were expecting my call, her secret exposed.

As a child, "Jimmy" exhibited "extreme social phobia" and was "basically terrified of everything." He had problems adjusting to a new school after the family relocated from a small town to San Diego. She'd taken him for counseling but insisted there had been no underlying psychological issues, just trouble "adjusting." I asked about other family members, whether there had been anyone else like Holmes. His father was an "introvert," she said, and nothing further. (Years later, she would testify that Holmes had *many* psychotic relatives.) I asked if she thought Holmes was angry.

"He was furious with me once," she said, her voice shaking a little as she described his obsession with video games following his initial rejection from the many graduate schools to which he applied during his senior year in college. Despite Holmes' impressive academic record, admissions departments were undoubtedly perplexed by his personal essay, which described his use of "clairvoyance" to solve complex scientific problems and boasted about his "infinite vastness of indefinite knowledge." No school wanted him, and no one would hire him for any entry-level science-related jobs. Discouraged, Arlene had ordered him to "get a job or move out," and he'd exploded at her, calling her "mean names" and causing her to withdraw, to "give up."

The pain in her voice was palpable. I imagined it must have felt like a betrayal to speak negatively of her son. At the same time, she must have felt rejected by her child, emotionally abandoned after years of support and nurturing. She wrote about her tremendous loss years later in *When the Focus Shifts: The Prayer Book of Arlene Holmes*, begging others to forgive her "for not knowing what was happening." She prayed for "those who had been written off as evil" and described her life in the aftermath: the death threats, like incessant "knocking, pounding, ringing, knocking, pounding, ringing, ringing." She'd pleaded with her readers, "How do I lessen the guilt of being alive?" And she found irony in protection: "I just put a password on my phone. My texts, my emails, my contacts, are now protected. How do I put a password on my life? No protection possible."

"I'm sorry I haven't been much help," Arlene said to me in farewell, her voice hoarse with emotion.

I called Sergeant Lynn Whitten at the University of Colorado's police station, a small white brick building on the edge of campus. What did she know about Holmes?

"He's clean," she said. "No criminal history, no military service, no weapons permit, and his driver's license has his apartment address. When he officially leaves the university, we'll need to deactivate his key card."

Key cards gave students access to secure areas. Holmes' gave him access to the sixth floor of the neuroscience building and the vast state-of-the-art laboratory stocked with test tubes, vials, fuel tanks, refrigerators, laptop computers, and electron microscopes where he studied the brains of fruit flies (and his own).

"Are you looking for anything in particular?" Whitten asked.

Evidence of imminent danger, a specific plan, identifiable victims, a reason to involuntarily commit him, but so far I had little more than a bad feeling. And it wasn't enough for a mental health hold.

CHAPTER 8

TARGET PRACTICE

June 12, 2012
[38 days before the massacre]

This town deserves a better class of criminal,
and I'm gonna give it to 'em.
—The Joker, *The Dark Knight* [2008]

FENTON

I met my friends that night for our monthly dinner at the Capital
Grille. After Holmes' last session with Steve and me, I thought he
might have schizoid personality disorder, intermittently functioning at a psychotic level, possibly on the autism spectrum and shift-
ing insidiously into a frank psychotic disorder such as schizophrenia.
Holmes *wasn't* an overt danger, and I couldn't commit him. Not for
his *thoughts*. Not when he planned to find a job, had money in the
bank and family support. I needed to let him go. Just then I caught
my reflection in the large wall mirror; even in candlelight I looked
like hell: too thin, wan, yellowing from stress. I'd been drinking
from nerves, letting the waiter top off my wineglass without regard
for the units.

"Don't second-guess yourself," Toby said as if reading my thoughts. "We've all been there." Gayle blew on her bowl of lobster bisque. "The 'should I, shouldn't I' and 'what if' scenarios we replay in our heads over and over."

They were right, of course. It did no good to ruminate, zooming in for close-ups, looking for cracks that might change my mind.

"We're trying to make you feel better." Kat smiled. "After all, we're psychiatrists."

I'd been seeing my own for years. Ironically, I'd once dismissed psychiatry as a real discipline, until my then husband, Steffen, half out of his mind with panic, practically dragged me to my first appointment with Dr. Daniel Edinberg, "the psychiatrist's psychiatrist." I'd closed my thriving private medical practice in anticipation of relocating with Steffen to San Francisco. In the few months before the move, I'd begun to dabble in day trading. I amassed significant wealth and an impressive portfolio—until the fickle stock market turned and I lost everything. Suddenly broke and despondent, I swallowed a sample dose of the antidepressant Luvox, had a bad reaction to it, and crawled into bed for several days, tangled in sweaty sheets, staring at the bladed shadows of a ceiling fan.

Edinberg had such kind eyes. I was a mess then, and I worried I'd made a bad initial impression, my story unraveling bit by bit, with its intricate plot twists dead-ending in sobs, all dignity gone. I wanted him to know the *real* me, not the crisis me, not the one reaching for tissues and giving him a play-by-play of my sudden plunge into poverty. Of course, I was in shock, the enormity of the loss, my security gone, the life I'd planned with Steffen upended. These things didn't happen to me. I wasn't that person. I so badly wanted Edinberg to see that, to understand who I really was.

And in that moment of crisis, I finally had clarity: *he did see me, in all my imperfections. More important, he understood me.* And slowly, slowly, he helped me emerge from that fog.

"He disgusts me," I said of Holmes, envisioning his spaced-out stare, as if he were looking *through* me, not *at* me. What I needed to know—what I'd been searching to find out—was whether he was so odd because he was truly psychotic or because he was just a strange human being. I'd treated many psychotic patients before and Holmes was not like them. Truly psychotic people did not merely *think* they were hearing voices; they *actually* heard them. Or they experienced unusual perceptual disturbances, like foul odors no one else noticed; one of my patients, for instance, convinced she was being poisoned, began to put soap in her nostrils. Prior to any of these psychotic symptoms, though, she'd had a prolonged period of depression. Holmes wasn't depressed. And as far as he'd disclosed, he did not find his voices intrusive or even alarming. The Holmes he let me see was one-dimensional, and searching for anything deeper had been like navigating a dark cave.

With Edinberg, I could discuss my reaction to Holmes not as his psychiatrist but as *me*. And in that capacity I didn't have to justify or edit my feelings. I could tell Edinberg the truth: Holmes made me uneasy, filled me with dread, made the hair on the back of my neck stand up. The more I talked, the more clarity I had. That was the power of psychotherapy; results manifested with consistency and hard work.

But sometimes I craved a shortcut, instant relief from the pressure building in my head. I white-knuckled it over Independence Pass in my Infiniti, windows down, sharp wind slapping my cheeks, engine vibrating through the steering wheel. I whipped around narrow curves, my grip strong, steady, and controlled, passing motorcyclists speeding in single-file formation, hugging the edges of sharp, jagged cliffs with no protective guardrails, feeling dangerously alive. I was aware of all my senses—touch, color, smell, focus. No mistakes, no sudden brakes. No second-guessing. Holmes' scattershot gaze loomed in my mind's eye as the road narrowed and dipped and switchbacked. My stomach lurched. Fog curled onto the road, so dense I pulled into an overlook, my heart pounding.

At twelve thousand feet the air was thin. I opened the door, walked to the cliff's edge, looked down the sheer rock wall dusted with clouds, saw the vast drop-off into nothingness, and screamed until I thought my lungs would burst.

June 13, 2012
(37 days before the massacre)

HOLMES

From an online supply company, Holmes stockpiled six thousand rounds of ammunition for his M&P 15 rifle, shells for his 12-gauge shotgun, and magazines for his Glock .40. As easy as ordering a book from Amazon. His arsenal consisted of jacketed hollow-point bullets boasting a higher muzzle velocity capable of penetrating microfiber and bonded leather (like the material found on industrial theater seats). He bought extra magazines for his rifle, a special high-capacity (100-round) drum magazine, and a Beamshot GB800M green-dot laser sight, which he installed on one of his pistols. His head pounding, he bought 250 "single slug" shotgun rounds (bird hunters typically used scattershot) and human-silhouette targets. *Practice. Practice. Practice.*

He ordered a bulletproof vest and tactical gear and disassembled his Glock, scattering the parts—frame, barrel, slide, spring—across his bed like guts. He put the pieces back together again and again, timing himself. And when all was reassembled he racked the slide, liking the "powerful" sound it made.

Terrorism isn't the message, Holmes wrote in his notebook. *The message is, there is no message.*

June 25, 2012
(25 days before the massacre)

Holmes applied online to join Lead Valley, Colorado's "most family friendly shooting range" and followed up with an "incoherent" voice message the owner described at trial as "guttural, very heavy bass, deep, bizarre on a good day, freakish on others." But even though he returned Holmes' call more than once and invited him to participate in a mandatory orientation meeting, Holmes had already lost interest. He didn't need an orientation; he needed supplies, specifically a Blackhawk Urban Assault Vest, a Be-Wharned folding knife, and two magazine holders from an online tactical gear store. Next, he purchased bullet-resistant pants and chaps and a neck and Kevlar groin protector. Also on his list of purchases were ignitable and electronic fuse materials, hollow plastic balls, and a missile launch control receiver from a site called CannonFuse.com. In chat rooms and forums, he asked about gunpowder and napalm, specifically, "What's your fav bomb and How do you make it?"

The black "possession lenses" he'd ordered several days earlier from an online theatrical supply company had finally arrived and he slipped them on, barely able to see through the pinhole pupils. He thought they made him look "devilishly evil."

June 27, 2012
(23 days before the massacre)

FENTON

At my annual faculty garden party, surrounded by thick bamboo, a gurgling, fully stocked pond, water lilies, and clusters of bright pink petunias, Steve sipped a glass of Merlot. "Have you heard any more from our guy?"

"Holmes?" A hummingbird hovered over the blooms of penstemons. "Only that he's left the university." But he hadn't left my thoughts. He'd lingered like a nightmare, the aftereffects as vivid and disturbing as those of Toby's "Butcher," except that Holmes' character was undeveloped, his story unfinished, his narrative disjointed, and his plot unsatisfying—with no beginning or end. The fact that he was just "out there" unnerved me. And after only six sessions, it was chilling to think maybe I *had* known the real Holmes and had only *hoped* I'd been wrong. It wouldn't have changed anything; what little I did learn wasn't enough. He was still a blank.

I waved to Gayle and Toby, who had just arrived and were making their way through the rose portal, balancing plates of speared shrimp.

"It always bothered me how that ended." He bit into a cracker.

"Me too."

I sensed a desperate quality in his voice, as if he'd somehow failed me, or failed Holmes, and had taken it personally.

Marilyn, in a pastel sundress and bright white Keds, tugged at Steve's elbow. "You have to see this. It's like something out of *Alice in Wonderland*."

Steve held up an index finger and said to me, "To be continued."

"I love what you've done to the place." Toby nodded toward the pond, spilling drops of wine as she did so.

"Beautiful renovations." Gayle grinned, swatting away a bee. "I hear you're pretty handy with a pulley."

"It was a labor of love." I meant it: I *loved* improvement projects, loved the physicality involved, digging deep, unearthing the foundation, the hidden potential, and making something entirely new. There were no disasters, just problems that had solutions—like people, landscapes and gardens were works in progress, inherently flawed and in need of attention and care. Time and use and the elements would inevitably take their toll.

"I want the grand tour." Toby took my arm and pulled me into the lush greenery. A soft breeze carried the sweet smell of roses.

June 28, 2012
(22 days before the massacre)

HOLMES

Holmes, now consumed by his plans to commit murder, spent most of his waking hours playing *Diablo III*, ordering ammunition and an MICH Level IIIA advanced combat ballistic helmet, and choosing a venue: *What better place to case than that of an inconspicuous entertainment facility?* he journaled, after ruling out alternatives:

Targets random. The cruel twists of fate are unkind to the misfortunate

Method: Bombs X (too regulated & suspicious)

Biological Warfare X (too impatient, repairs extensive)

Serial Murder X (too personal, too much violence, easily caught, few kills)

Mass Murder/Spree (maximum casualties, easily performed with firearms, although primitive in nature. No fear of consequences . . .)

Venue—Airport or Movie Theater?

Airports had "substantial security" and "too much of a terrorist history." But "Cinemark 16"[10] seemed feasible, "isolated," "Proximal," and "Large." He underlined, asterisked, and ranked the various auditoriums, noting "exit paths" for moviegoers, visibility, and number

---

10 Century 16 movie theater.

of doors. After drawing various diagrams, he determined "10 & 12 best targets in complex" and considered "3 options of attack":

—start at 12
—start at 10
—start at smokers escape J[11]

Next, he calculated the approximate response time from the Aurora Police Department to the theater ("ETA ~3 mins") and obsessively prepared his personal Armageddon.

He drove to the Century 16 movie theater to stake out the place, snap photos of the interior with his cell phone, and select the perfect auditorium. Some had "excellent spatial approach," while in others "visibility was marginal." The hallway smelled of stale popcorn and spun sugar. Holmes' shoes stuck to the dizzy, patterned circles in the carpet. He bought a ticket for the matinee showing of *Seeking a Friend for the End of the World*. Auditorium 9 had stadium seating, thick purple drapes, and cushioned seats.

He sat in the back and counted the number of steps up to his seat. He studied the placement of the exits and considered "best side of approach." He noted the lighting, the darkness of the theater before the movie started, the white flicker of the screen over the audience's faces during daylight scenes.

July 1, 2012
(19 days before the massacre)

Holmes dyed his hair clown orange from a box of Clairol he purchased at the supermarket and signed for his FedEx delivery of 170 pounds of ammunition. His mother recommended he get "stress

---

11 "Joking."

counseling," said *she'd* seen a psychiatrist while at UC Berkeley and she wasn't the only one; "the waiting room was full of students" who needed "help coping." She wrote that though she "felt weird" and "wondered if she wasn't normal," the sessions "helped her understand herself."

He returned to Gander Mountain sporting goods and bought a Vortex Strikefire Red Dot Sight (designed for close-quarters, low-light combat) for his rifle. At the range, he wanted to be perceived as a more dangerous version of his video-gaming avatar, "Sherlock-Bond," a kind of "James Bond man of action"—except that, unlike James Bond, *his* actions were real.

Goober wired him the last of his college fund to help him with his "downtime." Grateful, he used the money to register for an X-rated Internet dating service, AdultFriendFinder.com, that promised "world-wide sex dates, adult matches, hookups, and fuck friends." As "ClassicJimbo" he now only wanted flings or a "casual sex gal." He insisted he was a "nice guy . . . as nice enough of a guy who does these sorts of shenanigans." And while he waited for "winks" that he never received he bought another Glock .40-caliber pistol and journaled, *Death is life's fallback solution to all problems.*

July 2, 2012
(18 days before the massacre)

Holmes sped down Highway 40 toward the Byers Canyon Rifle Range near Hot Sulphur Springs. Two long gun cases stretched across the back seat. His crate of ammunition rattled on the floor. He cracked a window, wind whipping his shock of orange hair. In his rearview mirror he saw the wig wags, the swirling blue and red lights. Officer Donald Ransom of the Fraser Winter Park, Colorado, Police Department pulled him over.

"License and registration."

Holmes fumbled for his papers.

"Do you know how fast you were going?"

"Fast enough to get a ticket."

The officer released him with a warning.

The range was maintained by volunteer camp hosts with Colorado Parks and Wildlife.

"We don't have any licensing requirements to use the range," explained one host. "Shooters like to come here because we don't have the long lines and they can park right next to their target spots. Most come out here with their Marlin Model 60 .22 semiautomatics, elk hunting rifles, and Winchester Model 70 7 MM Rem Mag," but "Red—that's what we called him because of his orangish hair—came out here with his bad hair job, pasted smile and loud pistol" and "didn't shoot clays."

"Shooters complained about the noise. He alternated between the pistol and shotgun range and eventually only shot at the rifle range." At the pistol range he used a "riot gun" with a "shorter, sawed off barrel," a "black synthetic stock and shiny matte finish. A tactical gun for self-defense." But at the rifle range he used a Remington pump shotgun.

When he finished shooting, Holmes tossed his white plastic trash bags in the dumpster, each one containing more than five hundred spent .40-caliber Smith & Wesson rounds, 12-gauge shotgun shells, and .223 "super slick" brass shell casings.

"There were never any boxes," the camp host told police, "which means he bought his ammunition in bulk."

His life-size silhouettes of a "bad guy pointing a gun" and a "bad guy holding a woman hostage" were too large to hang, so he propped them against hay bales.

"I thought he must be practicing for the end of the world," said the range patrol, who drove a repurposed police car, a Ford Crown Victoria graffitied with the words "Zombie Outbreak Response Team."

The camp host approached Holmes one afternoon, curious about his "terrible dye job. It looked like he had spray-painted his hair."

She introduced herself, noticing his lack of eye and ear protection, and his "pasty smile."

"What's with the hair?"

Wearing dark clothes and a loose T-shirt underneath a long-sleeve flannel, he answered carefully, "I needed a change."

July 5, 2012
(15 days before the massacre)

Holmes snapped selfies wearing his ballistic vest and spirit lenses and holding his M&P 15 rifle and Glock pistol. He slid a black beanie over his head and pulled tufts of orange hair through the sides like devil horns. He grinned into the camera, enjoying his new "dangerous" image. He would later tell his court-appointed psychiatrist that he wanted people to fear him, to let them know he "wasn't someone to mess with," which was "unusual 'cause [he] wasn't normally a tough guy."

"He worked out at Lowry's twenty-four-hour gym," Hillary recalled. "Lifting dumbbells and sweating on the elliptical. But he wasn't what I would call fit."

Still, Holmes wanted to be remembered as such, explaining to Dr. Reid his reasons: "not so much a *for* or *how* . . . just that he wanted to be remembered visually . . . as James Holmes killer. This is what a killer looks like."

In his notebook, he recorded his "impulsive acts," and "periods of involuntary action" interspersed with "hyper speed." He jotted notes about his "possible interludes of catatonia . . . tired most of the time for about an hour, onset unknown." And he had other concerns as well:

Concern with cock. Suffered accidents as a child. Allergic reaction to soap—scarring. Excessive stimulation in response to "most beautiful woman in world" I had read in a book. Other event, a slab of skin tore away did not heal. Results of accident not prevalent to absent in appearance when erect. Despite my biological shortcomings I have fought and fought always defending against predetermination and the fallibility of man. There is one more battle to fight with life. To face death, embrace the longstanding hatred of mankind and over-come all fear . . . embrace the hatred, a dark k/night rises . . .

CHAPTER 9

TICK TOCK

July 6, 2012
(14 days before the massacre)

Nobody panics when things go "according to plan."
Even if the plan is horrifying!
—The Joker, *The Dark Knight* (2008)

FENTON

I couldn't help it. Though I hadn't seen Holmes in nearly two months, I thought about him. I pictured him, suddenly loose, like a wild animal, disoriented and forced to survive with only primitive coping skills. I worried, *Had I made the right call? Did I do enough?* I sounded like my attorney friend Jane, who, prior to law school, worked as a critical care nurse in the ICU. Tasked with disconnecting patients' life support, she'd struggled every day with their families' decision and eventually no longer wanted to end another person's life.

"I watched people die," she said, and "they became the ghosts I believed in." Now she managed other people's livelihoods: doctors in crisis, in medical malpractice suits. I wondered, *Had I become one—a doctor in crisis?* "When a patient harms a doctor who has taken an oath to 'do no harm,'" Jane said, "it's the worst kind of betrayal. The whole experience can leave a person shell-shocked."

I hoped I would never have to find that out. Still, I knew what she meant, had heard of cases like Wendell Williamson, a law student at the University of North Carolina who'd sued his psychiatrist after he chose to stop taking his prescribed medications. Several months after his last session, his persecutory delusions had returned in full force and he'd taken to the streets with an rifle, killing two strangers and a police officer before being shot by police. Later, a jury declared he was not guilty by reason of insanity. (He suffered from paranoid schizophrenia and believed he was saving the world with his random killings.) Williamson was committed to a state hospital, where he filed the suit against his psychiatrist (who had seen him six times) for negligence. A jury awarded Williamson half a million dollars before an appellate court reversed the verdict, finding the psychiatrist's "alleged negligence was not the *proximate cause*" of Williamson's injuries. Had the higher court ruled differently, Williamson's case might have discouraged psychiatrists from ever treating psychotic patients.

Even more alarming, and perhaps closer to home, was the case of Ms. B., a schoolteacher who drove herself to the emergency room and complained of having difficulty organizing her lesson plans. She told the psychiatrist on duty that, ever since her father's death four months earlier, she'd felt exhausted and sleep-deprived and was having trouble keeping her mind focused. On evaluation, Ms. B. denied having any history of mental illness. She denied feeling depressed and said she had never attempted suicide. The ER psychiatrist's mental status exam documented that Ms. B. was fully oriented and diagnosed her problem as "complicated bereavement" and referred her to a counselor. Within an hour of Ms. B's discharge, she walked to the top of the six-floor hospital parking garage and jumped to her death.

The ER psychiatrist's notes did not reflect an assessment of risk beyond the statement that patient "denied suicidal ideation." Ms. B.'s husband sued the psychiatrist and the hospital. The plaintiff alleged that had Ms. B.'s husband been contacted, the ER psychiatrist would have learned that over the past two weeks Ms. B. had twice been rescued by her family after walking into heavy traffic and had paced erratically through her house during the night, sleeping little if at all. At trial, the defense expert stressed the inability of psychiatrists to predict suicide as well as the impracticality of calling family members of every patient admitted to a busy emergency room. A psychiatrist couldn't be expected to know what a patient did not disclose, he said, or be held liable for the consequences of acts or omissions that were unforeseeable by any reasonable standard. Sometimes there were intervening causes.

Holmes had assured me, in his less-than-satisfactory way, that he was not depressed and had no suicidal ideation. But what did I really know of his history?

Even when psychiatrists followed every possible standard of care, their patients could *still* sue, but, as Jane pointed out, it didn't mean they were *right*. It just meant their lawsuits could still leave a psychiatrist feeling helpless and shell-shocked. Mr. D, a once-suicidal patient, had improved so much that he no longer required psychiatric care or constant observation. One night his spouse quite unexpectedly announced she wanted a divorce. The patient promptly went to his room, wrote her a brief note expressing his anger, and hung himself. His wife's rejection (not reasonably foreseeable) was an intervening cause of Mr. D's suicide. Nonetheless, Mr. D's family sued the psychiatrist for failing to schedule an immediate "follow-up" appointment with the patient, whom he'd been treating for depression, though he'd scheduled Mr. D for a check-in approximately two months later. The court ruled the psychiatrist was not liable.

July 7, 2012
(13 days before the massacre)

HOLMES

Holmes prepared to do harm—M&P 15 rifle, Remington 870 Express Tactical shotgun, two Glock G22 .40 caliber handguns, folding knives, full-metal-jacket bullets, ballistic gear. *The mind is a prison,* he journaled, *trillions of cells guard it for eternity. O' where art thou master key? Destroy the mind and be free . . . Why? Why? Why? Why? Why? Why?* His single question filled at least five pages in his notebook.

Hillary's text distracted him. I thought of you, working out on the elliptical, are you back in California?

Nah. Still here in my same apartment.
We should do another hike.

Have you ever met someone with dysphoric mania? he asked.

There was a pause—I'm looking it up, she said—then she read the definition: *a bipolar disorder with mixed features, symptoms or states. People experience mania and depression at the same time. This increases the risk of extreme behavior and means that the symptoms are generally more severe and longer-lasting . . .* Is it manageable?

It's in your best interest to avoid me. I'm bad news bears.
I struggle with stuff too.
The floodgates open now.

He circled July 19, 2012, on his wall calendar and marked it with his "Ultraception" logo. The calendar illustration for July was a peaceful pastel watercolor of an empty picnic table beneath a large elm tree; it reminded him of hikes with Hillary. He propped a blank shooting target against the closet and stabbed it with a knife next to a note from his mother about insurance.

He bought several cases of beer and six two-liter bottles of Sprite.

"That's some party you must be planning!" the checkout clerk joked.

"Yes." Holmes grinned.

But in the apartment he emptied the beer and soda into his kitchen sink and filled the bottles with gasoline. He stored the now nearly empty propane tanks in his bathroom next to his "little blow torch."

July 12, 2012
(8 days before the massacre)

Holmes biked to a nearby Walmart and bought several "fir tree" air fresheners and a padded envelope in which to mail Fenton his notebook. *Maybe she'd finally get it—that his mind was broken.* As he pedaled back to his apartment, he stopped at his bank's ATM and withdrew several hundred dollars in twenties. His apartment reeked of gasoline. He stepped over bowls of gunpowder on his kitchen floor and lit a burner on the stove. One by one he held the cash to the flame, charred the edges, and quickly blew out the fire. Ash littered the air. He tucked the bills inside the notebook, slipped it into the envelope, and addressed it in black crayon to "Lynne Fenton" from "James Holmes."

July 14–17, 2012
(6–3 days before the massacre)

Holmes purchased bomb-making materials from the Science Company, a Denver hobby shop: potassium permanganate (a common ingredient found in fruit preservatives), glycerin, ammonium chloride, and magnesium ribbon, petri dishes, and electrodes. At Walmart, he bought several cold packs, the kind used in kids' school lunch boxes, the kind that had once contained ammonium nitrate, which Timothy McVeigh had used to blow up the Alfred P. Murrah Federal Building in Oklahoma City seventeen years earlier. Holmes later shared with detectives that he had shopped at "five or six different stores" but the packs were "all non–ammonium nitrate based," "probably specifically because of this kind of thing." He purchased the packs anyway and sprinkled the white powder all over his apartment hoping to "scare first responders" into thinking they might explode on impact like "land mines." He created a "B-movie version of a sophisticated booby trap" by slicing the soda bottles in half and packing some with gunpowder and others with gasoline.

He poured his homemade "napalm" (gasoline mixed with Styrofoam chips) into large glass pickle jars and topped them off with rifle and pistol cartridges, hoping the intense heat would ignite an explosion. Next, he scattered his apartment with the green "fir" air fresheners, "the Christmas trees . . . the little thingamajigs that . . . hang from a rearview mirror?" He filed down aluminum rods and mixed the shavings with iron oxide from rusted metal to make highly flammable "dust" he called "improvised thermite." And in the same skillet he used to fry eggs and cheese, he cooked chemicals. After several hours, the gasoline fumes made him dizzy and he dozed off on the couch surrounded by a "tinderbox" of flammable liquid and explosives. But he "didn't feel any different, between going to sleep normally or with the stuff in the apartment."

July 19–20, 2012
(Near midnight in Aurora, aka "Little America")

It was nearly time. Detonating devices. *Check.* Fishing-line trip wire set to ignite upon entry and explode. *Check.* Computer synced to his boom box programmed to play forty minutes of recorded silence before loudly disturbing his neighbors. *Check.* Remote-control toy tank ("RC") on top of a white garbage bag near the trash can (because "people always leave their trash outside the dumpster"). *Check.*

Eleven forty-five p.m. and traffic was light. Holmes whistled as he held the steering wheel of his used Hyundai Tiburon with his left hand and drove the speed limit, stopping at every yellow signal so he could draw as little attention to himself as possible as he crossed each intersection. The last thing he needed tonight, of all nights, was a cop on his tail. He was on a *mission.* His body was slicked with sweat, an annoying side effect from the hydrocodone pill he'd swallowed to blunt the pain in case someone shot him. *Like that would ever happen with the armor he'd bought.* A car flashed its high beams and Holmes tapped the brakes; his rifle slipped off the passenger seat, into the pile of tactical gear, combat boots, ballistic vest, and pants on the floorboard. The muzzle pointed directly at his head. He smacked the tip away with his thumb and, momentarily distracted, drifted across the center lane. He abruptly overcorrected, nearly missing the turn for the Aurora Century 16 movie theater.

He'd memorized the entrances and exits and rolled slowly through the parking lot with its cars packed in tight, like empty aluminum coffins. Near the rear of the auditorium, he found the alcove with the single bald lamppost, pulled into a spot, and shut off the engine. He had a few minutes. It was only 11:50 p.m. He twirled his key fob around his index finger, opened the door, and, still dressed in his student uniform of jeans, black T-shirt, and long-sleeve open flannel, he tucked his newly dyed shock of orange hair underneath a knit cap and headed to the service kiosk to print out his paper ticket. As he waited in line the air smelled like sweet butter and made his nose itch. A kid behind him in line was dressed in a black Batman cape and plastic eye mask. She giggled and waved, looking pleasant and restful, her little brain so full of private thoughts and secrets, *like his was*, though it sort of pissed him off that she was there—he hadn't planned on kids being at a midnight show.

He punched in the transaction code from his iPhone and the machine spit out a ticket for the wrong theater. It didn't matter. It wasn't like he needed a ticket, not really. No one checked, and despite the fact that he'd already designated theaters 10 and 12 as the best, he planned to slip into theater 9. He hovered for a few minutes near the concession area, pretending to scroll through his phone. It was important he blended. Sheeple passed him, smiling, laughing, joking. Some were dressed in pajamas. One hugged a large flowered pillow. He envisioned the petals soaked in blood.

Quietly he slipped inside the dark theater just as the previews started. It smelled of fresh popcorn, pretzels, and warm cheese. He sat six rows from the screen in the aisle seat. Next to him, a couple held hands. The woman rested her head on the man's shoulder. Gold hoops threaded through her nose and clusters of scars branded her cheek in the shape of twin moons. In front of him two teenage girls cuddled beneath a blanket, just their heads showing. He resisted the urge to slice them clear off with his Buck knife. The light from the screen flashed over the rows and rows of soft white faces. Too many to count. Each kill was worth one point. His hands tingled. *It was time.*

He faked a phone call, speaking into his silent cell—"Just a sec, movie's about to start." He hoped at least he *looked* polite as he stood and headed for the exit. On his way out, he propped open the door with a plastic tablecloth clip, the kind he'd used to secure a tablecloth to a picnic table when on a date.

His car chirped when he hit the fob. The windows were heavily tinted and inside he was hidden in plain sight. In the cramped space, he wriggled into his body armor, relieved he'd preloaded his shotgun and semiautomatic rifle in the apartment, which he'd rigged with trip wires, gasoline, and napalm bombs. Fleetingly he wondered if they had exploded yet. He was about to put in his earbuds when he heard a clash of metal in the alley and froze. A theater employee was stuffing trash into a nearby dumpster; the lid clattered. Slowly, he reached for the spare pistol he'd loaded with hollow points and stashed inside the passenger door. He rested a gloved finger on the trigger, prepared to blow the fucker's head off. He envisioned the bullet striking the skull and sending bone fragments into the brain like sharp little knives. But before he had the chance to pull the trigger, the employee ducked back inside the theater.

He tossed the gun on the front seat, tugged on his ballistics pants, and, just before he fastened his gas mask, made another phone call, this time for real, to an operator at the University of Colorado. He cradled the cell between his shoulder and cheek. It rang and rang and after nine seconds he hung up. *This is it. I'm doing this. Armageddon, fuckers.* He scanned the parking lot for FBI agents, who he suspected had been watching him for weeks. They had showed up at the shooting range where he'd practiced blowing apart human silhouettes.

All clear. Now, fully dressed in his tactical gear, he opened the car door and accidentally dropped one of his two tear gas canisters. It rolled out of sight. He wasted precious seconds looking for it. His gas mask fogged. He jammed a gloved hand underneath and quickly wiped it clear. He caught his reflection in the car's side mirror and liked what he saw, a "dangerous" apocalyptic beast.

He activated the metal fuse on the tear gas; it hissed and sparked like a firecracker as he stepped inside the theater and hurled it into the captive crowd. *Shock and awe, shock and awe.* "Becoming Insane" by the techno band Infected Mushroom pulsed through his earbuds.

"I'm becoming insane, insane, insane, insane, insane, I'm becoming insane . . ."

He saw sudden movement in the back and fired, using his 12-gauge shotgun first because he didn't have to be accurate and he could kill large numbers with a single blast. With each muzzle flash, bodies flopped into the aisles. Shrapnel exploded a plastic water bottle. In seconds, the thin movie chairs were pocked with buckshot. A pregnant woman in sandals slipped in pools of blood as she dashed to the exit. He let her go. A man screamed into his cell, *probably dialing 911*; pieces of his face wound up warm and sticky on Holmes' boots. A couple cowered on the floor, clutching each other, their clothes wet and tight like bloody Saran Wrap. After he shot them, parts of them littered the ground like flesh confetti. He grinned at the woman whose blasted scalp hung like raw meat. Light from the projector cast a thick gunpowder haze over the auditorium.

Sweat and scratches on his brand-new gas mask visor blurred his vision, and he couldn't see clearly through the close-range infrared scope he'd installed. Still, bodies were piled up on the steps. His arm cramped from the weight of the shotgun. One man, wearing a blood-soaked Batman shirt full of holes, *grinned* at him. Another crawled toward him, the floor covered with spent shells. Holmes stepped over debris, crushed drink cups, wrappers, a purse, a silver jacket, lots and lots of popcorn. Alarms flashed, making his head throb.

When his shotgun emptied, he switched to his favorite "killer" rifle, the M&P 15. He remembered the sound it made at the shooting range when he'd pulled the trigger for the first time, a loud, ear-piercing *crack, crack, crack*. He jammed in a cartridge, causing it to misfeed. And in that pause, people rushed toward the exit.

His mission over, he left too, tossing his rifle onto the concrete outside. Sirens sawed the night. He headed to his car and rested his Glock on the roof, the luminous green dot beaming onto the far wall like a sniper's laser. He began to strip, struggling a bit with the ballistic pants. As two cops approached, he considered shooting them, but then reconsidered. . . . They looked like him, dressed in padded bulk and gas masks. Maybe they'd leave him alone if they thought he was one of them? But the cops quickly cuffed him, a magazine cartridge falling from his vest. After removing a large Buck knife from his belt, they cut off his multiple layers of clothing, leaving him only in boxers. As they shoved him into a hot squad car, he banged his shoulder against the cage. Cops' voices swirled around him, sounding far away; he heard "stink," "sweat drenched," and "huge pupils." Blue and red lights illuminated their faces. They smelled of sulfur; one, who resembled a small army tank, removed his gas mask and peered at him, his eyes like shattered marble.

"We need to move him."

An ambulance screeched.

He was put in a new patrol car, the floorboards soaked in blood. Clumps of hair clung to the separation cage. On the seat lay a child's torn shoe. Mumbling, Holmes tried to say something about the "improvised explosive devices" set to go off in his apartment "if tripped," but no one listened.

At the police station, he sat in his underwear in a stark windowless room. A clock on the wall showed 2:45 a.m. All he could think of was sleep.

"Water's coming, sir." A different cop set his digital recorder on the steel table, wrapped Holmes' hands in paper bags to capture gunshot residue, and taped them to his wrists. "We're going to make this as easy as possible on you. Can I get you anything else?"

"Oxygen?" he said with a shrug.

Holmes overheard low whispers, almost like growls: "can't screw this up," "confession can't be forced," "a real monster." He was amused by the sounds his fingers made inside the "popcorn bags." They reminded him of hand puppets.

"What was the plan with that?" FBI Special Agent Bomb Technician Garrett Gumbinner asked him during his postarrest interview. He sat across from Holmes in a metal chair at a steel table in a small white room with blank concrete walls. Cameras tucked into the ceiling recorded every whisper, expression, explanation.

Detectives with the Aurora Police Department, faced with an

"extreme public safety issue," desperately needed Holmes' help with the "bomb situation."[12] They appealed to the FBI, which agreed and granted the detectives an unprecedented order allowing them to interview Holmes without his lawyers present.

Holmes said he hoped a passerby would "try to play with the RC," "press all the transmitter buttons," and "set off the fuses to the gunpowder and gasoline mixture," which would then "ignite the thermite."

"That tangle of wires on top of your refrigerator?"

Holmes nodded. "The receiver."

"And the launch control, where did you put that?"

"Behind Planty."

"Planty?"

"The only *live* thing in my apartment."

Gumbinner swallowed his now cold coffee and continued. "Walk me through this again."

"The music would draw the attention." Holmes explained his plan as calmly as if he were reviewing the rules of Monopoly.

"Right, coming from the boom box."

"The attention would jostle the door, tug the fishing line, and topple the thermos full of glycerin. The glycerin would mix in the frying pan with the potassium permanganate to create a flame, and the flame—"

"Would set the petroleum-soaked carpet on fire," Gumbinner said. "And the little black mortars all over your apartment that looked like cartoon bombs?"

"Diversion."

"So, you soaked the carpets in gasoline. What about the magnesium chips?"

---

12 Holmes' legal team would later move (unsuccessfully) to suppress the evidence as unlawfully obtained in violation of Holmes' Sixth Amendment right to counsel.

"For effect."

"If stepped on, will they ignite?"

Holmes smirked. "It doesn't ignite with pressure . . . you should know this."

"I don't know. That's why I'm asking, James."

"They teach all the firefighters magnesium fires need to be handled differently . . . spray water on magnesium fires and it creates . . . hydrogen."

"Yeah, I'm not a bomb guy or a fire guy," the agent lied, wanting to hear Holmes' explanation.

"I'm not a bomb guy or a fire guy either." Holmes stared at the agent blankly and a moment of uncomfortable silence passed between them.

"What about a timer? Are these bombs set to explode at a certain countdown?" Gumbinner charged ahead.

"Timing was supposed to be the music . . . the whole shindig."

"What else, James? What else do you have in your apartment that could hurt people?"

Holmes shrugged. "Nothing. *I'm* not in there anymore."

As quickly as Gumbinner extracted information from Holmes and relayed the details of his plot to authorities, the Adams County Sheriff's Department, Aurora SWAT team, fire department, and FBI bomb squad evacuated and secured Holmes' apartment building and surrounding structures. Snipers took up positions on rooftops. Bomb-sniffing dogs cleared cars in the nearby parking lots and alleys. Using the fire department's ladder truck, the FBI shattered a window to Holmes' apartment and extended a pole camera through the crack.

Meanwhile, the SWAT team, using a remote-controlled robot, began a "slow clear" of the complex, beginning on the ground floor. Bomb technicians, wearing heavily armored suits, sealed visors, and self-contained breathing apparatus, investigated unsubstantiated citizen reports of military-grade explosives ("C-4") strewn on the roof.

At dawn, the robot arm extended into Holmes' dimly lit apartment. Cameras illuminated the zigzag streaks of white powder on the carpet and the eerie glow of fishing-line trip wire thumbtacked to the front door, leading to an open plastic jug filled with glycerin and tilted over a skillet of potassium permanganate. The tiniest of spills would have ignited a violent spark and, in a room full of gasoline fumes, cause an inferno.

The cameras panned wider to reveal flashing LEDs labeled "Launch Kontrol Pyrotechnic system" and red and blue bulbs illuminating the living room. In the shadows, gallon-size pickle jars filled with gasoline, homemade napalm, and rifle cartridges were balanced on chairs with magnesium ribbon and detonating wires connected to their tops. Nearby were several black spheres filled with gunpowder and homemade thermite. Fresh motor oil stained the rug. Even Holmes' bicycle, propped against the wall, had electrical wire tangled in the spokes that connected to explosives. Over the course of several hours, the first bomb specialist slowly disarmed the fishing-line glycerin-potassium-permanganate booby trap.

By late afternoon, the agents were once again consulting with Holmes, now dressed in an orange jumpsuit and shackles, slumped over in his chair in a small, sterile room in the Aurora city jail. One of the agents tucked a micro digital recorder between the pages of his notebook and slid it toward the middle of the table but, so emotionally drained and exhausted from the ordeal, forgot to press "record" until several minutes into the interview.

"We need your help," he said, and, appealing to Holmes' purported concern for children, added, "We don't want to endanger any children in the building."

This suggestion seemed to flip a switch in Holmes, and he began to methodically answer the agent's questions; for more than thirty minutes, his monotone nearly a whisper, he detailed his more than thirty homemade grenades, gallons of gasoline stored in his kitchen cabinet, chemicals "frying" in pans on the stove, and elaborate detonating devices. But he did not tell anyone about the package he'd mailed to Dr. Fenton a few hours before the shooting: no one knew to ask.

Holmes' setup was so complicated, it took agents four days to dismantle the bombs.

PART II

In Memoriam

July 20, 2012
(Just after midnight)

I took the blood that wasn't mine to take.
—James Holmes

Alexander Jonathan Boik (aka "AJ"), just eighteen years old, warm and kind, "made people laugh" and aspired to someday open his own art studio after graduating from the Rocky Mountain College of Art and Design.

Alex M. Sullivan (aka "Sully"), celebrating his twenty-seventh birthday, was a "cherished, gentle giant" whose father returned often to the movie theater to sit next to the empty seat where Sully lost his life.

John T. Larimer, a twenty-seven-year-old naval petty officer third class, stationed at the US Fleet Cyber Command station at Buckley Air Force Base in Aurora, was an "outstanding shipmate" with a "quiet gentleness" and "rapier wit" who will be forever remembered.

Jesse Childress, a twenty-nine-year-old Air Force cybersystems operator based at Buckley Air Force Base, was an avid Denver Broncos fan, adored by all who knew him.

Jessica Ghawi, twenty-four, "sharp-witted and funny," was an aspiring sportscaster who believed "every day was a gift."

Matt McQuinn, a twenty-seven-year-old hero, died protecting his girlfriend.

Veronica Moser-Sullivan, a vibrant six-year-old, was enchanted by life and all things "sparkly."

Jonathan Blunk, a twenty-six-year-old aspiring Navy SEAL, was a "true American hero" who died the way he lived, protecting those he loved.

Micayla Medek, a twenty-three-year-old college student attending Aurora Community College, graced many lives with her kindness.

Rebecca Wingo, a thirty-two-year-old "happy, bubbly" mother of two young children, was "fearless" and an "amazing spirit," a "Rock Star" in her own right.

Gordon Cowden, a fifty-one-year-old "true Texas gentleman," was the devoted father of four children who were "the focus of his life"; the world is worse without him.

Alexander Teves, a twenty-four-year-old aspiring psychiatrist, died a hero protecting his girlfriend.

CHAPTER 10

MADNESS AT MIDNIGHT

July 20, 2012
(And so it begins . . .)

FENTON

"Are you seeing this?" Steve's voice over the phone sounded far away, like he was in a wind tunnel. "It's our guy, Lynne! He did it, he really did it. Jesus, I can't believe it!"

His call woke me from a sound sleep, the panic in his voice making my heart pound as I scrambled out of bed, padded barefoot to the living room, and switched on my computer. I felt suddenly light-headed, unsteady on my feet. Blood pounded in my ears, and there was a shrill ringing in the back of my skull. I couldn't believe it. *Holmes.* A reporter described the massacre as "Madness at Midnight. Gunshot after gunshot. Hundreds of people just running around." Disembodied voices recounted the horror, the words assaulting me.

Something flew across the screen and exploded nearby with a sound like a soda can, *pop, pop, pop.*

Possibly a prank.

A whistle hissing, then the overwhelming smell of gunpowder.

Sulfur and burning flesh.

The shooter, a blocky figure in the doorway, wearing a mask, carrying a long barrel with a scope, yelled *"hey you fuckers"* and then *boom, boom, boom!*

The air was so thick it was hard to breathe.

Some considered playing dead.

Run! Run! Run!

One survivor, eyes tearing, recalled smoke billowing out from beneath the chairs; something stung her thigh and she heard "little beads falling around her." Gunfire sprayed, and in her mind she repeated, "Spray and pray, spray and pray."

Tearfully, survivors spoke of how they'd slipped over bodies in the aisle, their hands sliding on the bloody railing, their ears ringing, as if they had been hit in the head with a firecracker. Another heard loud bangs, saw sparks, and then, in the serene calm that followed, had the sensation she was going to die.

A reporter's voice droned in the background.

In the span of a few minutes, hundreds of people in an Aurora, Colorado, movie theater were terrorized when a masked gunman entered an auditorium at the Century 16 multiplex, threw a gas canister, and opened fire . . . Moviegoers tried to run or crawl for cover. Twelve people were killed and over fifty-eight injured.

I couldn't breathe. I was transfixed by the scene of carnage, the theater now a makeshift grave. The white movie screen was draped over several rows of seats, riddled with bullets, spilled popcorn, and fresh blood, punctuated by the eerie sound of cell phones ringing and ringing. A lump formed in my throat. Outside, more chaos as police cars and ambulances jammed the parking lot, stricken moviegoers collapsed on the curb, in the grass, draped in heavy woolen blankets, shell-shocked. Strangled cries echoed as witnesses searched for their missing loved ones.

"Lynne!" I'd forgotten Steve was still on the phone. "You should come in. They've set up a command center at the campus police station."

I couldn't believe what I was seeing. It didn't seem possible. His mother's haunting statement played over and over in my head: *"He was terrified of everything."* And so, he became the monster he feared. *This was my Virginia Tech* . . . surreal, life altering, the horror of it all jolting me like cold electric shocks.

"Lynne?"

"I'm still here." I barely recognized my own voice. "I'm . . . okay." *I wasn't. I was free-falling over a cliff.* I clicked off my computer, ended the call, and sat in eerie silence for what seemed too long. A darkness crept across the floor, a rushing heaviness that felt like a physical punch to the gut. And suddenly I was right back there in a night air drill, crawling on my belly beneath a canopy of barbed wire, dragging a fake injured patient to safety, wearing a snug gas mask, barely able to breathe, the simulated desert battlefield now a smoke-filled haze. Though my instructors had always been kind to me, I knew they could be stern; new recruits needed to feel the terror, that sense of helplessness, that tunnel vision, and to know the only way out was through, through that darkness, one foot in front of the other. Just keep going. Do the next right thing. Go on.

A shiver coursed through me at the knowledge that when I left my house, I would not be myself anymore.

Gayle's text in the blue-lit dawn was almost surreal as my world suddenly narrowed. "There's been a bomb threat at Building 500, we've all been evacuated."

Heart pounding, I stared at my phone, almost paralyzed.

"I'm heading your way." Another text. "Hard to do this with one hand." I called her, told her not to come, that I was heading to a safe place, the irony not lost on me.

"Lynne." Gayle was choked up. A car honked. I heard a siren chirp and it sounded like she was being pulled over. "Hang on," she said, her muffled sobs making *me* tear up. And for the first time in many years, I felt helpless, alone, like the morning after an apocalypse, like the whole world had changed but I was still trying to function in some kind of normal. "There's been a shooting," I heard Gayle tell the officer, and soon they were both crying. "We're in this together," he told her, his words hitting me hard. We weren't in this together, I realized. I was very much alone.

I made my way to the makeshift campus "command center," where pots of fresh coffee brewed, clippings and maps of the university covered the walls, police radios blared, and members from the legal department swarmed around large conference tables, looking ashen, disheveled, and unshaven. Surrounded by half-empty boxes of doughnuts, they noisily chattered into their cell phones. But as soon as I entered, the room grew suddenly quiet.

"You look like a ghost." Steve, the only person there I recognized, elbowed his way through the throng of police and bear-hugged me, his voice trembling in the shell of my ear. "You'll get through this."

I didn't believe him. It wasn't real yet. How could any of this be okay? How would I *ever* be okay? In that moment, I felt sick.

As the horror replayed on the television, news reporters struggled for answers and debated "why" Holmes had slaughtered an auditorium full of moviegoers: *Was he mentally ill? Did he have a history of violence? Was he on the FBI's "gun watch list"?*

Steve took my elbow and guided me to a chair. Sitting down suddenly seemed important.

The police had questions, of course. Did Holmes ever tell me about possible targets, accomplices, other bomb-laden traps?

"No," I said repeatedly, "he never said a word."

He barely talked. And when he did, he said nothing. The police looked a little incredulous; they probably thought I was in shock, unable to think clearly or remember details from our sessions, but that wasn't the case. Holmes was like a permanent stain on my psyche. And though he'd physically spared me his bullets, I hadn't truly *survived* him. . . . I hadn't *stopped* him, and no matter my reasons, or the legal restrictions, I had to live with that knowledge. His darkness had seemed so impenetrable, each session with him like an exercise in opening my eyes, hoping to *see* something, even a thin band of light beneath a locked door. But I never did; I only ever *sensed* him.

And how exactly was I going to explain that?

Somehow, I drove home later that afternoon, though I didn't remember starting my car or finding the freeway; usually so adept at compartmentalization, invulnerable to crisis, this time I succumbed to the horror of the massacre, my hands trembling on the steering wheel as I navigated in full-on freak-out mode. *Was this my fault? Could I have done anything differently? Did I make a mistake?* My mind racing, I replayed all the sessions I'd had with Holmes, his strange, robotic presentation, almost inhuman sputters and non sequiturs. *I could not have done anything differently . . . could I?*

Once home, I paced my living room, closing the curtains, fearful I'd been followed, staring out at the busy street, wary of every car that slowed at the intersection or honked its horn, though Steffen, whom I still considered my best friend, gently reminded me when I called him that no one knew who I was; still, I insisted he not hang up until I'd finished most of the Beaujolais and swallowed a sleeping pill. The next morning, it started again, the unreality of it all making my head throb as I absorbed news updates of the carnage and the growing public outcry toward psychiatrists as pill-pushing, quick-fix mechanics unwilling to look under the hood and *see* the person inside.

But what if there was nothing there? What if the patient was a complete blank?

CHAPTER 11

JUST SAYING

July 22–26, 2012

I don't respond to threats, I make them.
—The Joker, *The Dark Knight* (2008)

FENTON

Steffen, likely drained from listening to me ruminate for hours over the weekend, insisted I contact Jane, who not only specialized in malpractice litigation but whose firm, Hall & Evans, also regularly contracted with the university, accepting their overflow and conflict cases. Reaching out to Jane seemed a reasonable precaution, "damage control" in the unlikely event someone actually sued me personally for malpractice, and since I was insured through the university, Jane's legal fees would be covered.

She called me right away, interrupting her Sunday bike ride to say how "sickened" she was by the news accounts of Holmes' massacre. She wanted to see me first thing Monday morning and told me to bring "everything" I had.

I canceled my Monday patients, dreading the return to campus and the inevitable barrage of questions from colleagues and students still reeling from the shooting. I would have to comfort patients who either knew Holmes or knew his victims, all the while quietly imploding.

I met Jane at her law firm, Hall & Evans. We sat across from each other at a large conference table littered with paper and electronic records, including my notes and reports, Holmes' medical files, and all the information I'd stored on servers, computers, flash drives, and disks. My body of work sat exposed like guts ready for autopsy. Then it occurred to me that if Jane had already received my materials from the university, they, too, had begun scrutinizing my interactions with Holmes. And I envisioned my department chair consulting with experts, assessing the damage, gauging how much of a liability I'd become, and I felt utterly sick.

"No one has sued the university *yet*," Jane said, looking crisp in her navy pin-striped suit, thick designer-framed glasses, and stylish gray cropped hair. "But potential litigants, including families of the victims, will likely file pre-claims, called legal holds, so they don't run any risk of missing the statute of limitations." She slid a cup of fresh coffee my way. I dumped packets of sugar into the liquid, unable to get the survivors' screams out of my head.

It had only been three days since the massacre, and if *I* was still reeling from the aftermath of it all, I was pretty sure the victims' families were as well. They were probably more focused on making funeral arrangements than suing the university. *And why target the university at all? What possible connection did it have to this horror other than Holmes having once been a former student?*

"I've asked for reinforcements. Rick Murray, one of the firm's senior lawyers, has agreed to help." Jane cupped a hand over mine in a gesture of support, her face softening, registering my shock.

"The public will want a scapegoat," said Rick as he breezed into the conference room. Towering over Jane, he was a slender man with an open, Irish-looking face complete with full red mustache and piercing blue eyes. And after an hour of interrogation, I could see how he'd gotten his reputation as Hall & Evans' "super lawyer." He didn't just ask me what happened; he grilled me on every detail, pinning me down on dates, times, chart notes, observations, exchanges, what Holmes *said* and *didn't say*, what I did and didn't do and why. Soon, it became clear to me, he didn't just want information; he was preparing me for every possible litigation: criminal, civil, malpractice. Wiping his round-framed glasses with a soft chamois, he brought up the law related to the famous Tarasoff case. Didn't I have a duty to warn others? *Yes.* Didn't Holmes repeatedly tell me he had homicidal thoughts? *Yes, but no specific targets, no plan, no intended victims.* Why didn't I place him on a mental health hold? *He didn't qualify, as he wasn't suicidal and had made no direct threats to harm others.* The more we talked, the more anxious I became. I felt the room shift, as if everything was going in and out of focus.

Rick, perhaps sensing my distress, said, "I think we've done enough for one day."

I felt a sinking feeling in my stomach. I couldn't imagine spending *more* time talking about this. My life was now consumed by Holmes. I'd practically memorized the actions I'd taken and had thought about nothing *else* since the massacre, retracing my steps, reviewing my notes, line by line.

I escaped at the first opportunity, hiking a flat, rocky trail that looped for miles through expansive meadows and fields of flowers. But the sunset looked bruised and swollen, and the clusters of Alpine fireweed and fairy trumpets popped around me like spots of blood.

When I returned to campus that first week, nothing felt the same—though I had a full schedule, met patients, prepared course materials, supervised at the outpatient clinic. I was on autopilot, distracted by racing thoughts as I grappled with the magnitude of Holmes' brutality and all the lives he'd forever changed. My department had implemented a "check welfare" system as support for psychiatrists whose patients had committed suicide or threatened bodily harm . . . or committed mass murder. Well-meaning colleagues dropped by frequently to check in on me, bring me food, make sure I was "okay." But I wasn't, and I wasn't sure when I ever would be again. At some point I realized I was functioning but not fully present. And though my department chair had reassured me that the experts he'd consulted had all supported my decisions, I still worried about my job security. I had Gayle and Steffen on speed dial, obsessively discussing over and over the precautions I'd taken to prevent exactly this disaster. Talking was release, like vomiting words; when I'd finally hang up, I felt better for a while, until the sickness returned and I needed to talk again.

"Let's start with the basics. Give us your credentials." Rick bit the cap off a black felt-tip marker and drew several vertical and horizontal lines on the whiteboard to record a timeline of events. I went through my professional history—bachelor's degree in genetics from the University of California, Davis; medical degree at Chicago Medical School; four-year residency in PM&R (physiatry) at Northwestern; chief of physical medicine at Wilford Hall Medical Center at Lackland Air Force Base. After leaving the Air Force, I took a job with a group practice in the Denver area, then opened a private practice, where I became known for employing acupuncture as a way to treat chronic pain.

Patients seemed to recover more quickly when we incorporated acupuncture, even better than they had with their local Chinese medicine experts. I knew it wasn't my acupuncture skills. I was applying a kind of untrained psychotherapy to my patients' problems. Having specialized in the physical, I had become fascinated with mental health, how thoughts and expectations affected physical outcomes—so much so that I completed a second residency program in psychiatry at the University of Colorado, becoming chief resident of the outpatient clinic and, soon after that, a research fellow at the Veterans Administration, studying the effects of psychotherapy on the brain. I then served as the director of the Anschutz Medical Campus mental health service for students and now was an associate training director of the psychiatry residency program.

Rick smiled his curiously asymmetrical smile, which made one side of his face droop. "Yet somehow Holmes managed to elude *you*, one of the most brilliant and qualified mental health experts in the country."

It was a sobering fact, but Holmes' evil wasn't obvious; it defied explanation. He fit none of the more than four hundred categories of mental health disorders listed in the *DSM*. He was unique. His weirdness had come on gradually, over time, appearing after the end of childhood when so many other disorders first manifested.

"Tell me about BETA," Rick said, spelling out BEHAVIORAL AND ENVIRONMENTAL THREAT ASSESSMENT on the whiteboard in large block letters and underlining it several times. I'd helped form the campus-wide team after the Virginia Tech massacre five years earlier, as a better way to share information between faculty, police, Student Mental Health, Legal, and other university departments. I'd informed them all about Holmes. About my fear regarding his potential violence.

Rick's questions began, easy at first, a back-and-forth volley that gradually sped up like in a Ping-Pong game, the hits becoming harder, followed by power slams, errant balls, and missed points. Jane played referee, keeping score, calling fouls, cheering me on. "Again," she'd cry, "it's like muscle memory." Well, maybe it should have been, but my notes got jumbled in my head, my sessions blended together, and I saw only Holmes, his bug-eyed stare, his monosyllabic speech, his unease. I stumbled over my words. Jane wasn't worried; "We'll keep practicing," she said.

Three hours into the interrogation, my body ached with fatigue. Rick's questions pinged in my ears. Did homicidal thoughts necessarily lead to murder? He'd ask the same questions over and over in slightly different ways, testing my memory, my cool under pressure. It was all so surreal. One minute I was treating patients, the next preparing for litigation. Why did Holmes want to kill? *Killing was his solution to his biological problem, but he said it was flawed because he couldn't kill everyone.* Jane poured me some water as Rick asked, "Did he elaborate?"

"Not really," I said, feeling suddenly shaky from low blood sugar.

"Did you *ask* him?" Rick's question reverberated like an echo in my head. *Did I ask him? Of course I asked him, but he didn't answer.* At that point, my relationship with Holmes had been tentative, and I was still trying to build rapport.

Rick seemed to be losing patience, prompting Jane to jump in and point out that Holmes had all but dismissed the idea of homicide as an effective solution to his problems, meaning I couldn't point to any imminent violence. That should have brought me relief, but it didn't. "Let's move on," Rick said, and pivoted to medications: Why had I prescribed sertraline (aka Zoloft), a common antidepressant, if Holmes wasn't depressed? *Because it worked for anxiety and could help with OCD.* And Klonopin? *Holmes needed immediate relief and sertraline could take too long to be effective.* Had I considered antipsychotics? *Yes, I thought he might have a cluster A personality disorder or be at the beginning of a psychotic disorder, but I needed more information and had brought Steve in as a consultant.*

My life was not my own anymore. Every word I said, every pill I prescribed, every thought I had, was up for review, and paradoxically, the more exposed I was, the more protected I was supposed to feel. "What we don't know can hurt you," Rick said, convinced it was never too soon to mount a malpractice defense.

Jane squeezed my arm. "Break time," she said. "How are you holding up, kiddo?"

My head throbbing, I swallowed a Tylenol dry. "I'm fine," I said. *I wasn't really.* I was pretty sure I was living every psychiatrist's nightmare.

"You're the only one I know who could handle this kind of scrutiny and pressure and not implode."

I wasn't so sure about that. "How do *you* think I'm doing?"

"Let's go for a walk."

Once outside, the traffic noise and high-rises of downtown Denver did little to soothe my nerves.

"Rick means well. He just has a more . . . aggressive style," Jane apologized, probably sensing my distress. I wasn't sure I understood the point of his "style"—hostility had never been a motivator for me—but I held my tongue as she rattled on about paperwork, reviewing my notes, and the importance of memorization. *It felt like medical school all over again. Only worse, because this time there would be no relief, no end to the mounting tension or dull ache.*

HOLMES

At Holmes' first court appearance, heavily armed guards escorted him, in his jail jumpsuit, orange hair, handcuffs, and shackles, into the Arapahoe County Justice Center, where he was formally arraigned on 165 criminal charges, including twelve counts of first-degree murder. In addition to his parents, who held on to each other as if each was the other's life raft, pockets of media, and rows of victims' relatives, defense groupies (called "Holmies" by the press) also crowded the gallery. Dressed in black goth, they had dyed their hair bright orange in solidarity, claiming they, like Holmes, "were all Jokers." One later told the press that she supported Holmes in part because she hoped to "better understand her bipolar brother," but mostly because she was "in love with him."

Judge William Blair Sylvester (who later recused himself once the prosecution announced it would seek the death penalty) issued a gag order prohibiting the disclosure or dissemination of any information related to Holmes and sealed his medical records. Since both the prosecution and defense had a right to ask for preclusion of certain evidence, crop their own snapshots of Holmes, develop their own theories of what happened and why, if information was prematurely leaked it could jeopardize the entire case, resulting in a possible change of venue, mistrial, or undue prejudice to Holmes' constitutional right to receive a fair trial.

But three days after the shooting, Holmes' heavily stamped white envelope arrived at the campus mail room. Suspecting it might contain explosives, campus police cleared the building, cordoned off the perimeter with yellow crime scene tape, and called in the Adams County bomb squad with its five-ton truck and robot. Clusters of environmental safety personnel joined them, along with members of the Aurora Police Department and even an FBI weapons-of-mass-destruction expert. All watched as the robot carefully pinched the package in its metal claw and slid it inside a hooded container where it could be X-rayed for biochemical hazards and possible explosives. After detecting no imminent threat, a bomb technician, dressed in gas mask and plastic head cap, carefully opened the package and removed its contents—a brown spiral notebook titled "Of Life."

Fox News reporter Jana Winter, in an exclusive article, disclosed its contents: details of how Holmes planned to kill people, violent drawings, "gun-wielding stick figures blowing away other stick figures." When pressed for her sources, she remained vague, describing them only as "law enforcement" and Holmes' "intended recipient" as "a professor who also treated patients at the psychiatry outpatient facility," stressing "it could not be verified that the psychiatrist had had previous contact with Holmes."

Winter's disclosure, just five days after the massacre, violated the judge's gag order; "law enforcement" later testified that they may have "inadvertently fanned" the pages of the notebook, unlawfully revealing its contents and risking preclusion of the one piece of evidence that provided insight into Holmes' murder plot. Holmes' defense team demanded Winter, who lived in New York, reveal her sources. Judge Sylvester agreed and ruled Winter was a necessary witness to Holmes' prosecution. But in order for the Colorado court to enforce Winter's subpoena, it needed the approval of a New York judge.

New York's "shield law," unlike Colorado's, unequivocally protected reporters from having to reveal their sources "no matter how crucial the information." After a sixteen-month legal saga, it was affirmed that the law covered New York journalists reporting on crimes in other states, and Winter was never compelled to testify or to name her sources.

Meanwhile, the gag order did little to protect *me*.

CHAPTER 12

"GOTCHA!"

July 27—August 2, 2012

A fish with his mouth closed never gets caught!
—The Joker, *The Dark Knight* (2008)

FENTON

"You've been outed." Leslie Stephens Wallman, one of the university's risk management attorneys, burst into the office of Bob Freedman, chair of the Psychiatry Department, and interrupted my afternoon consultation with him. She marched to the window and peeped through a slatted blind. "The press is salivating. The building is already crawling with reporters. They're outside your office, looking for you. It's a feeding frenzy."

At first, I didn't register what Leslie was saying. I couldn't fathom how I'd been "outed" and hadn't yet grasped the gravity of all that implied.

"Your name is all over the news—we need to get you out of here!" She snapped her fingers at me. "Give me the keys to your office; I'll get your purse and whatever else you think you'll want. I'll be back in two seconds. Stay away from the windows."

Sweat began to trickle down the back of my blouse. Freedman put a comforting hand on my shoulder and said, "You'll be okay, Lynne; it's going to be okay."

How exactly was it going to be okay? The public's anger at this sense-less massacre would now be directed at me, like a massive army levying tanks, artillery, and bombs in my direction.

Freedman ushered me quickly into a wing of administrative of-fices near the back elevators. Heart pounding, I focused on loose threads in his suit jacket, the skin at the back of his neck, his glossy black hair. Ordinary things. Normal things. And as the floor shifted and lurched beneath my feet, my thoughts drifted to my packed schedule, my teaching, my patient load of eighty-plus students, and the many sessions I would now have to cancel or postpone.

"Don't worry about your appointments." Freedman's voice sounded like tin in my ears. "We'll work it out."

My patients would be upset, though, perhaps start to mistrust me, and, with their treatment delayed, might relapse. *This was a nightmare.* What would they think of me now that they knew I was the psychiatrist of a mass murderer? Would they even want me to continue to treat them?

In an empty conference room, I shut the door and stood hold-ing on to the knob as if somehow it was my only support. Finally, I let go and, shaking, called Steffen, still the only person who could comfort me.

"You can't go home. It's not safe. Stay at our place. We won't be there until later. Pull into the garage; there's an extra house key hid-den inside."

Leslie found me, tossed me my purse, held on to my keys. "Let's go," she said. "Campus security is going to distract the press, give them a decoy so we can get you out of here."

Flooded with adrenaline, I hurried after her toward the eleva-tors that led down to the alley behind Building 500, my only dis-guise a pair of sunglasses. The whole experience was otherworldly, like a dream I couldn't wake up from. It felt like it was happening to someone else. Only it wasn't. It was happening to me and I couldn't stop it, couldn't get off the ride, which just rushed faster and faster, taking my breath away.

A colleague held open the doors to the elevator and peeked in, then gave us the all-clear signal. I rushed inside, suddenly light-headed from the oppressive warmth and the unnatural glare of the fluorescent bulbs. At street level, we hesitated at the double exit doors. Through the small vertical windows, I caught glimpses of reporters, fuzzy microphones, and news vans parked askew on curbs, in the street, and in the grassy patches between buildings.

"Predators," Leslie muttered.

"It's about a three-minute run from here to my car," I said, staring at the stretch of sidewalk that snaked to the garage. It was going to feel like a marathon.

Leslie gave me a thumbs-up and we dashed into the bright afternoon sun and ominous quiet; distracted reporters were now storming the front entrance. My world shrank to tunnel vision, jagged gravel beneath my wedge heels, broken chips of glass, labored breathing, concrete columns, license plates.

"Get in and keep your head down!" Leslie hit the key fob, climbed into the driver's seat, shifted my car into gear with a crunch, jammed her foot on the pedal, and peeled around several corners to exit the garage. I crouched down, heart pounding as I directed Leslie to Steffen's house. Wind buffeted my little car. Every bend and dip in the road made my stomach lurch. I drew in a breath, a silent gasp of shock as if someone had dumped a bucket of ice-cold water over me, jolting me awake. I had spent so much of my career helping people in crisis, helping them process that exact moment that forever changed them. Never did I imagine that I might one day experience the same crushing sensation.

Just then, my cell phone lit up with a text from my brother. "Your Facebook has been hacked. Someone knows our names. What the hell is going on Lynne?" Nausea roared in the back of my throat. *It had begun. Like a shock wave, the impact of Holmes had spread to my family.* Horrified, I didn't know what to say, didn't know how to reduce my brother's panic. It wasn't okay; it wasn't going to be okay. Nothing was okay anymore. I'd been exposed. My life, my family's life were now under a microscope. *Nowhere to hide.*

"We're here." Leslie idled the car. "Do you have a key?"

"It's open; just pull inside." My voice, so full of emotion, sounded throaty, clogged.

"You have that look."

"What look?"

"Like you've just aged a hundred years."

As the garage door rolled shut behind us, we sat in silence for what seemed like several minutes until Leslie whispered, "How long can you stay here? You shouldn't go home for a while."

Panic surged through me. I couldn't just *not go home*. I had cats! And I needed clothes, toiletries. I felt like my flight had just crashed and I was sifting through the debris for my belongings, my survival reduced to simple comforts.

Jane called. "The press is all over your place. We'll have to sneak you inside," she said. "Go through the back entrance. I'll create a diversion." She offered to watch my cats.

I sat at Steffen's kitchen table numbly watching the small television on the windowsill, absorbing snippets of mostly replayed interviews with first responders:

"It was taking too long, ten minutes for us to get to the scene."

"No one could get through. There were people, moviegoers from the other theaters leaving, police cars blocking exits, civilians running, just running. Complete pandemonium."

"Officer Justin Grizzle spoke through tears as he described how he'd walked into Theater Nine, his gun drawn, slipping on pools of

blood, his nose running from tear gas. Strobe lights whirled above him, alarm bells sounded, the movie still blared. Through the fog he saw bodies, checked corpses for booby traps and steered two of the wounded into his patrol car. With his siren blasting, he sped off for the Aurora South Medical Center, violating protocol, transporting the pregnant and bleeding Ashley Moser, whose six-year-old daughter had been fatally shot."

"I didn't want anyone else to die. No one else could die."

"He made multiple trips in the early morning hours of July 20th and, as other emergency rooms in the area filled up, he took the injured to the University of Colorado Hospital, the very facility where Holmes was a graduate student just a few weeks earlier."

My cell rang and, thinking it was Steffen, I answered. "Fucking murderer!" I heard before I hung up, my heart racing. Calls continued to come in from unknown numbers and I let them go to voicemail.

Steffen arrived home, balancing bags of groceries. He left them on the counter, gently pried the remote from my hand, and shut off the voices. "Can I make you some soup?" Though I knew he was trying to be kind, food was the last thing on my mind.

"You can borrow a pair of my pj's." His wife, Mara, lay several choices on the bed. Silky boxer shorts, lace-cuffed cotton Ts, an elegant flowing nightgown.

What did it possibly matter what I wore to sleep?

"Well, at least let me get you some wine." Mara started to pour each of us a glass of Chianti, then reconsidered. "Fuck it, we're going to need the whole bottle."

In the quiet dark of Steffen's guest bedroom, I lay awake despite the sleeping pill I'd swallowed, my thoughts full of Holmes and his empty, bulbous eyes. Eventually I sat up, bunched several pillows behind my back for support, and switched on my laptop to read my emails. As long as I was *doing* something I could focus.

In the screen's white glow, reporters shouted at me. The *Denver Post* and Fox News wanted simply to talk "off the record" for "just a few minutes." They wanted information "from a first source at the University . . . The mail room found a package from James Holmes containing a notebook spelling out his plans, want to talk about it?"

I enlarged the dates: two days ago, *before* I'd been publicly outed in the media. My heart thumped in my chest. *How had they known? Who had leaked my information to reporters?*

I scrolled through the multiple emails I'd received that day from reporters with Dow Jones Newswires, CNN, the Associated Press, the *Denver Post*, 9News, Thomson Reuters, and the *New York Times*. "Hello, Dr. Fenton, looking through court documents on James Holmes and saw that he referred to you as his psychiatrist. I wanted to confirm." *Court documents?* I felt suddenly dizzy, like laughing or maybe crying. I took a deep breath and pinched the bridge of my nose, trying to get ahold of myself as I read another. "Can you tell us how long you were treating him? The filings from Holmes' attorneys also said Holmes sent you a package." *What filings?*

The more emails I read, the louder the reporters' demands seemed—*Dr. Fenton, Dr. Fenton, Dr. Fenton*—until soon I was addressed simply as "Lynne."

"I gotta ask," a reporter from 9News baited me. "Anything you wanna say?"

Plenty, but I'd been gagged, and it was like screaming in a wind tunnel. The *New York Times* was apologetic: "I assume you can't say anything in response to the court filing . . . but my job obligates me to ask, just in case . . . take care . . . I'm so sorry this is happening to you." A correspondent for the *Sun* ("the British family newspaper") hoped to circumvent the "gagging order" and have me "speak broadly" about my role at the college, something of "international interest."

My eyes stung a bit from the glare. The *Denver Post* was "doing a profile" on me for the newspaper and had "reached out to many people from my past." *Dear God.* My chest tightened.

> I know you are under orders not to talk to the press because you are intricately intertwined in this criminal case. I also know the judge's gag order and HIPAA limits what you can say. But I am trying to do a profile on who you are, your history and life and career. Not about the criminal case . . .

Bullshit. The only reason he was interested in me was for the criminal case.

Blood rushed to my cheeks. I was suddenly at the mercy of predators whose constant challenge was to find fresh food. I thought about basic instinct, survival of the fittest. I was running for my life, and I was out of breath.

Some colleagues reached out. One, a nationally renowned psychiatrist from the Jed Foundation, which was dedicated to preventing suicide in college students, wrote, "I can only begin to imagine what you must be going through. I'm so sorry. If I can be of any help . . ." Another, the dean of the School of Pharmacy, wrote about my "incredibly difficult situation," "certainly thinking about you and appreciate everything you and the Student Wellness and Mental Health team has [*sic*] done . . . I'm sure that this has been personally very difficult for you and may get worse . . . The media can be unrelenting . . . I have a big house, if you need to have a place to stay, away from your home . . . or rotate between safe houses . . . If there is anything I can do to make your life a small bit easier (errands, ironing, cooking, gardening or anything) . . . I really mean it."

Safe houses? Had it really come to that? Was I in physical danger?

Former residents' well-wishes also flooded my in-box. "Just thought you should know your kind nature and delighted intelligent curiosity shaped my practice to this day, you were one of the very best parts of my residency experience, and a big part of why I am able to be so happy and successful today . . ."; "my heart goes out to you"; "you are totally wonderful and terrific . . . try to keep this in mind during this ridiculous and horrible time." Another criticized the university for not issuing a general statement "defending my skills, professionalism and competence . . . perhaps reminding the public that psychiatrists are not mind readers and future tellers? Must be hard to have your hands tied by gag orders and HIPAA, such a helpless feeling." *It was.* Others slammed the media for their lack of compassion, suggesting it might be time to broadcast my board scores "(weren't you #2 in the nation!) and glowing reviews from patients and residents who have worked with you!"

Then there were the more condemning emails from ignorant reporters who somehow felt compelled to educate me on Holmes:

I'M A REPORTER. JAMES HOLMES' BEHAVIOR IS LOGICAL IF HE DEPLOYED BIOWEAPON, AUTHORITIES' BEHAVIOR ISN'T.

I understand his behavior (see below) if he wanted to show everyone that he is smarter than them and used his microRNA research to develop a bioweapon (like a motor neuron retrovirus) . . .

Behaviors

1. Instead of shooting those closest, shot those trying to escape gas.

2. Use of the gas itself. Smoke bombs are used to obscure you from sight of enemy shooters. Tear gas made people scramble . . . targets harder to hit . . .

3. If blood borne disease, use shotgun pellets to create wounds so the disease carrying gas droplets can infect them.

4. Took every precaution to make sure he lived to see the spread of disease.

5. Spit on guards to spread disease. Sheriff dept did not deny this until I emailed them.

6. Signed up with AFF to spread blood borne disease. Prostitutes usually take more precautions then [sic] swingers.

7. I predicted based on the most likely bioweapon he could have developed given his background that he would be twitching if he infected himself. Reports of him twitching and his appearance back up my prediction.

Others, just as insulting, demanded to know my "role" in the mass shooting and "WHAT COMBINATION OF PHARMACEU-TICAL DRUGS" had I prescribed?

But one in particular, from a "Microsoft Certified Systems Engineer" who claimed to have "beheld Satan," made me sit bolt upright in bed. He asked whether I'd treated Holmes "for mental illness, paranoia, or schizophrenia," as he planned to get an "FOIA request" on "any/all information" from the university pertaining to Holmes, and "BTW -Tell whoever took down your profile . . . nice try!"

"I know it's late," I said to Jane on the phone, my voice sounding shriller than I would have liked, "but this is starting to freak me out." I told her I'd been receiving multiple hang-up calls and voice-mail messages from "concerned citizens" wanting to know how I'd allowed this to happen, hoping I'd had no knowledge of Holmes' "plan." One breathed heavily, another scolded me, "Yikes! I wouldn't want to be you," and others referred to me simply as "Lynne." "Hard to believe you didn't know, *Lynne*, really hard to believe."

"Forward everything to me. Let me be your filter. From now on you'll be on a 'need-to-know' basis, which means if there's a new development or something critical concerning your case, I'll make sure you read it. Otherwise, don't open the emails, don't respond to anyone, don't answer your phone, and for God's sake don't delete anything. It could be evidence."

We hung up but I was still holding the phone to my ear, having an out-of-body experience, when I saw the email from Daniel King, Holmes' public defender:

> Dr. Fenton,
>
> I hope this email finds you as well as possible considering recent events. I am very sorry that the Court decided to release our pleading, which made reference to you, to the public. This came as a complete surprise to us as the court file had been previously sealed. Please accept our apologies for any difficulties this may have caused you, had we known the pleading would be made public, we never would have included your name.

Was he kidding?! My whole world had imploded. I dropped the phone and switched on the bed lamp, the glare hitting me like a slap. *Jesus, what if he'd done it on purpose? What if outing me wasn't just thoughtless or reckless but a deliberate act to deflect attention from Holmes? What if it had been the defense's strategy from the beginning? What better way to defend a monster than to shift the blame, make someone* else *the monster?*

Shaking, I forwarded the lawyer's apology to Jane, who replied simply, "We need to get your email address changed."

I wasn't aware of drifting off to sleep, or what suddenly shot me into consciousness as if someone had stabbed me in the heart with a syringe. But I lay there gripped with fear, momentarily disoriented, my heart pounding. *Repeat after me: you're fine.* I checked my phone: three a.m., five missed calls from unknown numbers. *You're in a safe house—*I almost laughed out loud at the way it sounded. *No one knows where you are. No one can get in. No one can reach you.*

I checked my voice messages and heard a throaty whisper: "How can you even sleep at night?"

"It might be best if you left town for a while," Jane said later, pulling the blinds in Steffen's house and shutting off the lights. Dust particles floated in the air. A porcelain replica of a West Highland terrier crouched by the fireplace. Steffen's real Westie whimpered in the quiet gloom. "It's only a matter of time before that reporter from the *Denver Post* across the street knows you're hiding in here." *So . . . I wasn't safe?*

"She's at the door," said Steffen as he squinted through the peephole.

I felt a surge of panic and instinctively dropped to my knees, piling throw pillows on top of me and pressing my forehead to the floor. I shut my eyes, welcoming the dark, suddenly painfully aware *that I was alone, completely alone.* My mind flashed again to the Capezio robbery, to the sickening helplessness. Trapped on that floor, in a place I didn't belong, in a scenario I'd interrupted and had wanted desperately to leave. Although this time the gun wasn't literally pointed at my head, the impact felt just as real.

I heard Steffen open the front door and say, "She's not here and even if she were, she's not talking."

I called Freedman, my department chairman.

"Where will you go?" He sounded far away, as if he belonged to another place and time.

"I'll stay with family for a while . . . just until things die down a bit."

"Are you sure about this?"

"It's for the best." *Even as I said this, a part of me died.*

"Don't stay away too long."

I chewed my lower lip, feeling sick. "I'll need to transfer my caseload." It was the last thing I wanted to do, but I didn't have a choice.

Holmes' bomb-laden apartment building on Paris Street.

PHOTO CREDIT: Getty Images

The infamous notebook detailing Holmes' theory on "human capital."

PHOTO CREDIT: Provided by the Eighteenth Judicial District Attorney's Office

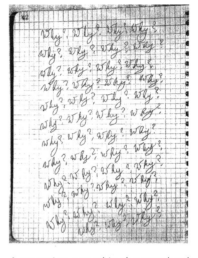

A question posed in the notebook.

PHOTO CREDIT: Provided by the Eighteenth Judicial District Attorney's Office

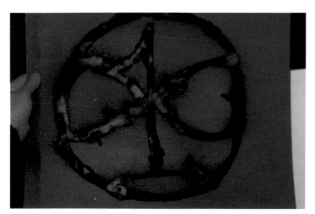

Holmes spray-painted his "Ultraception" logo on a piece of cardboard paper for the cover of his notebook.

PHOTO CREDIT: Provided by the Eighteenth Judicial District Attorney's Office

Guns, gas masks, and ammo spread out on Holmes' red satin bedsheets.

PHOTO CREDIT: Provided by the Eighteenth Judicial District Attorney's Office

Bomb experts took four days to dismantle all the bombs in Holmes' apartment.

PHOTO CREDIT: Getty Images

Holmes' apartment was extensively booby-trapped with makeshift bombs and shell fragments.

One of the jars of homemade napalm.

Inside the booby-trapped kitchen full of homemade bombs.

"Holmies" sent James a Valentine's Day card.

PHOTO CREDIT: Provided by the Eighteenth Judicial District Attorney's Office

Holmes took a gleeful selfie wearing his "possession" lenses.

PHOTO CREDIT Provided by the Eighteenth Judicial District Attorney's Office

First day of trial, James Holmes in court with his lawyers, Daniel King, Katherine Spengler, and Kristen Nelson.

PHOTO CREDIT: Getty Images

Inside the movie theater, destroyed seats and scattered bullet holes.

PHOTO CREDIT: Provided by the Eighteenth Judicial District Attorney's Office

Police marked the trajectories of the bullets that pierced the movie theater seats.

PHOTO CREDIT: Provided by the Eighteenth Judicial District Attorney's Office

James Holmes' jail cell where he launched himself off his bed.

PHOTO CREDIT: Provided by the Eighteenth Judicial District Attorney's Office

A seemingly bored Holmes yawns during survivor testimony.

PHOTO CREDIT: Getty Images

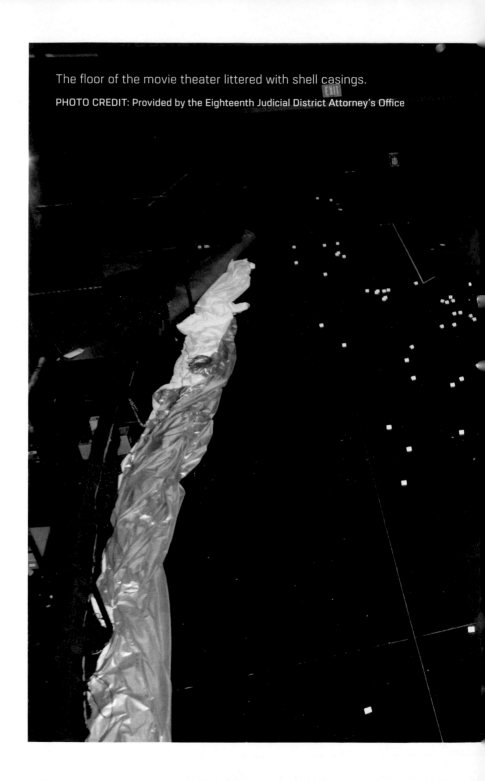
The floor of the movie theater littered with shell casings.

PHOTO CREDIT: Provided by the Eighteenth Judicial District Attorney's Office

Lynne's garden—with its redbud and royal purple smoke trees, oregano, and sage—where she once found peace.

PHOTO CREDIT:
Steffen Andrews

Makeshift memorial dedicated to the twelve movie theater shooting victims built across the street from the Century 16 Theater in Aurora.

PHOTO CREDIT:
Getty Images

Lynne Fenton, MD

PHOTO CREDIT:
Author's Collection

I wasn't myself. And I needed space to fall apart for a while, and not just in the shower, fully dressed, as hot water pelted my head, blending with my tears.

"But your patients love you."

"It's not fair to them if their psychiatrist is in hiding."

Jane pulled into Steffen's garage and, for the second time in several days, I slid into the passenger seat, hair piled into a baseball cap, dark shades covering my eyes, and ducked down as Jane sped off.

"They won't recognize my car," she said. "I can pull into your garage, enter the house from the backyard so they won't see me, and distract them at the front door. That will be your cue to sneak inside."

That's good—a foil, a decoy. Was this my life now? Hiding, sneaking around?

"Incredible," Jane muttered as she approached my house. "They're everywhere, smoking on the curb, hiding behind your bushes, leaning against your fence, like little trolls."

Once inside the milky gloom of my bedroom, I shakily packed clothes for a month, though I had no idea when I would return. I formed sad piles on the bed, T-shirts, jeans, sweatshirts, cardigans. All fit into a small carry-on separated by luggage organizers, bags within bags, neatly stuffed into a vacuum-like seal. My gaunt face in the dresser mirror startled me. It wasn't just the lack of sleep or the deep circles under my eyes; it was something else, something unfamiliar, an emptiness, a look I associated with orphans.

CHAPTER 13

"WOULD YOU RECOGNIZE ME?"

August 3–10

In their last moments, people show you who they really are.
—The Joker, *The Dark Knight* (2008)

FENTON

In between booking flights, packing, and coordinating with my colleagues to cover my classes, I fixated on the news, obsessing over the headlines, clicking from station to station, seeing Holmes' arraignment photo over and over again: his glazed, absent stare and fiery hair. I'd received more hang-up calls and jarring voicemails—"Watch your back, Fenton," "You're the real Devil," "It should have been you in that theater!" "Hope you get what you deserve!"

"She's getting death threats," Steffen shouted into the phone at Jane. "Can't you do something?" He paced as he talked, cradling his Westie in his arms, his face flushed with anger.

"What would you have me do?" Jane argued.

"Defend her! Be her voice! Tell these assholes what she did to try to stop this."

"I know you're upset—"

"Upset is not even close." Steffen hung up and stood at the window, his large frame blocking the sunlight.

"She can't do anything about the threats." I was sitting on the couch, head in my hands, thinking about buying a book called *How to Be Invisible* by J. J. Luna. Though the book focused more on protecting one's privacy and assets, I found the idea of disappearing very appealing right now. Just to check out for a while, release this tension, take a breath.

A vein in Steffen's neck bulged. "If she were doing her job, she'd be out there salvaging your reputation, telling people how you tried to stop this, how this isn't your fault. People might not want to kill you if they knew what really happened. . . ."

"It's complicated."

Steffen snorted. "No, it's not. Jane's your advocate. She should be advocating. Not telling you to become Lynne 'I have no fucking comment' Fenton."

"Would *you* recognize me?" I asked Steffen on the way to the airport, and though I was "disguised" again in my baseball cap and sunglasses, I wasn't referring to my physical appearance. It was more than that; something had shifted inside me. Such sudden, massive change in every area of my life had left me off-balance.

"Ever since this happened, you've been unrecognizable."

I nodded, adding, "I don't know when I'll be back."

"I know."

"Thanks for everything."

"I know."

"Tell Mara. . . ."

"I will."

We drove in silence to the airport; I stared out the window, mostly at other drivers, envious of their seemingly normal lives, wishing desperately I could reverse time and be one of those people again, driving to work, parking in my spot, seeing patients. But I realized the futility of that kind of thinking. I just wasn't ready to accept my new life. I hadn't prepared for this. I didn't know how to do this. My life had gone so far off the tracks, it was like I'd been dropped at the wrong station and in the wrong time period. Steffen double-parked at departures. It was a bright Monday afternoon, and so far we'd eluded reporters. He put a hand on my shoulder. "You're tough, Lynne."

The way he said it, I realized he needed me to be okay so that *he* could be okay. Trauma, like grief, made people uncomfortable, which changed their behavior. Suddenly, they didn't know what to say or how to act and, feeling guilt racked, they censored their positive emotions.

"You're going to get through this," he continued.

"Mm-hmm. Thanks."

With my heart hammering in my chest, I headed toward the metal detectors, feeling exposed, half expecting reporters to suddenly spring out from the airport waiting area or be disguised as security guards, cashiers, or flight attendants.

I felt eyes on me, the hard, accusing stares of strangers. We were all just passing through on the way to somewhere else, hoping to make a connection, searching for the right terminal, rushing, then waiting, to take flight. A woman pushed past me, bumping me in the leg with her suitcase, and I nearly fell off the escalator. My hand shook when I paid for my coffee and again when I gave over my boarding pass, my name clearly printed in bold.

"I would have used a pseudonym," Toby said when I told her.

"I thought about that," but it wouldn't have mattered; everyone knew who I was, and changing my name would have felt like one more loss. I cradled the cell to my ear, the irony not lost on me that I was now slumped in a chair, hiding behind a *People* magazine, when all I wanted now was to avoid people. After a while, feeling a little paranoid, I moved into the restroom and squatted on top of the toilet seat so that no one would see my legs and know the stall was occupied. In a conversation repeatedly interrupted by the sounds of flushes and hand dryers, Toby grew increasingly alarmed.

"Maybe you should reinvent yourself, enter witness protection or something?"

"I don't think I qualify."

"That's bullshit."

"I'll be fine." *Was Toby right? Maybe I should have worn a wig.* "Besides, it's just for a few weeks." *I wasn't sure I could do this for too much longer.* I hadn't realized until I lost my freedom how much I'd taken it for granted. Now every decision I made seemed to have a thousand implications, nearly paralyzing me. Never had I prepared for *fleeing.*

"You're like a celebrity—everyone knows who you are, or at least they think they do because they know your name and know you treated Holmes, and the rest they just make up."

"They hate me."

"They hate who they *think* you are or what they *think* you've caused."

Intellectually, I knew she was right, but it still hurt. It felt personal.

Toby kept apologizing. *I'm so sorry, I'm so sorry, Lynne. I can't imagine what you're going through.* But truthfully, she *could.* In fact, I was pretty sure I was living her worst nightmare, that she looked at me and thought, *This could be me right now; this could be me losing my life.* It struck me how courageous she was, to watch me go through this with Holmes, all the while fearing the worst for her *own* case, knowing she was potentially only one step behind me.

"You're a good friend," I said fervently.

"I'm a phone call away."

I boarded the plane, slid into my window seat, and pressed my face to the glass. Cool air soothed the tension in my forehead. I was breathing too fast again. *What if someone recognizes me?* Thankfully, the seat next to me remained empty. I'd purposefully flown in the middle of the afternoon, hoping to avoid business travelers. I ordered a glass of wine, gulping it down so fast it made me choke. The warmth of the alcohol spread through my blood, instantly relaxing me.

"You can pull down the shade." The flight attendant smiled, her overly made-up face a little too large, too close, disjointed like a Picasso painting.

"I'm sorry?"

She pointed to my sunglasses. "If the sun's too bright."

My brother hugged me at the airport, his grip so tight I thought I might never breathe again. "You look pale. When was the last time you slept?"

"Thanks for taking me in."

Slowly, he released his hold on me, held me at arm's length, arched a brow, and said, "Hope you don't get sick of me."

In his cul-de-sac, pink hibiscus dotted the driveway and a lush mimosa tree with its fernlike leaves formed a canopy over his sweet terra-cotta–colored single-story home. Once inside, surrounded by cream walls, pastel watercolors, and warm slate tile, I finally exhaled. A slight breeze blew into the living room through the open windows. No reporters. No thick blinds.

He led me down the hall to the room that would be my temporary home. "I'll let you settle in." My brother's eyes watered as he shut the door. I dropped into the puffy white chair next to the Murphy bed piled high with decorative pillows and sat motionless on the edge, absorbing the silence that closed around me, profound and womblike. *This was my life now.* Quiet nothingness. Time moved on around me, but I felt as if I were enclosed in a bubble where everything stood still. My life had shattered but my face had no marks. My hazel eyes stayed startled open as if I'd just discovered I was still alive after a horrific accident.

That first night, I curled up on the bed, knees to chest. The night breeze flirted with a tendril of my hair, blowing it against my cheek. I had never felt so alone in my life. My body was exhausted but my mind was still racing. I imagined I felt the way most of the survivors did: in limbo, a twilight space where one life has ended and another is waiting to begin. Only I hadn't a clue what mine would look like in the end, or even if there ever would be an "end."

The next morning, when I stayed too long in my room, staring out the window at families of quail trotting single file across the lawn with their babies close, my brother knocked on my door.

"Breakfast?"

I joined him at the kitchen table, picked at my scrambled eggs, and scrolled through my phone, feeling my blood pressure rise with each email. So much hate. Why was it taking so long for the university to supply me with a different address? *It wasn't as if I could have patients or students email me at my personal address—our communications were confidential and often privileged.*

"Might be wise to stop reading for a while. Maybe watch comedies?" my brother gently suggested.

After another restless night of ruminating, I took his advice. I helped myself to wine and chocolate and switched on *The Tonight Show with Jay Leno.* His guest, Jeremy Renner, spoke about receiving hate mail after portraying serial killer Jeffrey Dahmer on film. He was berated, called a sick monster, an asshole, told "we know what you did." He had to stop reading about himself, he said, because the experience was too painful.

Maybe I should try that, simply shut out the hate, lose myself in orchids and lilies and poppies.

The next day I patted soil in a pot with one gloved hand and smiled, amazed that the five minutes of mindfulness I'd vowed to achieve had stretched to hours.

"It's nice to see you up and about," my brother said.

"Plants always make me feel better."

"Our house thanks you."

But at night I once again paced my bedroom barefoot, looking out into the twilit street, into the gaping windows of neighbors' houses, their televisions blaring, dinner steaming on the table, garage doors clicking open and shut. The world was happening without me. I called Toby, told her I was afraid to dream, afraid my mind would go again to that dark theater and the rows and rows of seats riddled with bullets. I told her that sometimes, in the thick quiet, I recited the victims' names like a long prayer, refusing to forget the horror they'd faced, how many had died as human shields protecting their loved ones, how several had served in the Navy or Air Force and trained for combat but had never imagined Holmes, how many were parents, how many were lovers just starting out their lives. And how one, just six years old, had died before hers had even begun.

Toby shared how much the Butcher had changed her, how much Holmes would change me. She'd once loved the smell of fall, the orange leaves as if the trees were on fire. Now she hated the month of October, the month the Butcher murdered his girlfriend. I wondered if I would now hate the month of July. I'd grieved before, but not like this; what I felt now was an overwhelming sense of loss, of disconnection, as if the world itself didn't feel right anymore.

I decided to resign as head of Student Mental Health. I needed to be available to my students, to counsel them through crises; how could I do that when I was in hiding and barely functioning myself? My voice shook when I told Bob Freedman. It was absolutely the last thing I wanted to do. I loved my work, loved being a psychiatrist, loved my patients. But I was still receiving death threats on a weekly if not daily basis, and the stress of it all was distracting. For the first time in my life, I found it difficult to compartmentalize. Holmes seeped into my every thought.

"Lynne, are you sure . . ."

Yes. It was the right thing to do. I suspected I'd become a liability to the university. Jane was doing her best to hold up the wall, to keep potential lawsuits at bay, but I knew it was only a matter of time before the whole building came down and the university would be sued. It wouldn't help if I was still counseling students.

"You're an asset."

"Maybe I used to be, but now I'm a lightning rod."

"We can discuss this when you return."

"There's nothing to discuss. I need to step down."

"When are you coming back?"

Never. I never want to go back. I could stay here, in this lovely, quiet place, forever.

"You should report these to the police." My brother stood over my shoulder and read the latest emailed death threats, five in all since that morning.

Saw your picture on CNN, you're smiling after what you did! Were
you happy about the whole thing?

It was my university profile picture taken years ago, years before Holmes. . . .

Another came from the Daily Stormer, a Nazi website, calling me a "fucking Jew" and condemning "all Jew psychiatrists." I wasn't even Jewish, but that was beside the point. Jane had assured me she was "creating a media file," then asked whether I was still "tucked away" in my safe house. Part of me wondered whether this was all just a little too "thrilling" for her.

"Why haven't they given you a new email address?" *Why indeed?*

My brother scooped a ball of tuna fish onto a plate of fresh spinach and drizzled it with lemon juice. But I'd lost my appetite.

Instead, I checked my voicemail, feeling anxious and somewhat guilty that I hadn't responded to so many. One from Jane left me unsettled: the university had enlisted a "big gun," former US attorney Robert Miller III, to investigate "all actions" taken by its employees in relation to Holmes. "They'll want to interview you," she said.

"They may have to take a number," Steffen said after I told him the latest development. "I just picked up your mail and the *National Enquirer* wants you."

I returned Jane's call. "What does this mean exactly?" She explained that the university was launching an internal review and had retained the law firm of Perkins Coie to assess whether I had committed malpractice in my treatment of Holmes.

"How long will it take?"

"They don't have a deadline."

"Who requested this?"

"The chancellor of the Anschutz Medical Campus with the endorsement and support of the Board of Regents and president." Jane paused. "You have to brace yourself. Perkins Coie have a ruthless reputation."

I felt a little nauseous. Though it made sense that the university would want to protect itself against possible liability, I didn't want to be the scapegoat, the one blamed if victims' families sued. This would not be a "friendly" internal review; it felt like Perkins Coie was the university's firing squad, hired to take me out.

"You'll need to return, Lynne," Jane said. "We have to prepare."

I wasn't ready. I liked being tucked away in my brother's retreat, in my own room, in another state where no one could find me, where I could go outside and not be accosted, or stay in my pajamas all day if I wanted, roam his garden barefoot and watch the plants grow. In part, I couldn't imagine what I was going back *to*. An indescribable emptiness? It wasn't as if I could just resume life where I'd left off, and I didn't have the energy to pretend I wasn't shattered. Holmes was a collective ache. And, as one of his survivors, I still had to *be* in the world, to function. *I just didn't know how to do that yet.*

"Steve and I are so pleased to know you'll be heading back soon. We've missed you. The residents need a strong female role model. Steve is a poor substitute." Freedman was on speakerphone trying to be positive, though I heard the concern in his voice. I assured him I'd missed work and would return as soon as I could, after I'd secured my safety first. The university had finally assigned me a new unlisted work email, 08012012@ucdenver.edu, a combination of random numbers that ominously reflected the day I was outed.

"We're getting fitted next week for bulletproof vests," Steve said, and explained that he'd already researched various vendors.

"'We'?"

"Marilyn wants one too. She's worried some crazy freak will break into our home, kill her first, then shoot me."

I tried to picture it, Marilyn the life coach, meeting clients in body armor.

"Would you like one too?" Steve asked. "Might be good to have protection."

CHAPTER 14

SAFE

August 15, 2012

I need new haters. The old ones became my fans.
—The Joker, *The Dark Knight* (2008)

FENTON

"Are you sure this is a good idea?" My brother idled the car at the departures terminal.

"No, but I have to take care of my life." I opened the passenger door. I was again dressed in my full disguise, hair tucked into a baseball cap, baggie gray sweatshirt, jeans, sneakers, sunglasses. *I still hadn't figured out how to hide.* "Thank you for everything."

"You bet. Hey, happy birthday."

"Your new fans left you some gifts." Steffen handed me the stack of mail my pet sitter had collected.

"I liked my old fans." I thumbed through bills, university mail, and a slew of business cards, mostly from reporters who'd scribbled little notes to me on the back. *I LOVE your garden,* one wrote. I stared at it now; it looked the way I felt, worn-out, abandoned, dull. My pond had a thin layer of algae skimming the surface. I wanted so badly to fix everything, dig up the weeds, trim back the overgrown paths, restore the whimsy. But instinctively I knew my garden would never be what it once was; I wasn't that person anymore, and I had lost that sense of peace. My contemplation bench took on a more ominous quality after a reporter promised to wait for me every day across the street, in the school playground: "I'll be on a bench. Just want to talk."

"What the fuck!" Steffen screamed at Jane later. "Lynne needs security!"

"I'll let the reporter know that he needs to delete Lynne's number and stop contacting her."

"I feel so much better—let's tell all the nasty reporters to just stop."

Though the university had sent security to inspect my house, install extra locks on the doors and garden gates and motion cameras throughout my property, I still felt violated. It reminded me of friends who'd installed invisible fences around their property to protect their dog from escaping and others from their dog. *But would any of it deter a sniper?* The university's "psyops" agents spent half a day reviewing my Wi-Fi and Internet and installed firewalls.

"We want to keep you safe." One agent winked, as if technology was the problem.

"Police are doing drive-bys," I told Toby later that afternoon, glancing nervously at the bus stop across the street, where several seemingly homeless people loitered outside the gated elementary school parking lot typically crowded with parents collecting their children.

"At least you have eyes on you."

I felt like I was wearing a large sandwich board: DR. FENTON HERE.

August 16–20, 2012

"We thought it was a good idea to move your office," Freedman said, almost apologetically. "You were too isolated on the fourth floor. It just wasn't safe." He led me down a narrow hallway to a barren boxy space directly across from his large, inviting office and main reception. A lump formed in my throat as I surveyed my new rectangular room with its sliver of window. The executive desk looked like a shipwreck in the middle of a lonely sea. This was my life now, sealed off, closed in, protected, invisible. I was thinking about what kinds of plants would survive in this artificial light, when someone rapped on my door.

"We're here to take measurements."

"Measurements?"

"For your bulletproof vest?" *More encasement.*

As one officer recorded the dimensions of my chest, the other reviewed with me the many protective tactical "options"—to deflect heavy artillery and rifle rounds, I might like to add ballistic plates, which were ultralight ceramic ("ideal for petite females"). Extra steel plates, on the other hand, could prevent knife attacks, "stabbings with machetes, even bayonets." And would I like a plate around my heart?

"I look like a box." I had met Toby for breakfast at the mostly empty corner diner near my home. It was a risk to be in public, but I needed air and the place felt safer than most. We sat on the patio under large spotted umbrellas that looked like mushrooms.

"Think of it as trendsetting." Toby poured ketchup over her plate of scrambled eggs and smothered a smile.

"It's awful, isn't it?"

"It's really not that bad." She chuckled.

"None of my clothes fit over this." I shifted uncomfortably in the bulletproof vest—without plates. "And the edges are cutting into my flesh."

"But you're protected."

"Sure, as long as no one shoots me in the head."

Toby put down her fork, wiped her mouth with a napkin, and said thoughtfully, "I'm sorry, Lynne. I don't even know what to say. You *do* look like a box."

"And the Kevlar is making me sweat."

August 24–26, 2012

Maybe I did need protection? I spent a few days absorbed in varieties of firepower, scouring the Internet to learn all I could about the "well-armed woman" and the types and models of weapons and ammunition "women might love." Top ten choices included: Glocks (models 42, 43, and 19), the Smith & Wesson M&P Shield, SIG Sauer (models P238, P365, P938), Ruger LC9s, and the Springfield XD-S. Revolvers were best for concealed carry and for women with weak hands unable to rack a slide on a semiautomatic. But they looked too bulky. I was leaning toward the SIG Sauer—small, simple, with a smooth trigger.

In the Air Force I'd never been required to do weapons training. Had I been deployed I would have had to know how to at least handle a gun. But I was there to treat patients; the Air Force paid me to go to medical school. Basic training consisted of treating the fake injured and learning how to march and salute properly, which, admittedly, I didn't take very seriously. Once, for fun, I did a do-si-do square dance in the middle of a marching exhibition at the parade ground. I found the whole saluting thing awkward too, sometimes forgetting to return the salute of a lower-ranking airman and discovering, minutes later, that he was still standing where I'd left him, waiting with his hand pressed against his forehead.

"It's not a joke," said my friend Heath. He was the only colleague I knew who had gun expertise, and he sounded a little worried when I told him of my plan to buy one. "If you're going to own one, you'd better be prepared to kill." He insisted I "test try" some models. I envisioned him handing me a rifle, the weapon heavy and nearly as tall as me as I practiced in a flowery field, fifty feet away from life-size dolls filled with water, the firepower nearly knocking me backward, my face drenched and my hair full of bits of rubbery flesh. I started to have dreams about shooting. I even smelled the gunpowder like rotten eggs, heard the bang in my ear, and felt the cool metal of the trigger. I dreamed I was wearing my Air Force uniform inside out and with the wrong insignia; targets "jump-scared" me the way they had in simulated exercises, at first ghoulish and faceless, and then in the shape of headstones. I'd startled awake, heart racing, sweaty. *I can't do this.*

Toby looked horrified when I brought it up and reminded me how suicide rates increased in households with guns. I assured her I wasn't suicidal, not even close. Our group met again for dinner, this time hidden, seated in a dark, secluded room surrounded by wall-to-wall mirrors. *Was it for my safety or the restaurant's?* I wondered. A waiter slid a large appetizer platter of lobster and crab cakes onto the lazy Susan and winked at me.

"He knows who you are," Toby said.

"Everyone knows who I am—hence the gun," I said, though I still wasn't convinced I wanted one. It seemed like a lot of responsibility. I'd need to schedule regular times at a shooting range to practice, buy ammunition and targets, apply for a concealed carry permit, get a gun safe, buy special accessories like a "gun purse" with a hidden pocket. Never mind the stress of having a weapon so accessible. Where would I keep it? In my nightstand, under my pillow, in a closet, on a shelf, in my car? Would I keep it loaded? I'd mentally practiced how many seconds it might take for me to reach for it in the dark, point it at an intruder, and try to stop my trigger finger from shaking. What if it jammed? How many seconds would it take for me to reload? What if I couldn't find the extra bullets? And what if I forgot about it, took it in to work with me, and set off alarms in the building? All that worry would probably *attract* violence.

Gayle pointed out the obvious, that I'd *already* attracted people who wanted to hurt me.

She was right; anyone could order a gun off the Internet without a background check. And they could easily get "ghost guns" self-assembled from parts purchased online or at gun shows, missing serial numbers so the Bureau of Alcohol, Tobacco, Firearms and Explosives couldn't classify them as "firearms" and couldn't regulate them. Not to mention the guns that were transferred or loaned between family members, none of which were registered or traceable.

"I *don't* think I'm going to get a gun," I said just as a table in the next room popped champagne. Applause and a chorus of "Happy Birthday" reached a crescendo. A heavyset woman lifted her cell phone, her white ruffled sleeves trailing through a dish of Hollandaise sauce. She snapped a photo, the flash momentarily blinding me. Toby bolted from her seat, napkin still tucked into her collar, ready to snatch the woman's phone and toss it into her wineglass. "Better not be taking her picture!" said Toby, glaring at the woman, her voice so loud the whole room froze as if some director had just yelled, "Cut!" A tough Philadelphia native, she'd chased a bully down an alley with a tire iron because he'd verbally assaulted her friend. *I was lucky to have her in my life.*

Just then our waiter returned, balancing plates of prosciutto-wrapped mozzarella with vine-ripened tomatoes, garlic shrimp, and pan-fried calamari with hot cherry peppers.

"Did we order all this food?" I laughed, hating the spasm in my voice that made me sound perpetually nervous.

"It's dystonia, a condition that's worsened by stress," I'd confided to Jane once during one of our many prep sessions. Involuntary muscle contractions made my voice and my head shake. I'd shared this with Toby too, complaining that people likely thought I sounded feeble.

"That's ridiculous. You're one of the most accomplished women I know," Toby had reassured me. "You've had more professions in thirty years than most of us have even *thought* about. It's a good thing I like myself or our friendship would probably leave me suicidal."

There were some who didn't believe I'd had all of the professions I'd had. Incredulous colleagues in medical school, challenged with finding one skill I lacked, had teased me, "Bet you can't balance on a chair with one leg over your head." I knew it must have sounded like I was perpetually bored or restless or noncommittal, but it wasn't that at all. I learned from my father, who died when I was in my first year of internship, that life was fleeting, that plans reserved for another day, season, or year might never happen. Fear was restrictive and it was pointless to put off all the things I wanted to accomplish: I could be a dancer *and* a doctor *and* endure a second residency. I *could* do it all *if* I didn't waste time or get bogged down in the planning. He and my mother had had such plans for when they retired, for when they had "time," and sadly it never happened. Ironically, my father lost *his* father at the age of ten and then lost his mother to work as she struggled to support him. When he was just seventeen, he built a house for his mom so she could rent it out and earn extra income. He dreamed of flying planes, and though there was no money, he found a way; he joined the Navy and made it happen. *Anything was possible.* It was all about reinvention, one foot in front of the other. *Resilience. Strength.*

Gayle stared wide-eyed when the bill came. "It's zero."

Toby snatched up the folder. "How can it be zero? We ate an entire festival."

Kat smiled. "There are some perks to being married to the general manager." It was more than just a "perk"; it was an act of kindness, acknowledgment that I was going through an ordeal and reassurance that I was not alone.

CU PSYCHIATRIST WHO TREATED HOLMES IS HIGHLY RESPECTED, LIKED. Reporter Jeremy Meyer's article in the *Denver Post* opened with a large headshot of me.

> *So far, information about Fenton and her connection to Holmes has been a tightly held secret, protected by the judge's gag order . . . [but] friends and ex-colleagues described her as a highly intelligent physician with an easy ability to connect with her patients. "You don't meet people quite as brilliant and amazing and caring and thorough as her," [one reported, and another said,] "I am sure she did everything completely the right way. I am sure of it. . . . Her history shows that is what she does. She is ethical, caring and brilliant."*

"Why would you do this?" Jane called Steffen later, irate. "I asked you specifically not to talk to the press. There is a gag order—"

"I thought it was important to balance the hate."

"By going rogue?"

"Someone has to be Lynne's advocate."

"I appreciate you looking out for me," I said as I backed out of my garage, cradling the phone to my ear, "I really do, it's just . . ."

"What?"

I was suddenly distracted by a man at the side of my house picking through my garbage. I described him to Steffen, homeless, scruffy, unshaven, dressed in holey jeans and a trench coat (in the middle of August?).

"A reporter?"

"I don't think so."

"Call the police."

My hands froze on the steering wheel as I watched the trench coat flap in the breeze and wondered what he might be hiding underneath. Heart pounding, I began to calculate how many seconds it might take for me to jam my foot on the gas, reverse into oncoming traffic, or accelerate into my garage, hoping to steer clear of the bullets I was sure he was going to fire at me. I wasn't wearing my vest; most mornings it was part of my costume, but lately I'd found it cumbersome and hot and . . . frankly, I was tired of looking like a box. But now, as panic gripped me, I wished I'd put it on. I remembered the officer's warning when he'd fitted me: *It will happen when you least expect it. One morning when the sun is shining and you let your guard down, he will come out of nowhere and you won't have time to reflect.*

Instinctively, I braced for the sting that would feel like several hundred hornets as I envisioned the side-passenger window shattering, my blood and flesh sticking to the steering wheel, the seats, my hands. Only I wouldn't see this because I wouldn't exist anymore, gone, obliterated in less than two minutes, the time it took for Holmes to shoot up an entire theater and murder twelve people. Panicked, I revved the engine, startling the man. He dropped the garbage can lid and it clattered to the pavement. We stared at each other for what seemed like several seconds, our eyes locked in terror, as if I'd just startled a bear and had forgotten to breathe.

"He's leaving." I watched him cross the street with his stash of recyclable aluminum cans and head to the elementary school. Heart pounding, my right leg shaking uncontrollably, I took my foot off the gas pedal. *Suddenly, I didn't feel like going anywhere.*

"What happened to your security?" Steffen asked.

Once so independent, I now had to "check in" randomly with friends and colleagues and broadcast my whereabouts to campus police. No sneaking out, even to get milk. The university had deployed extra security to guard the outpatient clinic where I worked. But all the added safety measures instilled nothing but panic in my students, who worried their mere association with me would make them "sitting ducks."

"We just want you to feel safe," everyone kept repeating.

I didn't. Instead, I felt contagious.

CHAPTER 15

SLOW AND STEADY

September 24, 2012

You look nervous, is it the scars?
—The Joker, *The Dark Knight* (2008)

FENTON

"Can we do anything about the tremor in your voice? My insider thinks you suffer from Parkinson's." Jane looked at me over her glasses at our next prep session.

Insider? Since when did Jane have a press confidant? Hadn't she drilled it into my head for months that communication with reporters was forbidden? If I said *anything*—if I so much as breathed the wrong way—I'd risk violating the judge's gag order.

"It's not what you're thinking," she said a little too dismissively. "I've cultivated this clandestine relationship for a while, to try to get information."

The whole idea left me unsettled, like I was being spied on, and suddenly I wondered what deals she'd made with her "insider" in exchange for this information. Living under a microscope was stressful enough without also having to worry about optics.

"Is it possible they know something you don't?" Steffen challenged me after another grueling session with my lawyers. "Why the endless preparation? Are they protecting *you* or themselves? What are they so afraid you'll say?"

He got irate with Jane over the phone. "You think an inquisition is in her best interest?"

"The university is entitled to an investigation," she said calmly.

"I can see why that would be important to you."

"What is that supposed to mean?"

"The university is your client."

"*Lynne* is my client."

"You're on the university's payroll."

"Who pays me has nothing to do with my representation of Lynne."

"Doesn't it? Sounds like a conflict of interest to me."

"Don't be ridiculous."

"What's ridiculous is that you've done nothing to protect your client. She continues to receive hate mail and death threats, which you simply collect. The public defender outs Lynne, practically ruins her life, and there's no retribution, not even a spanking."

"It's a little more involved than that."

"The hell it is."

Afterward, Steffen, probably feeling a little helpless to ease my stress, made me a cup of mint tea and offered me a plate of chocolate biscotti.

"Tell me why you need to meet with your lawyers incessantly to prepare a full month in advance for an interview with the university's hired guns, Perkins Coie?"

"I don't know. Why don't you ask them?" I said, dunking the edge of a biscotto into my steaming mug, though being forced to relive the same four months over and over *was* becoming a special kind of insanity. The endless loop of interrogations only magnified my sense of isolation, that I was little more than Holmes' psychiatrist.

"Why aren't they more confident that you did nothing wrong? The university's own consultants concluded weeks ago that you followed protocol. . . ."

"It's—"

"Harassment."

October 22—November 27, 2012

"I've taken every precaution with your file," said Jane, flashing a small silver key at me the next time we met. She explained in great detail how the IT department had created an electronic record, which she locked nightly in a cabinet, in case reporters broke into the building or paid someone from the cleaning crew to steal my information.

"Is that really necessary?"

"We can't be too careful." As always, she seemed to be enjoying the stealth.

"We've put together some talking points," Rick said as he slid a laminated document across the table. "And we've prepared a timeline of events to help jog your memory."

I skimmed my folder, titled MD [medical doctor] SESSIONS. Each date was color-coded to match my abbreviated notes, with action items bolded in blue. I couldn't imagine needing reminders after I'd gone over and over the details in long, tedious "prep meetings," but I appreciated the gesture.

"If all else fails, just remember SIS, *serious* threat of *imminent* physical violence against *specific* persons. That's Colorado's law on duty to warn." Rick wrote the acronym on the whiteboard and underlined it several times in red marker. "All answers lead back to SIS."

"Or IOG," Jane interjected. "*Imminent* danger to *others* or himself or appears to be *gravely* disabled."

I nodded—the tenets were obviously familiar to me—but the letters were scrambling in my head, and as they grilled me, I felt that familiar foglike dizziness take over, the white walls closing in, Rick's voice ticking in my head like a dull metronome: steady as she goes, stay laser focused, be calm, no sudden moves. His questions pummeled me like fists. Sometimes I took too long to formulate my thoughts, get my words out, and then I'd see Rick's face tense, his brows pull together, his glasses slip to the edge of his nose, eyes cast down. When Jane cleared her throat, it sounded like a chair scraping on hard tile.

Rick sighed deeply. "The answers need to come more quickly." He snapped his fingers. "No hesitation."

The spacious room felt suddenly oppressively cramped. "I'm trying. I just want to be accurate and sometimes—"

"Just refer to the chart. Rinse and repeat. The goal here is to look solid."

I tried again, my voice unsteady, distracted now by the look of alarm in Jane's blue eyes. She poured me a glass of water, splashing it onto the table.

"Time out." Rick motioned for Jane to join him in the hall. He left the door ajar and I could hear them whispering frantically. "What's happening to her?"

"I'm sure this is traumatic."

"All she has to do is repeat SIS or IOG."

"Maybe we're pushing her too hard?"

"We're not pushing her hard enough."

"It's making me jumpy." I was in Edinberg's office again. I'd been seeing him more regularly since I'd begun the endless prep sessions with Rick and Jane. I needed him to listen, needed his support, just as my patients must have needed me. Having Edinberg sitting across from me, nodding (or not!), was comforting. Rick's grilling had left me withdrawn in ways I'd never been and could never have imagined. By keeping Holmes front-row center in my life, I couldn't move on. I thought about him day in and day out—my sessions with him, how he looked absent, detached, almost nonhuman. He'd left his impact in other ways too: the outpatient clinic now had NO WEAPONS signs posted on the doors and walls (precautions that did little to deter the knife-wielding patients who sometimes entered and threatened their psychiatrists), and Steve had started doing active shooter drills, in which fake masked gunmen stormed the building, took hostages, and role-played.

Police posing as the fake gunmen would enter the clinic, guns drawn, and pretend to take hostages. They dragged their fake participants in choke holds through the hallways, kicking in doors, scouring the twenty offices for targets, while residents, doctors, and pretend patients scrambled to take cover. Those who were too slow, too terrified, or too reckless were "shot" and pronounced "dead." Others, who obeyed the captors' instructions and huddled on their knees, hands behind their heads, were mocked and hectored into pretending to jump out the windows.

"They carried it too far," I said to Steve after one of these events. "Several of the doctors felt traumatized by the drills. The officers had them cowering in the corner, crying, shaking." On the other hand, one colleague had complained the scenario had not been real enough. He claimed he was a martial arts expert and leapt on the backs of the fake invaders to try to wrestle them to the ground and take *them* captive. He karate chopped the guns right out of cops' hands, chanting, "What do you think of that? What do you think of that?" and then pointed the guns at the ceiling, pretending to shoot into the drywall.

When I recounted all of this to Edinberg, he looked a little alarmed. "I hope *you're* not participating in these drills."

I'd been excused. But even isolated in my office, with the door closed, I still heard my colleagues' real screams. These jolted me back to Holmes, to imagining the theater, the victims he'd ambushed row by row. And I realized, no matter how many drills, rehearsals, or simulations Steve enacted, *nothing* would ever prepare any of us for the senseless annihilation of human life.

"We've brought in reinforcements," said Jane after introducing two other lawyers from her firm. "We're going to try some role-play."

We practiced several simulated trial exercises in the firm's mock courtroom; although I would be interviewed by lawyers in a conference room, Jane wanted my experience to simulate trial testimony so she could better evaluate me as a witness and, she reasoned, prepare me for the criminal prosecution. I sat on a makeshift stage in a metal witness chair, dressed in a sensible brown ensemble I thought made me look grounded, confident, emotionless—exactly the opposite of how I felt inside.

Rick and Jane assumed the roles of judges, frantically scribbling their critiques on legal pads, occasionally shouting out words of encouragement. The People, represented by a fierce-looking woman in her mid-forties, dressed in muted charcoal and round-framed glasses, stood at a podium and doggedly fired off prepared questions, quickly dispensing with my credentials and expertise and going straight for the jugular: my sessions with Holmes. The acronyms SIS and IOG swirled in my head as the People went over each session and interrogated me about all my conversations with Holmes and especially the medications I'd prescribed. A major area of concern was why, on April 17, while Holmes was taking 100 mg of sertraline, I noted he'd had an increase in obsessive homicidal thoughts, and a few weeks later, on May 1, "clearer indications of psychotic-level thinking," even though I'd increased his dose to 150 mg. Though I knew she was playing devil's advocate, her tone reminded me of Holmes when he'd accused me of being nothing but a "pill pusher."

Jane had warned me that Holmes' lawyers might use as a defense "My medicine made me do it,"[13] claiming the medications I'd prescribed Holmes had actually aggravated his psychosis by reducing his anxiety enough for him to (albeit irrationally) theorize about killing people. Whatever link the defense hoped to establish between sertraline and violence, however, was squarely rebutted by Dr. Reid, the court-appointed psychiatrist, who interviewed Holmes nearly *two years* after the shootings and learned Holmes *still* believed in his theory of human capital and warned that people should continue to be "worried about him."

The People mentioned the fact that, coincidentally, both Eric Harris and Kip Kinkel had been prescribed Luvox and Prozac before their mass shootings. In reality, though, instances of antidepressants causing violence were rare. In fact, several studies analyzing the correlation concluded it was far more likely that violent behavior was driven by *under*medicating these individuals, who were taking antidepressants during times they were feeling more anxious, depressed, or angry to begin with and thus were at higher risk to act out violently.

"You're doing great," my cheerleader, Jane, crowed from the shadows. "I like the way you handled that line of questioning."

"I think you can improve on the response time, though," Rick put in. "We don't want any hesitation. Steady as she goes."

The People moved on to Steve. "You enlisted his help. He's a codeveloper of violence and suicide risk scales and an expert in this area?" I repeated how he and I had taken turns talking and taking notes. He'd focused more on mentalization and transference and I thought Holmes might relate better to a man.

"He at first described the sessions as 'reassuring' but during subsequent interviews said they were 'worrying' and there was a 'general tenseness' in the air. Would you agree?"

"I would not characterize the sessions as 'reassuring.'"

---

13 Holmes' lawyers ultimately decided not to pursue this defense.

"How are you feeling after today?" Jane asked as we walked to our cars.

"Pretty beaten up."

"We need to see how you'll hold up as a witness."

"Do you really think I'll have to testify if there's a malpractice case?"

Jane shook her head. "Not a chance."

Steffen wasn't pleased when I called and told him.

"Then why put you through all of this? Why can't you just refuse to participate?" he said.

"I guess I didn't think I had that option." Between the Air Force and medical school, I'd gotten used to going with the flow, doing what was expected of me. It had never occurred to me to rebel. And it never crossed my mind that I could refuse the inquisition or that it wasn't necessary—or could even be harmful to me.

"You can tell them all to fuck off. Be your own best bulldog."

When I didn't respond right away, Steffen softened. "At least come over for dinner. I baked key lime pie."

November 11, 2012

HOLMES

"I'd rather be dead," Holmes announced to one of his many jail psychologists, prompting concerns he might be suicidal. During his first few days of incarceration, he'd refused to talk to them, saying he had his "own psychiatrist." He was (mistakenly) referring to the defense team's neurologist, Dr. Jonathan Woodcock, who, accompanied by a defense investigator, had interviewed him four days after the shooting. When the jail psychologist explained she was there to see how he was doing and whether he needed anything, Holmes was a little irritated. "Well, thanks for checking on me," he said, "but I think one psychiatrist is enough."

Adding to the confusion about caregivers was the stance taken by senior jail administrators, who also erroneously concluded that Dr. Woodcock had been tasked with Holmes' welfare. As a result, for nearly four months the staff ordered the jail's clinical psychiatrist not to examine Holmes or prescribe him any medications. Untreated and unwell, Holmes nonetheless insisted he was "fine."

Indeed, according to jail notes, in those first few months following the shooting, Holmes appeared "normal," a "model prisoner"—nonconfrontational, disengaged, quiet, "Just James." His orange hair faded to brown; he grew a beard, had decent hygiene. His family, with the exception of his sister, corresponded with him periodically, though Holmes didn't write back; he said he "didn't have much to talk about." And though his university "friends" had not contacted him since the murders, he insisted they were "secretly supportive" but probably reluctant to be "lumped in as related to a killer."

As a precaution because Holmes had hinted at "suicidal ideation," jail staff again moved him to an isolation cell in the medical ward ("administrative segregation"), where they could carefully monitor him (and keep him alive long enough to be tried and possibly executed). "He was on 'suicide watch' for his own good," jail staff noted. But Holmes "behaved normally . . . ate well, drank plenty of fluids and took his medication as prescribed . . . no odd movements . . . no signs of psychosis . . . no banging of his head against the wall." When asked how he felt about his isolation, his future, his parents' perceived abandonment, he stared blankly at his doctors and said repeatedly he "didn't understand the question."

In a sparsely furnished cell equipped with an emergency intercom and cameras secured in corner ceiling pockets, the twenty-four-hour fluorescent glare condemned him to perpetual daylight. His heavy wool blanket lay on the floor like a rug next to his wooden bunk; in a corner, his stainless-steel toilet and sink resembled salvaged parts. A jail-issued plastic vomit bucket contained several empty Doritos bags, his favorite commissary snack. Small metal carnival mirrors (the kind that distort a person's reflection) hung above his bed next to photos and letters from his female "fans." They addressed him as "Sweetie," "Darling," "Babe," and "Hon"; one wrote, "I want to be with you so bad I can taste it, sexy man. Love always." Some of them sent money orders, donations that, over the next three years, would exceed $4,000.

Women attracted to dangerously unhinged criminals shared a core belief (however misguided) that the killers' misogyny was fleeting, that *their* love could transform the convict from cunning and cruel to caring and compassionate. Katherine Ramsland, a professor of forensic psychology and criminal justice at DeSales University, wrote extensively on the subject of hybristophilia, asserting that women who sought men incarcerated for life enjoyed rescuing people they pitied, convinced that the "wounded child nestled somewhere inside the killer could be healed through a devoted nurturance that only they could provide." Cognitive neuroscientists Ogi Ogas and Sai Gaddam posited a more cynical reason for the women's attraction: that they wanted to share the killer's media spotlight, thereby emerging from their own anonymity into infamy. They wrote, "Killing people was an effective way to elicit the attention of many women: virtually every serial killer, including Ted Bundy, Charles Manson, and David Berkowitz, received love letters from large numbers of female fans." These women were either incapable of finding love in "normal ways" or enjoyed perpetuating a "romantic ideal" with a partner who would always need them, who would never stray, and whom they could control.

In addition to the love/lust mail, Holmes also received letters from "kindred spirits," "murderous soulmates" who were convinced he'd been "framed" or "railroaded" by the "System." Some even suggested he might suffer from a brain tumor that caused his violence.

Holmes exercised for an hour daily in a walled-in concrete "yard" with a netted ceiling or "lounged" in a nearby cell and watched television. To pass the time, he played with his jail-issued Hacky Sack and sometimes juggled socks.

But mostly he journaled his "philosophical musings" about "Galactic Colonization," his self-described "Ultraception" (an exaggerated form of perception), and death as a "dreamless sleep."

Galactic Colonization

Locate hospitable planet . . . evolve human species on earth to niche environment, a replica or unhospitable [sic] planet, small scale . . . Design pseudohuman w/features enabling life on unhospitable [sic] planet but still retaining the human spirit or essential essence of being human . . . devise machine that can create human life when destination reached. Did god do this w/humans as machine to create god?

Awareness

the state of awareness changes from wakefulness to sleep, from life to pseudo death. States of awareness are as fundamental as space/time, hot, cold, or solid/liquid.

Then, on November 11, 2012, video captured Holmes standing on his bunk facing the wall, arms crossed, momentarily pensive, as if mustering his courage—before he fell straight backward, slamming his body to the concrete floor, reflexively extending his arms to brace his impact, his skull narrowly missing the ground. Once on the floor, he writhed side to side for several seconds, knees to chest, then shot his legs out, crossed his arms, and closed his eyes. Within minutes, guards rushed in and circled him, wary of his fluttering lids and limp movements. Holmes would later offer a curious explanation to psychiatrists: that he fell off his cot because he had been inside a puzzle game of his own making that involved Peter Pan in a green vest. In any event, guards helped him to his feet and escorted him to a special safe cell in "BC" (behavior control), where the jail housed violent and suicidal offenders "for their own good."

This safe cell (known as the "Rubber Room" or the "Hole") contained nothing but a metal drain in the center of the floor. Naked, Holmes draped his crinkly "suicide blanket" around his shoulders and promptly defecated on the floor. Later, in his pretrial interview with Dr. Reid, he said that at the time he "thought other people were reading his thoughts . . . so he tried to, like, hide them, so he would say a bunch of colors like red, blue, green, red. And then, like, point in his cell and stuff in random locations . . . to get them to stop listening to his thoughts . . . to hide them."

His various jail psychiatrists observed:

Patient was noted to be talking to himself . . . told people he was not sure if they were real or not . . . when asked why he has not been eating/drinking, he said, "I don't know what the juice is" and "I was in a box without any juice and couldn't reach it." . . . When asked why he was in jail, he said "because I pulled away from the people I know" and "I drank their blood . . . I took the blood that was not mine to take . . . it was unfair . . . I was selfish."

Patient reports he is in a "shadow box" and voices tell him to "get water." Patient also reports when asked about self-harm that he has "bitten his arm for food" before; when asked what kind of food, the patient reported "proteinaceous."

Holmes' "odd, unpredictable behavior" continued several hours after being transported to "BC"; he barreled headfirst into the cell wall, explaining later that he needed to confirm he was actually *real*. Guards and nurses kept their distance as Holmes prowled his cell, stopping intermittently to point and whisper before falling straight back again onto the concrete floor. Staff watched him through the night as he slung his sack breakfast onto the drain toilet and "licked the walls," convinced the "suicide sack," labeled with the letters *SS*, had come from the Gestapo. Finally, after several more hours of starvation, Holmes slapped processed meat between two smashed paper cups, swallowing everything before performing backward somersaults, balancing a paper cup on his penis, and mashing his next slop into his suicide blanket.

Once again Holmes defecated on the cell floor, covering his feet in feces. When jail medical staff tried to intervene, he became agitated, his "eyes . . . bloodshot and tearful," and "assumed catatonic postures." Holmes was transported to the emergency room at Denver Health Medical Center for tests to rule out head trauma. He returned just two hours later, fully hydrated, naked, motionless, refusing water and food. Jail video showed Holmes pressing his fingers into his bouncy rubber enclosure as if assessing its hardness before launching himself headfirst into the wall. This time it took nine guards and medical staff to restrain him, and as they strapped him into a chair and lowered a spit guard over his head, Holmes shouted, "I see shadows. You're a shadow!" They jammed an IV into his arm and pumped him full of lorazepam.

Once the drugs wore off, his "bizarre jerky movements" returned, and after two days Holmes again refused food and drink. He lay naked on the floor, shivering and unresponsive. While jail staff prepared to implement a "starvation protocol" to force-feed Holmes, he again became agitated and staff strapped him into a restraint chair. But instead of transferring Holmes to the Colorado Mental Health Institute at Pueblo (nearly two hours away) for further psychiatric care, doctors recommended inpatient treatment in the special jail unit located in the basement of the Denver Health Medical Center.

Progress notes revealed:

Patient did require restraints on lower extremities . . . after using them to flip a blanket over his head . . . effectively obscuring observation of the patient. Patient reports he was trying to "hide from the shadows." Mr. Holmes experienced both a psychotic disorder and a delirium related to his metabolic imbalance. Patient no longer has visual hallucinations . . . auditory hallucinations have decreased to hearing minimal "shadow voices." He wants to "keep the hallucinations away."

FENTON

"I know we're not supposed to talk about this, but I saw Holmes last week when I was on call." Toby stabbed a cube of rare steak and popped it into her mouth. "He looked like a kid with schizophrenia. Severely dehydrated, starving, hearing voices, said he saw shadows, rammed his head into the wall to 'get his bad thoughts out.'" She took another bite, adding, "Apparently, we're the only two psychiatrists in Denver."

As Toby spoke, my risotto cooled on my plate. My thoughts had returned to the bleak, tunnellike basement of the hospital, where I could picture Holmes writhing in his sterile room behind double-paned sheets of clear bulletproof glass, strapped into a restraint chair bolted to the floor, with his one free arm flapping at his side like a chicken wing. Like Toby, I'd regularly served on rotation as the on-call doctor to assess the medications and care of patients admitted to the jail wing of Denver Hospital's psychiatric ward. In that limited capacity, flanked by guards, I reviewed their charts, talked to them for fifteen minutes *at most*, and learned their histories from the varied "medical team." There was no relationship, no nuanced exchange of information.

How much could Toby actually know about Holmes in the fifteen minutes she'd spent with him?

My Holmes, with his blank, penetrating stare, never met the criteria for schizophrenia. Schizophrenics predominantly experienced auditory hallucinations. Visual hallucinations like shadows were more associated with delirium. My delirious patients described seeing pink elephants or tiny munchkins. One pooped on the floor, poured bleach over the poop, and told me she was killing clusters of worms in her carpet.

Steve and I *had* suspected Holmes might be psychotic and suggested the antipsychotic medication risperidone, but he had refused. Now Toby had prescribed the same medication, and he was taking it. Faced with the possibility of the death penalty, was he making his case for insanity? Was he "overcoming biology" by refusing to feel hunger or thirst, or did he know that dehydration could cause acute delirium, agitation, even delusion? As a neuroscience student, Holmes had surely learned about schizophrenia. Perhaps he'd even identified with "misunderstood" geniuses like John Nash, the brilliant mathematician, or Brian Wilson of the Beach Boys, whose biopics dramatized how they felt "othered," their intellect on a higher, almost "mystical" plane.

Less mindful Hollywood portrayals, like *Psycho*, *The Fisher King*, *Shutter Island*, and *Donnie Darko*, sensationally depicted schizophrenics as completely disconnected from reality, lost in delusions they perceived as real, and compelled by their mental illness to commit heinous acts of violence. Holmes was smart enough to know the game. *Had he fooled Toby? Had he embellished?*

The whoosh of the double kitchen doors behind me reminded me of the thick, bolted steel doors in the psychiatric ward where Holmes (admitted under the pseudonym Brady Arkansas) was being treated for multiple suicide attempts, the very thing he'd assured me he would never consider.

Holmes later told Dr. Reid that "he was homicidal to protect himself from knowing he was feeling suicidal." But in his notes Dr. Reid wrote, "Holmes did not, or could not, describe any memory of actually feeling very suicidal, or of symptoms of severe depression, during the months before the shooting."

December 11–13, 2012

FENTON

My heart quickened a little as I described for Edinberg my two-day interrogation at Perkins Coie.[14] In the firm's gleaming conference room hung three canvas panels that looked like they'd been splashed with paint. A large bare window framed the Denver skyline. Voss water bottles chilled in a crystal bowl on a credenza, and the room smelled distractingly of disinfectant.

The senior partner, Robert Miller III, sat at the head of the table like an overdressed Santa Claus with his full white beard, fluffy tufts of hair, and chunky feet, which barely skimmed the carpet. His thuggish-looking wingman, T. Markus Funk, towered over him at six foot three and absorbed me with his light blue hooded eyes. The *Chicago Sun-Times* had dubbed him a "street-smart prosecutor with an Oxford pedigree." But to me he was just an asshole. He had spearheaded "one of the most important criminal investigation in American history," having once worked for the Department of Justice and prosecuted "Operation Family Secrets," the inspiration for the 1995 Mob movie *Casino*. Seated next to him was the "notetaker," a striking young blonde with a heart-shaped face and perfect white teeth. She looked as if she'd been popped from a mold.

Her specialty was patent litigation, intellectual property, nothing whatsoever to do with medical malpractice. In fact, I'm not sure she had any idea who was being interviewed or why. Her role was to mindlessly record, even though there were several cassette players on the table. Throughout, she looked bored and preoccupied and

---

14 The following scenes are re-creations culled from extensive interviews with several participants; a copy of the recording was never provided despite repeated requests for disclosure.

left the room to make phone calls, text, or answer emails. All of them seemed distracted and uninterested, as if it almost didn't matter what I said. They had an agenda and treated me like a hostile witness in a criminal prosecution.

The room seemed to be flooded with an unforgiving glare. I picked at the soft skin around my nails, feeling suddenly lightheaded, shaky, exposed. It was exactly how I had felt when federal agents had surprised me at my acupuncture clinic. A pharmacist had "tipped them off" about the "large quantities of the Schedule III Vicodin pills" he'd been called upon to refill by one of my employees.

"The DEA is here," my receptionist said softly at my door. "They have guns."

As I recounted the memory for Edinberg, the shame and humiliation of that ordeal resurfaced; just as I had been then, I was now being unjustly accused of wrongdoing.

The agents wore stark white dress shirts accented with deep-red ties and shoulder holsters jammed with twin SIG Sauers. Their predatory expressions unnerved me as I ushered them into my office and explained as calmly as I could that my nurse (who was also a friend) had suffered from migraine, and I'd written her a prescription for twenty Vicodin to manage her pain. No refills. Only later did I learn she'd called the pharmacist and ordered *hundreds* of pills in refills.

"Is that right?" The agents seized on this information as if it were some kind of confession. And as they inventoried my shelves full of acupuncture needles and electro-stimulators, they snarled, "What is it you do here?" One chewed gum like chewing tobacco, wadding a lump in his cheek and flipping it from side to side over his front teeth, all but accusing me of doling out "high doses of narcotics."

"Your employee gave us names," the agent said, his eyes pinning me to my chair. And then it hit me: they weren't there to ask about the nurse; they were there to investigate *me*—demanding to know whether I'd just "helped out my nurse friend, supplied a dealer or sold opiates."

"We're going to need to see your patient records."

In that moment I'd felt cornered. Like my whole world was imploding. I knew I'd done nothing wrong, but they were succeeding at making me feel guilty. "No." My single-word response left me winded and teary-eyed. I really thought I might throw up. Fortunately, I had the presence of mind to ask for a lawyer.

Edinberg looked at me thoughtfully, as if I'd just revealed something profoundly intimate. *Maybe I had.* The lawyers who'd attacked me at Perkins Coie were no different from the DEA agents who'd visited me those many years ago. All were accusatory, demeaning bullies. I felt violated, marginalized, *less than*, but mostly outraged, particularly since my entire motivation for becoming a psychiatrist was to help people. One of the things that irked me most about Funk was that he was unprofessional and appeared to be unprepared. He kept interchanging "psychologist" and "psychiatrist" and was (or pretended to be) ignorant of the fact that I was a medical doctor, often qualifying his questions with "Well, it's not as if you have a medical license." If I were being sued for malpractice, maybe then I'd have understood the disrespect coming from the university's lawyers. But this was merely an inquiry into the precautions I'd taken (even if it felt more like an assault).

"Isn't it true that patients with mental health issues can be ambivalent about treatment?" Funk demanded.

"That's why Steve and I noodled over options, discussed how best to treat Holmes."

"And while you guys *noodled*, Holmes put the finishing touches on his master plan to kill the human race."

"He never expressed any plan to me." My head throbbed. *How many times was I going to have to repeat this?*

"That didn't make it into your noodling?"

"Enough," Rick snapped.

"I'm just using her word, trying to be accurate."

"Move on."

"So, in all your multiple sessions with Holmes, you never got to the jugular?"

"I'm not sure what you mean."

Funk tapped the tip of his pen against his throat. "Jugular. The why? Why did Holmes want to kill the human race?"

"It wasn't so cut-and-dried. It was important for me to establish rapport—"

"Did you *ask* him why?"

"I explored his homicidal ideations—"

"Is that a yes or a no?"

"I'm trying to answer you, but I don't want to be misleading."

"I'm not asking you to be misleading. Just answer yes or no to my question, and if you can't answer it, just tell me and I'll rephrase."

"I'm trying—"

"I understand that you're anxious to get your opinion across and that you're a professional psychologist—"

"Counsel, your voice is rising to an unreasonable level. I'd appreciate it if you keep it down." Jane's irritation was palpable.

"I want Dr. Fenton to hear me."

"She can hear you."

"Can you repeat the question?" My voice wobbled.

Funk cracked his knuckles and asked it again. When I shook my head, Funk cupped a hand to his ear, leaned forward, and said, "I didn't hear you."

"No."

"See how easy that was? A one-word answer and then we can just move on."

Robert Miller interjected as if he'd suddenly startled awake from a long nap. "So after Mr. Holmes left your office that last time, you just let him go?"

"Bet you were glad to be rid of *him*. Not your problem anymore," Funk piped up, making a dramatic show of wiping his hands. The notetaker snorted.

I started to recite again all that I'd done to assess Holmes' potential for violence, all the reasons why a mental health hold had not been possible, when suddenly lunch arrived, and the smell of onions and French fries wafted through the room. I was distracted by the noisy rustling of paper bags, ketchup squirts, and loud chewing, and my voice halted, cracked. I blanked, stuttered. The pressure brought me back to medical school, the hazing and humiliation I'd endured as a first-year resident. We were sleep-deprived, forced to work thirty-two-hour shifts, pounced on in the hallways by seasoned colleagues, and quizzed to "name five things" about an illness or a procedure, and if you didn't spit out the answers fast enough—or, worse, answered wrong—you were condemned to be accosted again, grilled, ridiculed, chastised, told to go home, told that "if we'd listened to Dr. Fenton, this patient would be dead."

"Why'd you prescribe sertraline?" Miller bit into his Philly cheesesteak, unaware that his beard was collecting crumbs.

There it was again, that accusatory, belittling tone. My ears rang as I again explained my reasons for prescribing the drug.

"Was he depressed?"

"No, he was—"

"Isn't it true sertraline can actually *cause* depression?" said Miller, seemingly distracted by his cell phone.

"Let her answer the question," Rick barked as he plucked tomatoes from his sandwich.

"So basically," said Funk, ignoring Rick as he bunched his sandwich wrapper into a tight ball and lobbed it across the table toward the trash can, "you got the whole thing wrong!"

I was pretty sure that if I hadn't already had years of psychoanalysis, I'd have been suicidal. I said as much to my lawyers in the hallway during a break in the interrogation.

"I know none of this is easy," Rick soothed, his hand on my shoulder like a slow burn. "But you should be proud of all that you did. You had the courage to get Steve involved professionally. You didn't just let a patient walk out the door without continuing to think about your professional obligations. You will get through this. Stay steady."

But I didn't need Rick's pep talk, and when the university's counsel and secretary of the Board of Regents joined us in the hallway for the debrief, I thought they could have prevented the whole thing or at least have found a more respectful approach and wondered if the university had ever intended to *clear* me of wrongdoing— or whether it just wanted to make me their scapegoat.

Though Jane assured me none of this was personal, it sure *felt* personal, like I was the enemy and posed such a threat to my university that, according to an article in the *Denver Post*, it had invested a million dollars in investigating me, even paying one of its lawyers an unprecedented $844,000 retainer.

"That would explain the preparation overkill." Toby was outraged when I told her. "Why haven't you blabbed to the press about your ordeal? You *could*. You have the contact information of every major news network. Why isn't the university afraid of *that*?"

Even if she was right, revenge wasn't my style. I just wanted my life back, my name cleared, my career intact.

A sliver of moon poked through the fading twilight as I sat on a stone bench in my garden, which was now overgrown with weeds and nettles. The pond was too still; dragonflies skimmed the surface, where there was a thick layer of algae. Rose petals littered dirty patches of lawn. The topiary had lost its shape. The honey locust tree's leaves were curled and spotted. The rust-worn iron gate and chain now creaked open into narrow walkways lined with crimson splashes of wilted geraniums in pots on the low walls. *This was so unlike me, to let my garden go.* When it warmed up, I'd have to do the annual treatment of my bamboo for heart rot, a fungus that lived inside the stems, weakening the plants, gradually taking over like a personality disorder. I couldn't help it—my mind went straight to Holmes, the weirdness living inside him like an incurable fungus. *You got the whole thing wrong.* Funk's accusation replayed in my head like a dull roar.

"Do *you* think I did?" I called Jane, still reeling from the afternoon's ordeal.

"You went beyond the textbook."

"Did they treat Steve that way?" I traced an *X* in the loose dirt with the heel of my shoe. I already knew the answer, but the double standard still frosted me.

"He wasn't on the hot seat."

"Margaret?"

"They insulted Margaret Roath about her age, implying she was too old to still be working."

Had they interviewed the others only to make it appear as though they'd conducted a thorough review?

"Was there a point to all of this?" I kicked off both shoes and sank my toes into the dirt.

"We won't know how this all shakes out until the end."

"The end of what?"

"The university's investigation."

"Wasn't I the end?"

"They just want to be thorough; it's not personal," Jane assured me, though it felt personal.

"Will they let you and Rick know the results?"

"Only if they have to."

"What does *that* mean?" As darkness fell, I switched on the white tea lights on my trellis.

"You will only know the results if they don't exonerate you."

That night I dreamed Funk's mouth was sealed with black electrical tape. The door to his office blew open into a hall of mirrors that smelled of sweetly rotten strawberries. I glimpsed my reflection, a flap of skin stretched taut like a stocking over my eyes, nose, and mouth. *You're doing well,* Jane's disembodied voice whispered in my ear. *You're doing so well. Now salute! Salute your superior.* My arms felt heavy, weighted as if underwater. My uniform, creased and stained and tight around my throat, cut off my air.

I never did learn the official outcome of the university's investigation—all documents mysteriously vanished, including any recording of Funk's interrogation. The lack of closure felt like a gut punch, a disappointing nonending to the university's relentless scrutiny of me. They offered no apology or explanation, maybe hoping I would just forget, resume my life where I'd left off. *But how could I?* For *months* I'd worried I'd be fired, my reputation ruined. I wasn't even sure I'd still *have* patients when it was all over, and if it was never over . . . what would I *do? Who would I* be?

As it was, even though my career remained intact, I was like a newly released criminal who, after wasting years of her life imprisoned for a crime she didn't commit, suddenly had to be in the world again, live *as if* nothing life changing had happened. But it *had* and there was no relief or remedy the university could offer to repair my damaged reputation—only stark awareness that nothing would ever be the same.

CHAPTER 16

TUNNEL VISION

December 14–20, 2012

A new monster is among us.
—The Joker, *The Dark Knight* (2008)

FENTON

Wearing my bulletproof vest, I sat in my office in the outpatient clinic surrounded by cards and flowers from concerned patients and tried to ignore the alarms and flashing red lights streaking the hallway. Steve had initiated another of his active shooter drills, and fake gunmen prepared to storm the building. But as staff cowered in the waiting area, ducked into doorways, barricaded their offices with furniture or their own bodies, and hid in elevators, I heard Steve suddenly yell, "Stop! Stop! There's been a *real* shooting."

Heart pounding, I joined the others in the reception area and listened as Steve, ashen-faced, gave us the details. At Sandy Hook Elementary School in Newtown, Connecticut, twenty children and six teachers were dead, plus the shooter, twenty-year-old Adam Lanza, and his mother. After stockpiling weapons for some time, he first killed his mother, then gathered his Bushmaster XM-15, two semiautomatic pistols, a shotgun, and several hundred rounds of ammunition and drove to the school, where he shot his way through the locked security door just after nine thirty that morning.

"We're murdering children now?" Steve's eyes watered behind his glasses.

The news so rattled me, I canceled my appointments for the rest of the day and left campus, unsure how to quiet my thoughts. Sandy Hook happened just four months after Holmes' massacre. I found myself wanting to blame someone—my mind replaying my own sessions with Holmes, how his presence each time had left me with a mental chill, a kind of inexplicable dread, as if the air around us had actually become poisonous. Had Lanza's treating professionals experienced the same tangible evil I had in Holmes' presence? Were they secretly grateful Lanza had shot himself and there would be no trial, no public scrutiny, no death threats?

Gayle had always marveled at my "strength" and assured me that none of my colleagues would have survived "a Holmes." I'm sure she meant it as a compliment, but I didn't want to be the chosen one, didn't want the burden. There was great relief in thinking, *Better you than me.* Easy to detach, become a spectator outside the ring at a boxing match. But I was in it, getting pummeled, beaten down, unable to catch my breath, no breaks between rounds, no relief, and no guarantee that I would ever fully recover.

I obsessed over Adam Lanza, absorbing news reports and articles about him, comparing him to and distinguishing him from Holmes. Maybe I wanted validation, more assurances that I had done everything possible to avoid exactly what had actually occurred. Both had suffered from social anxiety, a trait Lanza's doctors had attributed to his diagnosis of Asperger's syndrome and, later, to a sensory processing disorder that made him "hypersensitive to touch." He'd lived an isolated existence in a town that resembled a Norman Rockwell painting. Ironically, Sandy Hook prided itself on being a safe school, implementing the motto "Safety first," and, like my own mental health outpatient clinic, had even implemented "gun drills" and "lockdowns" and installed new security measures—a doorbell, exterior cameras. Parents had to show photo identification before collecting their children. *How was it possible that a school with such safety precautions had allowed Lanza inside?*[15]

Lanza's history, obtained after his suicide, reinforced how critical it was to know the backstory of a patient, details that could only be known with the patient's consent or, as in my case, by violating HIPAA privacy laws. As a first grader, Lanza was odd, aloof, and "never quite fit in." Some described him as the kid "who scared other kids." His second-grade teacher told reporters that Lanza "was a frail little fellow who rarely spoke." His mother was attentive and protective and at times "came off as extremely overbearing." When, at thirteen, Lanza refused to go to school, his mother ex-

---

15 Southwestern High School in Shelbyville, Indiana, is now deemed the "safest school in America." Teachers wear panic buttons (special "key fobs" that when pushed alert police to an active shooter); the school has smoke cannons in the hallways; and has installed cameras with a direct feed to the sheriff's office, and installed bulletproof windows. Nate Shute and Justin Mack, "How an Indiana School Protects Against Mass Shootings As the 'Safest School in America,'" *Indianapolis Star*, February 21, 2018. Mason Wooldridge, the cofounder of Our Kids Deserve It, identified five key factors in mitigating school shootings and helped to implement them in Shelby County in its "Safe School Flagship":

Immediate Notification: On average a 911 call is received two to four minutes after the shooting has started.

Stronger Doors: Law enforcement can't protect "soft targets" inside a public area when doors are vulnerable.

Cameras: Law enforcement has no ability to locate, track, or identify a threat while in progress.

Communication: Knowing the status inside classrooms—whether people are wounded, safe, or under attack.

Action: It takes seven to fifteen minutes on average for law enforcement to respond to a call; this is typically time when law enforcement can't help.

plained her son's newfound video game obsession as his way of "working through" his parents' separation. But soon even she grew alarmed at Lanza's outbursts, fearing "something was very wrong with him." She rushed him to Danbury Hospital's emergency room, but when Lanza denied experiencing suicidal or homicidal ideations, the physician concluded he was "not a danger to himself or others and said he was free to leave."

Like with Holmes, Lanza's neighbors described him to reporters as "different, with a weirdness about him. He wasn't a normal child." His only friend enjoyed shooting at paper bull's-eyes and other targets in the shapes of woodchucks or crows. By all accounts, from an early age Lanza was comfortable with firearms. With his mother's encouragement, he shot his first gun—a lightweight aluminum Ruger 10/22—at the age of four. Apparently, she "enjoyed target shooting [and] was very strict about it . . . very, very detail oriented," patiently reviewing step by step the proper hold and technique. She enjoyed watching her son practice with his "little rifle," acutely aware that if she left him alone "for even a moment," a "switch could flip."

His mother suspected her son "possibly suffered from a neurobiological condition," and as he aged he became a target for bullies who picked on his quietness. In fact, so distraught was she by her perception that the school failed to protect him that she insisted on accompanying him to school as his bodyguard. She was willing to do anything to protect her son, a "most strange and unsocial person," with an alarming hatred toward "normal" people and ultimately toward the world.

In the wake of Lanza's massacre, some mothers of mass shooters spoke out, "praying for grace," courageously sharing their stories, hoping to highlight the "problem of mental illness." One spoke at a TED Talk about her mentally ill son, how his unpredictable and violent behaviors frightened her; she was using her real name, she said, because, without it, "mental illness became somebody else's problem." In an impassioned speech she told the audience, "I am just like you. I am Adam Lanza's mother. I am Dylan Klebold's and Eric Harris's mother. I am James Holmes's mother. I am Seung-Hui Cho's mother. These boys—and their mothers—need help." She didn't want to talk about guns; the topic was mere deflection. Instead, she recited alarming statistics, such as "1 in 5 children (and 1 in 4 adults) in the United States has a serious and debilitating mental disorder and more than 4600 children between the ages of 10 and 24 will take their own lives." She finished with an even more sobering fact. The largest psychiatric treatment centers in the United States were Cook County Jail in Chicago, Rikers Island in New York, and the Los Angeles County Jail.

January 2013

Holmes' notebook became the subject of multiple pretrial hearings. While Holmes' lawyers fought valiantly to preclude his violent drawings and theories of human capital on the basis of privilege and patient/psychiatrist confidentiality, the state argued that my relationship with Holmes had officially ended six weeks prior to the massacre, thereby making his journal admissible and the best evidence of premeditated murder. It also, the state insisted, proved Holmes was sane, highlighting his elaborate plans to kill and his long-standing hatred of mankind. As yet, the defense had not revealed its strategy—that Holmes would plead insanity.

Jane insisted I come in to prepare for the hearing, and once again I found myself seated at the end of a long conference table in Hall & Evans, surrounded by cups of fresh-brewed coffee, water with slivers of lemon floating near the surface, and bowls of bright strawberries. As I was the intended recipient of the notebook, the critical question for the court was whether my relationship with Holmes had ever officially ended, putting at issue the disclosure of *any* information between us. The familiar grilling began, with Jane and Rick doing their "good cop, bad cop" routine, asking me what

I knew about the notebook (*nothing*), what it said (*no clue*), why Holmes had addressed it to me (*no idea*), and what the "Infinity" and "Ultraception" symbols on the cover meant. I truly didn't know. But a thought occurred to me: Had he bastardized the word "ultracrepidarianism"—"the habit of giving opinions and advice on matters outside of one's knowledge of competence"[16]—as a way to undermine me, to show me that he was superior, that I would never know what he didn't want me to know?

Rick's lobs kept coming, underhand, overhand, corner shots, spins, until finally, exhausted, I called match point.

"Get some sleep, kiddo. I'll be over at the crack of dawn to pick you up," Jane said.

But sleep was the last thing I wanted. Charged and stressed, I needed release. Padding barefoot into my home gym, I pressed "play" on the small boom box in the corner. Wall-to-wall mirrors glowed in the soft light as I swayed methodically to the robot-funk beat of Donna Summer's "I Feel Love." With each trancelike pulse, I jerked my body faster until I was whipping around the room with eyes closed, the hypnotic repetition of Summer's minimal lyrics helping me to focus, my body expressing what words could not. Power. Determination. Resilience. *You've got this!* Arms raised high, drenched in sweat, heart pounding, hair matted to my cheeks, in that moment I was ready to take on the world. But the euphoria was short-lived; the next morning my hand shook slightly as I unlocked the dead bolt on my front door to let Jane inside.

"Don't turn on the lights," I said. "I'm beginning to like the dark."

"You look . . . rested." Jane offered me a steaming Starbucks coffee.

"I was going for unflappable." My suit fit like a snug costume over my bulletproof vest. And I remembered what the officers had

---

16 -Ologies & -Isms. S.v. "ultracrepidarianism." Retrieved March 2, 2022 from https://www.thefreedictionary.com/ultracrepidarianism.

said about getting shot: *The force will knock you back, probably leave a bruise but no lasting marks.*

I was pretty sure I already had lasting marks.

We drove in silence to a Walmart parking lot. The morning was overcast, the sky wet and heavy with the promise of rain. In the passenger seat, I felt exposed, stiff, and filled with a foreboding of impending danger. Sleep deprivation in the military and in medical school and especially my years of grueling residency had instilled in me a steely resolve, exactly what I needed to survive Holmes.

After we idled for a few minutes, my heart pounding, a deputy sheriff in an armored black Expedition pulled up next to us and ordered us into the SUV, which smelled faintly of bleach.

I strapped in, my mouth dry as the deputy sped through stop signs and red lights on the way to the courthouse. Police had set up orange cones to slow the flow of traffic in the surrounding streets. As we approached the entrance, black-banded SWAT teams dressed in full riot gear—tactical vests, helmets, and face shields—armed with rifles, guarded long lines that had formed, like a perverse reenactment of the crowds that had waited outside the movie theater the night of the massacre in anticipation of seeing the premiere of *The Dark Knight Rises*. I later learned these were mostly survivors and family members who would watch the proceedings via a closed-circuit feed. It would be the first time they received detailed information about that horrific night.

The deputy ordered me to get down in case someone wanted to "take me out." It was hard to move in my armor, the vest cutting into my ribs as I wedged between seats, trying to make myself small, the way Holmes' victims must have crouched in shock behind cushions already riddled with bullets, seeking protection from the chaos and bloodshed, from the monster who wanted them dead. The van dipped underground into a long tunnel beneath the courthouse. "This is how we typically transport prisoners," he said. I certainly felt like one. It was as if I'd already been condemned to solitary confinement. In the flickering darkness, my chest tightened and for a moment I almost couldn't breathe as I realized I was being transported through the same tunnel Holmes had been, his evil lingering like a vibration.

Once out of the SUV, we were escorted by a deputy into a long rectangular hallway flanked by wall-to-wall windows. Our heels clicked in unison on the black-and-white checkerboard linoleum tiles. It felt familiar, like I was back in the military, marching. I glimpsed snipers on the courthouse rooftops squinting through scopes and felt like prey, hunted by strangers who wanted me dead, protected by strangers who wanted *them* dead, like a scene out of Richard Connell's short story "The Most Dangerous Game," in which one character enlightens the other, "The world is made up of two classes—the hunters and the huntees."

Outside Judge Sylvester's courtroom, Jane slid onto a lone metal bench and pulled a framed photo of Winston Churchill from her briefcase. "Rick wanted you to have this. He autographed it with his favorite saying, 'Steady as she goes.'"

As I took the witness stand, I faced Holmes for the first time in six months. His cold, detached stare still chilling, he now had a team of public defenders representing him, including Tamara Brady, whose face held the stress of a soldier back from the trenches. She reminded me of myself, tasked with the impossible job of helping a man whose single-minded mission was to hurt. And, like me, she had become the object of public hate. Holmes' parents sat in the audience looking stoic, perhaps afraid to show their anguish, as if their pain was somehow less important than the pain of the victims' families and survivors. Holmes didn't acknowledge them or even seem to care that they were present.

There was a heaviness in the room. Time slowed, as if we were all pushing through water. I tried not to look at Holmes, not to let him rattle me. For three and a half hours the lawyers engaged in heated debate over whether I continued to have a patient-doctor relationship with Holmes, thereby making the notebook and all our sessions privileged (and inadmissible) communications. Brady argued in the affirmative, saying Holmes had dialed the health services hotline ten minutes before the massacre, "maybe hoping to connect with his psychiatrist."

But patients didn't have a direct line to me (though they could always reach my voicemail), and though the switchboard *had* received a call at 12:31 a.m., the operator heard only seven seconds of silence before the call disconnected. Brady theorized that in that silence Holmes "meant to say, 'I'm feeling bad. Please stop me. Do something. Help me.'"

"That's illogical," the prosecution countered. "Holmes didn't see himself in a future relationship with Dr. Fenton because he planned to be 'dead or in prison.'"

Ultimately, the defense convinced the judge that the notebook was protected by patient-doctor confidentiality and would remain inadmissible unless and until Holmes waived that privilege by pleading insanity.

CHAPTER 17

POSSESSED JAMES

Spring 2013

The greatest prison we live in is the
fear of what other people think.
—The Joker, *The Dark Knight* (2008)

HOLMES

He did exactly that following district attorney George Brauchler's announcement in early spring that the state intended to seek the death penalty. Colorado had executed 101 people in its history, but since the Supreme Court reinstated the death penalty in 1978, only one person had actually been put to death (Gary Lee Davis, in 1997).[17] Victims cheered at the news, telling CNN reporters that Holmes deserved the exact same mercy he'd shown his victims, "extermination."

On May 13, 2013, Holmes' lawyers alleged he was not guilty by reason of insanity (NGRI), a difficult defense, since it required

---

17 The death penalty was repealed in Colorado in 2020.

Holmes' confession, and one that risked alienating jurors, who might erroneously conclude it allowed Holmes to "get away" with murder. In fact, most people acquitted spent more time institutionalized than did those found guilty of the same charges. In Colorado, a defendant could be found "criminally insane" if, at the time of the alleged crime, he suffered from a serious "mental disease or defect" that rendered him incapable of understanding that what he did was wrong. In most states, the *defense* had the burden of proving *in*sanity by a preponderance of the evidence, but in Colorado it was the prosecution's burden to prove the defendant sane beyond a reasonable doubt *at the time of the offense*. If it failed to do so, the jury would have to find Holmes not guilty by reason of insanity.

His trial began "offstage," with the judge ordering a sanity evaluation. By advancing an NGRI defense, Holmes necessarily waived all confidentiality and privilege concerning his mental health. Psychiatric records and sessions were now discoverable.

By the time the defense announced its NGRI defense, it had already retained Philadelphia psychiatrist Dr. Raquel Gur, a professor of neurology, radiology, and psychiatry, to evaluate Holmes. Her research specialty was schizophrenia. After reviewing his voluminous records and conducting four interviews with Holmes (during the first few weeks after his psychotic jail episode when he'd begun psychotropic medication), she was "quite certain" Holmes suffered from schizophrenia and was insane at the time of the shootings.

Though not forensically trained or board-certified in any field, Dr. Gur nonetheless insisted she felt "comfortable talking about brain function and MRIs," having twice testified in criminal matters before, once in 2009 (as an expert in "fitness for execution," not insanity) and fifteen years earlier in a federal insanity case. No state court in the country had ever qualified Dr. Gur as an expert on insanity (or on Colorado law); she would later testify that she lacked certain certifications because she had taken "the scenic route in psychiatry," meaning it had taken her a long time to specialize.

Nonetheless, Dr. Gur believed Holmes' delusions about human capital and the meaning of life had a "nihilistic flavor" similar to those of the Unabomber, Ted Kaczynski, a diagnosed schizophrenic. The prosecution objected to the comparison, finding it to be "utterly reckless" considering her "inferior qualifications." Though Holmes had been obsessively preoccupied with killing, I had never sensed his thoughts were disorganized like those of most schizophrenics, who jumped from topic to topic, their speech jumbled like a kind of word salad. But in her report, Dr. Gur described a completely different person. With her, and *no one else*, Holmes presented as an emotional "train wreck," "grimacing, red-faced as if he were crying, shaking, breathing hard, unable to talk." Similarly, she was the first (and only) person to whom he expressed remorse. She reported his "hopelessness, despair, pain" toward the family members of those he'd killed. She said he'd confided his fear of people, "all people," and spoke of seeing shadows, shadows he hoped would "catch him when he hurled himself off his jail cot." Considering schizophrenics mostly experienced auditory hallucinations, it seemed strange that Dr. Gur accepted Holmes' statements about shadow people.

Was Holmes really that different with her than he had been with me—or anyone else?

Could Holmes have been faking it, for hours, when he spoke to her?

Curiously, Dr. Robert Hanlon, a neuropsychologist also retained by the defense, reported that Holmes' "executive functioning was normal," there was "nothing physically wrong with his brain's ability to express things verbally, find words, generate responses or accurately comprehend oral or written material."

Holmes divulged to Dr. Gur that his mission to kill was a "call to action," a phrase he'd apparently repeated to her six times (though he never said it even *once* to any other expert). He didn't elaborate on what he meant except to say that a "master power" controlled him. He couldn't help having homicidal thoughts and wanted someone (perhaps me) to stop him. Death seemed a rational solution—his "call to action" wasn't inspired by anger or revenge—it just "had to be done."

His reference to an all-controlling "master power" suggested the possible rare defense of dissociated identity disorder (DID), the claim that more than one fully developed personality inhabited a single human body and that a criminal act was committed by a destructive "alter" of whose actions the dominant personality had only limited or no awareness. The legal community was conflicted as to the extent to which individuals with DID could or should be held responsible for their actions.

Since the trial of Billy Milligan, who was found not guilty by reason of insanity in 1978 after claiming one of his twenty-four personalities kidnapped, robbed, and raped three women, few dissociative defenses had been successful. In March 2012, just a few months before Holmes' massacre, Pamela Moss unsuccessfully claimed her "host" personality "Caroline" had murdered a man in self-defense. She'd lured the victim, a businessman, to her house and beat him to death with a hammer because she'd already spent the money she owed him and didn't want to go to jail. According to the defense, Moss wasn't even *there*. "Caroline" told police she was in fear for her life. Moss had been diagnosed with DID sixteen years earlier, after she deliberately overdosed her mother for an insurance payout. The defense urged jurors not to punish Moss for what "Caroline" did, since "Caroline" was legally insane at the time of the offense. But the prosecution argued that "alters" who allegedly killed in self-defense were not likely to hide their kills under the porch afterward. Moss was convicted and received a life sentence.

With Dr. Gur, Holmes dropped his flat affect and became talkative, a "phenomenon" she described as like a "train derailing," then later "an earthquake, shaking, slowly, slowly almost like a tornado, that accumulated and wandered and gained power." His "personality," she insisted, had "decompensated" over the seven months leading up to the shootings, and his social behavior and affectual difficulties were merely undiagnosed schizophrenic symptoms. But I knew that Holmes' "shadows" had other possible explanations that Dr. Gur didn't consider, such as visual illusions exaggerated by schizotypal obsessiveness, hypnagogic presleep phenomena, or "micro psychotic" episodes, none of which were symptoms of schizophrenia.

Dr. Woodcock, the board-certified neurologist hired by the defense team, met for two hours with Holmes in the jail on July 24, 2012, four days after the shooting; he concluded Holmes was "so psychotic he couldn't tell right from wrong." Though his specialty was dementia, he had more knowledge and training in psychiatry than Dr. Gur. But, like Dr. Gur, his information was limited to Holmes' own "blunted" statements, his "dissociation of affect." His opinions and diagnoses—like mine—were only as good as the information Holmes reported and were, at best, incomplete. Like me, he, too, had been subjected to Holmes' "emotionless" state—though, with Dr. Woodcock, Holmes disclosed that he'd been "suicidal" and that his "compulsion" (killing) was "Plan C," the only way to deal with his problems.

Holmes' self-described "catatonia" apparently caused a kind of "mental paralysis," a condition he "limited to his lunch hour," because he "needed to work and study." Dr. Woodcock reported no signs of anxiousness or depression; instead, Holmes complained he was "bored." He believed he'd become "manic" after I prescribed him Zoloft, because he'd embarked on "spending sprees" (buying large quantities of weapons, ammunition, and ballistics clothing). Strikingly, with Dr. Woodcock, Holmes denied having *any* hallucinations. Woodcock said his mental illness rendered him "tremendously emotionally flat," with a "twisted orientation" that made his "very essence" psychotic and "illogical."

There was "no point," Dr. Woodcock advised, "in trying to understand him or why he would hide behavior he wanted others to stop him from carrying out." He had interviewed Holmes twice, for a total of less than three hours. Neither session was recorded or videotaped, and though he asked Holmes nothing about his notebook or the crime itself, he nonetheless concluded that Holmes suffered from schizoaffective disorder, antisocial personality disorder, and an anxiety disorder.

Other experts would later explain Holmes' symptoms in jail as related to post-shooting stress caused by memories of the killing; or extreme isolation and deprivation in the "Hole," which triggered his natural anxious and paranoid schizotypal traits; anticipation of his trial and sentencing, including worry about the death penalty; and the metabolic effects of his starvation and dehydration.

The district attorney's office retained two rebuttal experts, a famous forensic psychologist and a psychiatrist, neither of whom the defense would allow to interview Holmes. All they had were his records, witness interviews, and the FBI's GAQ, a proxy for psychological tests, by which Holmes' friends and relatives answered questions about him in absentia. To make up for what the court determined were "inaccuracies and inadequacies," it appointed its *own* expert, local forensic psychiatrist Dr. Jeffrey Metzner, who interviewed Holmes for twenty-five hours over four days at the Colorado Mental Health Institute at Pueblo and found him neatly dressed in hospital clothing, alert and oriented in all three spheres.

Memory testing demonstrated a capacity to recall the past four presidents, spell the word "world" forward and backward and recall three out of three objects after five minutes . . . concentration was intermittently but not frequently impaired . . . he described himself as becoming "spaced out" when . . . bored . . . affect was generally flat . . . he expressed very little anxiety, conflict or regret regarding the shootings. He did smile at times . . . in response to the proverb, "the tongue is the enemy of the neck," he replied, "they are two separate things." . . . He frequently . . . answer[ed] questions with vague answers, which he acknowledged was similar to the "deflection" pro-

cess he described in his notebook . . . the content of his speech was sparse . . . a thought disorder (i.e. disorganized thinking as evidenced by poverty of speech and illogicality) was present as evidenced by his psychotic thinking re: human worth and transference of worth by killing others . . .

Holmes did not recall a history of auditory hallucinations . . . he experienced visual hallucinations . . . Paranoid thinking has been present in the past. For example, he perceived the FBI was following him during the time his homicidal thinking became "more realistic." Paranoid thinking was also present during November 2012 when Holmes thought that his food was being poisoned.

Throughout the psychiatric examination he was cordial in a distant sense . . . and on antipsychotic medication . . .

In his interviews with Dr. Metzner, Holmes described in meticulous detail how he'd designed the bomb system, studying "timing" so as to "divert police to his apartment" and "delay their response to the movie theater," leaving him "more time to kill." He'd researched Columbine and other mass shootings "to get an idea of law enforcement's response times and how much ammunition he might need." And he'd "cased the place," which involved sitting through movies in nine different theaters over a two-month period before he chose theater 9 for its "proximity and size," "limited number of exits," and "excellent spatial approach."

He said he chose a movie theater *not* because he liked movies, as Dr. Gur stated, but because a theater promised "mass casualties." He'd purchased three different tickets over a three-week period, hoping to get a ticket for theater 9, but his tickets were all for theater 8. It didn't matter; no one checked, and he slipped into theater 9 regardless. But the fact that he'd purchased so many over an extended period of time showed methodical planning, not an impulsive response to commanding visual hallucinations.

The fact that he'd ordered black "possession lenses" (the kind that darkened the entire eye, making him look demonic) "as a way to differentiate himself from his normal self . . . like he was possessed" revealed planning (and manipulation)—but true "alters" (dissociated personalities; Holmes did not have one) typically developed from dissociation to cope with prolonged early childhood trauma (something Holmes had not reported to anyone). Moreover, people with alters often referred to them as parts inside, aspects, facets, ways of being, voices, multiples, selves, ages of me, people, persons, individuals, spirits, demons, others, which Holmes didn't do.

Holmes took selfies, hoping he looked "dangerous" as he "stuck his tongue out, held a gun wearing his body armor . . ." He dyed his hair red "to differentiate himself from who he normally was . . . because he was not his normal self." He wanted to protect his "normal self," insisting "the other him," the "possessed James," "did everything." And, though the two selves were "distinct," he later reported that by June or July of 2012 he had trouble telling the difference.

He insisted to Dr. Metzner that his "possessed" self arrived at the theater around midnight on July 20, 2012, ten minutes later than he'd planned because he was fiddling with the bombs in his apartment. He was dressed in Kevlar chaps and a IIIA jacket (bullet-resistant clothing), an arm protector on one arm, a belt with ammunition (250 rounds for his handgun and six rounds for the shotgun), a groin guard, and a tactical vest that held 400 rounds of rifle ammo. He also wore a gas mask and helmet and was armed with a Glock pistol, M&P 15, and shotgun. He entered theater 9 and sat briefly in the front row before leaving during the previews because he "didn't want to appear suspicious to others and risk attracting the attention of a security guard." He propped open the exit door using a tablecloth holder and got into his car.

When he reentered the theater, he was wearing a wireless headset and listening to techno music at maximum volume "because he did not want to hear anything during the shooting . . . It wasn't personal." He didn't want it to feel like he was "actually murdering somebody." He admitted he'd worn the armor so he wouldn't get shot, since this "would have prevented him from killing more people." When asked why this was so important, he seemed irritated and replied, "If I could kill everybody in the world that would put an end to the question of why people needed to be alive in the first place. That was the question I wanted to answer ever since I was a kid. I was at rock-bottom—things couldn't get any worse."

In a sense, Holmes was conducting his own experiment—not only with the human race but with the experts. When Dr. Metzner asked why he had conflicting stories, he shrugged. "Things change with time." He insisted he'd never used the phrase "call to action," to Dr Gur. He said his targets were random and the shotgun "was optimal in that setting for killing people." When it was over, he felt "empty" and carefully laid his rifle on the ground and his handgun on his car roof because he was "being instinctual." He asked for a lawyer because he "didn't want to talk"; the very *act* made him anxious. He surrendered because getting shot might "hurt." He didn't participate in his own trial (opting instead to be interviewed endlessly by psychiatrists), putting his *brain* at issue and pitting expert against expert.

In the end, he killed when he did because he was afraid of being locked up, of having his murderous plot foiled, his childhood fantasy derailed. He admitted as much to Dr. Metzner, saying he didn't tell "Fenton his plans outright" because "Fenton was getting concerned"; she "seemed more nervous." That's when he began buying weapons and scouting for shooting locations. Though he knew he had a "broken brain" (as he put it in his notebook), the last thing he wanted was to be dismissed as "crazy." His linear, calculated thinking revealed anything but insanity. I was surprised to learn that he wrote me notes once or twice a week (after our sessions, after failing his exams) so that I and other psychiatrists could learn to treat people like him effectively. He admitted he was not "a communicative person," but "he thought Fenton wasn't trying either, because

Fenton had already prescribed drugs." He knew he was "difficult" but that "was just part of who he was." The notebook was his attempt to put in writing what he said I didn't ask him and what he "perceived he could not talk about," like buying weapons, wanting to kill people, thinking he was "crazy" because "killing people was crazy" and he was *not* crazy!

In fact, he went to great lengths to showcase his sanity. He'd briefed law enforcement about how he'd booby-trapped his apartment with firework shells, homemade thermite, napalm, glycerin, gasoline, and oil. And for four months, from July to November 2012, he sent grievances to jail authorities complaining about the food, asking for contact lens cleaning fluid and certain books, and refusing to eat or drink altogether. (This deprivation likely sent him into a delirium.)

Dr. Metzner received the most detailed explanation of Holmes' concept of "worth," of "how much a person's time was worth, for example a surgeon's time was worth more than a janitor's time, human capital was what would give him a more meaningful life." It was "more important for a killer to kill more than one person because it increased the worth of the person doing the killing in a mathematical way." He excluded the notion of killing children and friends—children were worth more than other people "because they had the rest of their lives to live." Friends were "real people," in contrast to "crowd people" (those he did not know).

His goal was to "kill as many people as possible."

He "only counted fatalities" because "the dead can't be repaired or come back to life or be normal again. Irreversible." The wounded were "collateral damage."

Equal = 0 No value
Equal may = 00 ultimate good
Equal may = 00 ultimate evil

Can a person have both no value AND be ultimately good AND/OR ultimately evil? What does the value of a person even matter?
*Justice
People are ultimately good or evil in value, then one may suffer from injustice.
If life has no value
—All is just
Moral imbeciles are those who side with 0 or −infinity [worthlessness or evil]. The ideals of society are founded on +infinity [priceless or ultimate good].
Why do persons commit to 0 or −infinity?
All men are created equal, and all men are uncreated equal but in between there is inequality.
My mind:——————
$$-00 \quad 0 + 00$$

Translation: violence can be used to solve problems—all problems.

PART III

CHAPTER 18

WHY?

December 13, 2013—January 14, 2014

People are starting to notice.
—The Joker, *The Dark Knight* (2008)

FENTON

On December 13, 2013 (one day before the anniversary of the Sandy
Hook massacre in Newtown, Connecticut), Judge Carlos Samour
postponed Holmes' sanity hearing (to determine if Holmes was
even competent to stand trial) until the end of January 2014. There
had been another shooting.

Karl Pierson, an eighteen-year-old high school senior, a self-
described "psychopath with a superiority complex," was enraged
after being demoted as captain of his debate team and opened fire
in Arapahoe High, a small suburban school in Denver (just a few
miles from Columbine). Days earlier he had apparently downloaded
several books on the subject of psychopathy, among them *Why Kids
Kill: Inside the Minds of School Shooters* by Pete Langman, *Confessions of
a Sociopath* by M. E. Thomas, and *Columbine: A True Crime Story* by

Jeffrey Kass. Pierson, who purportedly idolized Columbine shooter Eric Harris, entered the campus armed with a pump-action shotgun, three incendiary devices in his backpack, and a machete concealed in a scabbard. Scrawled on his arm were letters and numbers associated with five classrooms and the school's library. On the inside of his forearm, he'd scrawled the words attributed to Julius Caesar when he crossed the Rubicon: *Alea iacta est*, meaning "The die is cast."

"You look a little shell-shocked," Edinberg said, and shut the heavy paneled door to his office, sealing us in the quiet.

I welcomed my weekly appointments with him, finding comfort in consistency and familiarity. Even his waiting area was calming. Sometimes I came early just to sit, take a breath, and feel safe surrounded by potted succulents and silky white orchids and magazines that repeated each month. As strange as it sounded, I felt energized by the white noise.

This day, Pierson troubled me, so much so that I'd stayed up most of the night researching grim statistics on mass shootings, dismayed that the phenomenon had become a kind of epidemic. Since Holmes' massacre, America averaged one school shooting every ten days. There had been twenty-eight in all of 2013 and forty-four (an average of more than three per month) since Sandy Hook. Karl Pierson considered himself a "Grand exalted leader," and even had a URL on Facebook that announced to the world he was a kind of king: "Karl is boss."

Edinberg looked at me thoughtfully as I went on and on about Pierson. Finally, he asked, "Does he remind you of Holmes?"

"No," I said, a little too quickly. His question jolted me a bit. The only similarity between the two killers was that they had killed. I'd been looking for historical data on Pierson, signs and symptoms he may have exhibited long before the massacre, psychologists he'd

seen, childhood trauma, bullying, rage . . . all things that had been no-
ticeably absent with Holmes. Pierson's school psychologist had called
him a "low level of concern." *I'd been very concerned about Holmes.*

Pierson's mother had taken him to a mental health center,
where therapists all said he wasn't dangerous. He'd shown fellow
students' images of the gun and machete he'd bought but didn't
tell them about his upcoming plans. *Holmes told no one about the
weapons he'd amassed.*

Pierson wanted to kill his debate coach, a threat that was captured on a parking lot video but later erased.

His friends and family described him as a "dedicated and bright
student who came from a religious family that regularly attended
Bible study." He also kept a diary and wrote that he'd bought a gun:
*mom does not know about it . . . I will shoot up my school. . . . I am a psycho-
path with a superiority complex . . . I will do something I have wanted to do
for a while . . . mass murder . . . I alone will be judge, jury and executioner . . .
words hurt . . . they can mold a sociopath and will lead someone a decade
later to kill.* Pierson thought what happened at Sandy Hook was "hilarious." The day of the shooting he wrote, *today is going to be fun.
Holmes wasn't a psychopath, and he seemed indifferent to killing; he hated
all of mankind without motive.*

Unlike Holmes, Pierson left a clear map. He'd wanted to go to
West Point, applied to join the Air Force, had firearms training,
NRA qualification certificates, and a RAMS (Rifle Archery Muzzle
Loading Shotgun) ID badge, all the hallmarks of a good American
soldier. The debate teacher who demoted him said he'd never seen a
kid with such a look of hatred; it "haunted" him. In fact, the teacher
had even considered resigning from his position because he thought
it would be safer. *In sessions with Holmes, I didn't feel I was in danger; he
just made me uneasy and unsettled.*

Pierson had had a threat assessment; his psychiatrist concluded
he was a "narcissist." His mother reported her son had "deep-seated"
anger issues. *Holmes' mother recalled only one incident when Holmes*

became angry—when she asked him to get a job or reapply to graduate school.
Steve and I had *looked* for anger as a possible root cause of Holmes'
killing fantasies but found nothing. He *wasn't* angry; he just hated
people.

There were multiple reports of Pierson's anger; even by his own
admission he had "problems." He said, "I become a monster when
I'm mad." His parents tried to do the right thing, took him to a
behavioral health facility. He was prescribed medications, but he
wrote in his journal that the drugs were "a joke" and he "hated taking his pills." His "shrink appointments" were apparently a "massive
waste of time." At one point, he'd actually considered committing
his rampage at the mental health treatment center, said he "had an
interesting idea today. . . . I thought about shooting up the asylum
or whatever the fuck it was that my mother took me for that psych
evaluation . . . let the records show I lied through my teeth." *Holmes,
too, had withheld information.* But Pierson, who was so vocal about his
targets and plan—in writing, to friends, to parents; who threatened
violence; whom people locked out of classrooms because they thought
he was "scary"—was not reported, not committed for a mental health
hold. Pierson's debate teacher feared for his life, and yet . . . *no one did
anything.*

"The kid had a hit list, his journal described attack plans and
targets and a timeline. He planned to kill for revenge, even named
his shotgun Kurt Cobain."

Edinberg listened to my ramblings with a great poker face, betraying no emotion, revealing no information. For the first two
years, I'd found his nonresponsiveness a little maddening. *What was
I paying him for if not to tell me what to do, how to fix my problems?* I'd
never before participated in psychoanalysis, a type of therapy focused on how the unconscious mind influences a person's thoughts
and behaviors. Early in my treatment, when I wasn't sure how to
begin, Edinberg had prompted me to "just say whatever came to
mind. No matter how mundane or embarrassing or seemingly irrelevant."

Now, as I glanced at the prints on his wall of auks (flightless birds that looked a lot like penguins with spectacles and even more like Edinberg!), my mind wandered to *birds, guns, flight, blood,* and my latest disturbing death threat. I had received so many now I wasn't sure what to do with them all: keep them as evidence, forward them to Jane, shred them?

I felt shattered, angry, betrayed. My life had become unrecognizable. It was one thing to know a killer, or to study a killer's history and be able to connect the dots (or not, as in Holmes' case). It was quite another to have multiple hidden enemies *forever,* to know that, even when the trial ended, there would never be closure for me. Whether Holmes lived or died didn't take the target off my back. My safety would always be compromised. I'd always have to look over my shoulder, keep up my walls, park beneath streetlights, be hypervigilant about my surroundings, stay off social media.

When I left Edinberg's office that day, I cut my hair short; the act felt so freeing, impulsive, immediate, though I knew the reinvention of my physical self only created a false (short-lived) sense of control. I'd left jagged ends, and the style looked unfinished. But the more I tried to fix it, the shorter my hair became, until finally, I thought it might help if I just bleached it white.

April 2014

HOLMES

Meanwhile, for three days, experts on both sides engaged in heated debate over Holmes' sanity and his competency to stand trial. After reviewing Dr. Metzner's report, the prosecution's experts complained that his findings (that Holmes suffered from schizoaffective disorder, characterized in part by delusions) were biased. They insisted they, too, be allowed to interview Holmes. Offended, Dr. Metzner felt "blindsided" and "set up" and refused to cooperate further with the prosecution's experts. On April 14, 2014 (after another *thirteen* school shootings), the judge, fearing Dr. Metzner's hostility toward the prosecution would bias his trial testimony, appointed Dr. William Reid, MD, MPH, to conduct another evaluation of Holmes.

> *Pursuant to [Colorado statute C.R.S.] section 16-8-106(6), the report should include . . . (1) the name of each physician, forensic psychologist or other expert who examined [Holmes], (2) a description of the nature, content, extent, and results of the examination and any tests conducted; (3) a diagnosis and prognosis of [Holmes'] physical and mental condition; (4) an opinion as to whether [Holmes] suffered from a mental disease or defect or from a condition of mind caused by a mental disease or defect that prevented him from forming the culpable mental state that is an essential element of any crime charged; and (5) if [Holmes] suffered from such a mental disease or defect or from such a condition of mind, a separate opinion as to whether [Holmes] was insane, as that term is defined in article 8 of title 16 of the Colorado Revised Statutes, on the date of the offenses charged . . . The report must also address Holmes' cooperation during the examination. The new examiner shall not consider Holmes' competency to proceed or how any mental disease or defect or condition of mind caused by a mental disease or defect affects any mitigating factor in the death penalty statutes.*
>
> *Order C-94, pp. 2–4*

Just one month later, on May 23, 2014, twenty-two-year-old Elliot Rodger's "Day of Retribution" resulted in several dead at the University of California, Santa Barbara (he actually attended Santa Barbara City College). Rodger was a lonely, socially awkward, relentlessly bullied outcast who was obsessed with his virginity and wrote a detailed act of revenge against the women he violently hated because they'd rejected him. In his book-length manifesto titled "My Twisted World: The Story of Elliot Rodger," a writing more "verbally savage" than *Mein Kampf*, he wrote that women should be "destroyed," "incarcerated," or merely "tolerated for breeding purposes."

His parents' solution to his loneliness was to find him a psychiatrist; his was to buy semiautomatic pistols. His mission was to kill as many people as possible (surprisingly, not all of them women), then shoot himself.

Grieving victims' families demanded that the insanity stop, that *their* rights be heard, too, and not just those of the mentally ill or the gun enthusiasts. When was "enough, enough?" When were people going to finally silence the "craven, irresponsible politicians and the NRA?" The families received a response from Samuel Joseph Wurzelbacher (a figure who had become nationally known during the 2008 presidential campaign as "Joe the Plumber"). He said, "As harsh as this sounds—your dead kids don't trump my Constitutional rights . . . it is my responsibility to protect my family and I will stand up for that right vehemently."

On October 1, 2015, there was *another* school shooting. Christopher Harper-Mercer, an angry kid who had once pointed a shotgun at his mother, a night nurse, had by late adolescence acquired nine guns, including a rifle. For "fun" he and his mother target practiced. He used six guns to kill nine students at Umpqua Community College in Oregon before shooting himself. His motive: revenge against the bullies. Like Elliot Rodger (one of his "heroes"), he also wrote a manifesto "for all those who never took me seriously, this is for you . . . to quote Seung-Hui Cho: 'Today I die like Jesus Christ.'" He liked the idea of becoming somebody and wrote that when people like him "all alone and unknown spill a little blood, suddenly the whole world knows who they are."

Holmes wanted to be known as well—he'd wanted to survive his massacre so he could be a living archive—and Dr. Reid wanted people to know Holmes. Over the defense's strenuous objections, he documented twenty-two hours of video-recorded interviews (nine interviews over five days) at both the Colorado Mental Health Institute at Pueblo and the Arapahoe County Sheriff's Detention Facility.[18] Dr. Reid concluded that Holmes—regardless of "any mental disease or defect"—"clearly knew and appreciated at all relevant times that the shooting and killings he committed were illegal and socially wrong." In his report he elaborated that Holmes "knew that others, including psychiatrists and law enforcement personnel, would try to stop him if they realized what he was planning to do . . . and appreciated the likely consequences to others (e.g. death, injury) and himself (e.g., arrest and imprisonment or execution)."

He bragged before and after the shootings and wrote in his notebook that he expected to be arrested and/or killed by police and, if arrested, expected either to go to prison or be executed. He kept his plans secret from almost everyone and did not divulge details that might have caused others to interfere with his mission. Dr. Reid noted that Holmes broached the subject of killing with his girlfriend, but he'd kept the topic purposefully abstract, because he did not want to be "locked up." His "planning and practice was surreptitious," and "to avoid detection and interruption of the 'mission'" he purchased and stored weapons, material, and equipment in such a way that no one would suspect he practiced shooting at a faraway and unsupervised range. He kept his curtains closed to avoid being observed and implemented methods of distraction and escape, incendiary "booby traps" in and near his apartment, and Road Stars found in his car. Holmes "carefully chose a method of killing that he reasonably believed would result in maximum deaths with minimal chance" of being stopped. His chosen target, the movie theater, was a "contained and crowded killing field."

Calmly, Holmes explained how he'd planned to incapacitate his victims by using tear gas and handcuffing the upper exit doors shut. He walked through the lobby as if he were "an ordinary pa-

---

18 Reid was the only expert to video record his interviews with Holmes.

tron," exiting during the previews to "suit up." When he shot, he had no doubt his victims would suffer (he would not have wanted to be shot or killed), but he needed their deaths to increase his "value." Killing would alleviate his depression. "It was selfish." Dr. Reid found "little reliable indication in the record or descriptions from witnesses that Mr. Holmes suffered from severe clinical depression or significant mood instability during the months before the shootings."

> *Neither Holmes nor others described chronic or pervasive fatigue, . . . loss of energy . . . e.g. his activities of daily living, shopping, . . . driving long distances to practice shooting, playing video games, working on his "mission." There is no reliable indication that he felt particularly worthless or guilt-ridden. He appears to be able to think and concentrate sufficiently, . . . without . . . ambivalence, to carry out complex mission planning and implementation, as well as to attend classes and labs through the end of the school year and sit for his "prelim" examination . . . After the shootings, he referred to his homicidal thoughts as psychological defenses against suicidal thoughts, but he made it clear to me that the "suicidal thoughts" did not rise to a conscious level . . . and his "marginal response" to antipsychotic medication, low doses of Risperdal and moderate doses of escitalopram (Lexapro, an antidepressant) over 21 months had "little diagnostic significance." Holmes' thinking and behavior was not markedly different from his condition at the time of the shootings . . .*

After two days of intensive interviews, Dr. Reid concluded Holmes *intended* to commit mass murder and knew exactly what he was doing. He suffered from "schizotypal personality disorder" (just as I had diagnosed); Dr. Reid stressed that only a small portion of people with the disorder actually developed schizophrenia and cautioned against categorizing delusions, or "delusional disorder," as schizophrenia or schizoaffective disorder.

There was no reliable indication that Holmes manifested acute psychotic signs in any of his pre-shooting interactions, in many different contexts with clinicians, friends, former friends, professors or other people. He was able to perform school duties . . . shop, drive, [shoot] at the distant Byers Canyon range, order a complicated array of equipment, set up the attempted incendiary "diversion," carry out usual activities of daily living and prepare and implement his complex ruse and shooting procedure at the Century 16 theater, all apparently without significant impairment.

Reid found that Holmes *didn't* "psychologically decompose" in graduate school as Dr. Gur had suggested. Instead, he had untreated mononucleosis and continued to attend classes and labs in spite of listlessness, fatigue, and other related symptoms. And his so-called delusions involved his own philosophy of "human capital"—ideas *he* (and not a "master power") generated. Holmes, at all times, was in control of his thoughts and "made it clear that his statements existed because he believed them." And while he may have felt better because he was somehow "worth more" after killing twelve people, the "worth" he felt was arbitrary and idiosyncratic (i.e., it is whatever he decides it is); it did not make him stronger, imbue him with special powers, or extend his life. Holmes' views on the shooting were "part of an entrenched philosophy" rather than any significant mental disorder.

I see no firm indication that Holmes consciously thought that killing people in the ways he imagined or planned was "crazy." His view of himself in his notebook as "mad" was "literary hyperbole, meant to be read by others, rather than any particular insight into being delusional or otherwise "psychotic." . . . He did not indicate to me, nor does the record convincingly reflect, any consistent view that killing others was a sign of psychosis; however, there is good evidence in his behaviors, writings, and communications before and after the shoot-

ings that he knew his "mission" to kill was "wrong" and that part of him believed it should not be carried out. . . .

In the end, the judge ruled Holmes was competent to stand trial.

January 20, 2015

"MONSTER/MASTER" HOLMES

Nearly nine thousand prospective jurors filed into the Arapahoe County District Court for consideration in what promised to be the largest jury pool in the history of the United States. Selection lasted four months as the lawyers struggled to find jurors willing to be fair and impartial, sacrifice huge amounts of time to listen to graphic and potentially life-altering testimony that depicted indescribable acts of brutality, and agree to be "death qualified," which meant they would at least consider execution as a possible sentence. Those with religious, moral, ethical, or even *human* objections were automatically disqualified.

Initial prospects first completed lengthy questionnaires that probed their personal and criminal histories, employment status, educational background, family members, film preferences, bumper stickers, and any media exposure they may have already had to the charges, including photographs, television clips, and newspaper articles. Most, if not all, knew about Holmes, and some undoubtedly had already formed a preliminary opinion of him. A few knew survivors from the Columbine massacre and two claimed to have been "best friends" with the killers, Klebold and Harris.

Jury selection involved psychology; first impressions were critical, and attorneys were often trained to "read" the room, to observe a juror's facial expressions, physical appearance, body language—even body *type*. Were they late, panting, sweaty, overweight, too thin? Did they sport a Mohawk or orange hair, possibly in an effort to identify with Holmes? Did they seem rebellious and unwilling to follow instructions and apply the law? Were they distracted, texting during the questioning, sleeping, rolling their eyes, mad-dogging Holmes? Did they stutter, talk too fast or too slow? Eyelid fluttering denoted instability. Shifty eyes communicated distrust or dishonesty. Heavily made-up women were typically insecure. If they brought a book with them, what was the title? Had they ever been a mental patient? Prescribed antidepressants? Had a substance abuse problem? Had they ever been arrested? Or divorced? Had they ever lost a loved one? How did they feel about guns and gun control?

The lawyers tag-teamed. While one asked the questions, the others watched the jurors' reactions. And each side struck members for bias or "feeling," on the lookout for that foreperson, that juror most likely to persuade or lead (salesmen, engineers, accountants, surgeons, lawyers, doctors), and the lone wolf, the equally strong juror who was unafraid to hold out for a verdict of life. The entire case hinged on the jury panel.

The final twenty-four[19] (later whittled down to nineteen), along with reporters from forty media outlets, including television networks from Germany, France, and China, listened raptly as district attorney George Brauchler, looking like a young Brad Pitt, described "the horror, bullets, blood, brains and bodies" that filled a boxlike theater on a cool July night. While "four hundred people waited to be entertained one person planned to slaughter them to make himself feel better, to increase his self-worth." In what some reporters dubbed the *Star Wars* of opening statements, the prosecutor presented more than eight hundred graphic photographs, played choice portions of 911 calls, and struggled to lift pounds of ammunition,

---

19 One of whom was a survivor of Columbine and knew both shooters.

repeating after each grisly slide, *"Boom, boom, boom."* And as he spoke, Holmes sat calmly in his chair, bolted to the floor by a chain.

Brauchler, with more than 150 trials to his credit, had consulted with a priest before accepting the assignment to prosecute Holmes, a "career-defining case." As a military lawyer, he had deployed to Iraq in 2011, where he served as chief of military justice for the Fourth Infantry Division. His caseload included prosecuting an American soldier who killed a Taliban commander in an Afghan jail. Having once aspired to "attend a service academy and become a battlefield general," he enrolled at the University of Colorado on an ROTC scholarship instead and shifted toward a career in law, inspired by his mother, who, following law school, had worked as a civil rights investigator for the federal government. Like her, he, too, sometimes fell asleep on the floor surrounded by law books, cell phones, and laptops. Crime fighting was his "calling, his mission," so much so, his wife told the *Denver Post*, she'd had to "throw shoes away because they were covered in blood." He could not have known at least two of the biggest shootings in the history of the United States (Columbine and the Aurora massacre) would occur in his hometown.[20]

Holmes faced 165 criminal charges, including twenty-four counts of first-degree murder (twelve counts each for specific intent to kill an individual and reflection and extreme indifference [i.e., shooting blindly into a crowd], 140 counts of attempted murder, and one count of explosives possession. Among the dead were a former naval officer fatally shot while protecting his friend from gunfire, an Air Force staff sergeant on active duty, and an Air Force translator fluent in Mandarin. Holmes murdered a father and his two teenage sons, an aspiring sports reporter (who had ironically survived an-

---

20 Unfortuntely, since Columbine and Aurora there have been even higher victim counts (Pulse Nightclub, La Vegas/Mandalay Bay, Sutherland Springs).

other mass shooting in a mall just one month earlier), a petty officer third class serving in the Navy, a teenager hoping to study ceramics in college, and another who shielded his girlfriend and gave his life for hers. Veronica Moser Sullivan, just six years old, died before she ever had the chance to grow up.

The audience, filled with survivors, sobbed. Some left the courtroom, visibly shaken as the defense waved Holmes' twenty-nine-page manifesto at the jury. "This notebook," peppered with self-diagnoses, theater diagrams, and "theories on 'human capital,'" was, according to the defense, "proof positive that Holmes was insane."

It was the best play they had—and maybe the only way to make sense of something so senseless.

CHAPTER 19

THE WALKING WOUNDED

April 27, 2015

People need to know Aurora will never happen again.
—Mother of one of the slain victims

HOLMES

"Some had pellets all over their bodies, shotgun patterns, blank stares, like zombies," a fire medic said of the scene inside the theater. He was among the nearly one hundred first responders, investigators, law enforcement personnel, and survivors who testified in the first fifteen days of the trial. The medic had to choose between treating those who were just severely injured and those who were more likely to die. The experience left him "blank inside," like living was somehow a betrayal of the dead, like his life had been rendered "irrelevant."

One by one, survivors described a "heat sensation" as bullets shattered legs, hands, arms. "Everyone was screaming, I've been shot. I've been shot." "At first we thought it was theater antics, like bats flying over us" but then "we realized it was a gas" canister tossed over the stadium seats. Some, who had survived Iraq, were familiar with muzzle flashes like those from Holmes' weapons and knew right away they were being shot at. "There was gunfire, *boom, boom, boom,* then silence, eerie stillness as the gunman reloaded."

Instead of sitting in the courtroom while they waited to testify, some survivors huddled in an overflow room, where the proceedings were broadcast on a live video monitor; they couldn't bear hearing the nightmare recounted over and over. One suffered a bullet blast that left a "gaping hole in his calf, a burning sensation as if someone had taken a rusted railroad nail and jammed it into his flesh." The witness demonstrated with his cane how Holmes had aimed his rifle at him.

By the time police arrived, "smoke alarms blared, fluorescent blue lights, strobes," flashed like lightning over the dead, while the movie played on and on and cell phones, scattered on the floor, started to vibrate or ring. There was an overwhelming smell of gas, shit, urine, blood, and sweat as first responders cleared the theater, row by row, hunting for a possible second gunman. The courtroom grew quiet as an officer testified, "I knew there were going to be people who were not ever going to leave that building." Ambulances could not reach the wounded because of the roadblocks and choked traffic in the parking lot; "police were doing everything, hauling victims to their cars, driving over curbs, grass, making two and three trips to the hospital because there wasn't enough time." One officer cradled a teenage girl in his arms like a child, gently placed her inside his patrol car, and handed her his cell so she could call her mom. Another held a victim's airway open with his hands while his partner helped a woman who'd been shot in the stomach literally hold in her intestines. "There was so much blood, I could hear it sloshing in the back of my car."

"We thought initially there might be four or five victims," said a firefighter describing how he'd arrived in a hundred-foot-ladder truck and quickly realized how unprepared he was for the chaos and carnage; it had taken nearly ten minutes to get to a scene blocked by patrol cars, theatergoers trying to leave the crowded parking lot, civilians fleeing. Dozens of injured lay on sidewalks. "We asked the police to take them, to drive like hell." They weren't paramedics. They weren't doctors. They couldn't help the victims, but they could take them to the people who could. One officer choked up as he said, "It was a horrific privilege." Twenty-three of the victims rushed to University of Colorado Hospital arrived in police cars.

"I heard some of the most awful noises I've ever heard in my life that night," said an officer as he recalled helping Caleb, an aspiring comedian who was shot in the face. Paralyzed and unable to talk, Caleb was later wheeled to the witness stand by his father and testified by pointing to letters on an alphabet board. He had lost his right eye and suffered brain damage. Just two days before the shooting, he had performed in a contest at Comedy Works and had advanced into the finals. He and his wife, Katie, celebrated his win with a midnight showing of *The Dark Knight Rises*, their last date before officially becoming parents. His wife chose a seat close to the exit in case she went into labor. The scene that unfolded was like something out of a horror film. After being shot, Caleb, "pouring with blood," squeezed his wife's hand as if to beg her to run, save their unborn child. She ran from the theater, tripping in her flip-flops, slipping in pools of blood. With shaking hands, she dialed her cell—"Caleb's parents thought I was calling to tell them I was going into labor . . . instead I had to tell them their son had been shot and was probably going to die."

One Aurora officer tearfully described her last night working the graveyard shift as "surreal." She'd applied pressure to Ashley Moser's gaping wounds and "listened to her frantic screams for her daughter, Veronica. When she stopped breathing, I thought she'd died in front of me.

"I'd walked over her little girl four times in the theater as I searched for anyone still breathing." The officer let the tears fall as she testified about making six trips to the hospital, unaware that she'd transported the child's parents. "Her father, who'd been shot in the head, tried to jump out of my car, yelling 'I need to get my daughter.'"

Later, Sergeant Hawkins of the Aurora Police Department, a father of six, returned for Veronica; he ran out with her in his arms even though he knew she was dead. "It was important to me that the parents knew she'd been taken out by a daddy, that I have a daughter that age and that I am very cognizant of what was lost." Other survivors were racked with guilt that they lacked the strength to carry out their friends. "I hadn't even wanted to go to the theater, it had poor service and sticky floors. Then I saw Jesse Childress lying face down in a pool of blood. I couldn't lift him, just screaming Childress! Childress!"

One teen described how, in the melee, he lay flat on his stomach in the aisle, paralyzed with fear, pretending to be dead. His mother screamed in the dark, "Run! Run! If I tell you to run, do it!" As he did, he felt burning in his lower back, the bullet penetrating his flesh like a hot iron. His mother crumpled in front of him, shot in the leg and arm. "Leave me," she sobbed to her husband, "go with your son, I'm ready to die here."

Before the horror, the movie audience consisted of kids, teens, adults, people in costume, everyone "just really, really, really excited for the movie." Then the gunshots started. And the theater transformed into a war zone, body parts "fileted," organs literally "falling out," people suffocating.

"We set up a makeshift triage at a high school," an officer testified, "and tried to prioritize, treating those most gravely injured first. We color-coded the victims: Black for pulse-less; Red with pulse and breath rate, life-threatening injuries; Yellow, serious injuries but likely won't die and Green, the walking wounded." He paused. "We couldn't spend time on those in the black. Those shot in the back were tagged red. It was like a horror film."

"We risked a lot to save a lot," said another, struggling to maintain his composure. "We didn't know if there was another active shooter. We didn't think about ourselves. Our first thought, as we stepped over piles of spent ammo and blood, was get them out. There were mass injuries, ten bodies still inside, some missing parts, some with brain matter exposed, or half a head. Even if they were still breathing, we tagged them black."

May 30, 2015

FENTON

"I *have* to say something," I said to my colleague halfway through the twelve-week intensive group therapy we led at the clinic. One of the attending patients had lost her best friend to Holmes' massacre. She had been invited to go to the premiere that night but at the last minute had canceled. Now, haunted and guilt racked, she struggled with the aftermath, her grief all-consuming.

"It's not fair to her," I continued. "She doesn't know who I am."

Though I'd been seeing patients since October of 2012, I'd only ever had three ask me if I was *that* psychiatrist. And even then, they'd been respectful. "Mind if I ask you a personal question? You don't have to answer if you don't want to," said one, and another who had seen my picture in the paper noticed my "crinkly eyes" and thought I "looked cute." They were just curious, wanted to know what it must have been like to treat "such a monster."

But this time was different. I would be testifying soon and the last thing I wanted was for "Rose"[21] to learn my identity from some other patient or, worse, hear it on the news. Bad enough that my colleague had once inadvertently called her by the slain victim's

---

21 A pseudonym.

name, causing Rose, understandably, to go ballistic and spiral into a panic attack that lasted nearly the entire two hours.

My colleague nodded knowingly. It wasn't as if I could pull Rose aside, disclose my identity to her privately. Group therapy required that I reveal it to *everyone* so that *as a group* we could all discuss and process.

As the patients took their seats, I braced for the fallout, speaking slowly, feeling the room shrink and my words reverberate off the walls. Rose's face contorted, her eyes widened, and, flushed with anger, she screamed at me, "Murderer! I hate you. I hate you. You killed my best friend."

Her words hit me hard, but I let her unload as other patients intervened, holding her back, trying to console her, until after a while, shaking and tearful, Rose apologized. "I'm sorry"—her voice was nearly a whisper—"I know you didn't *really* kill her, I'm just so angry."

"I get it," I said. "It's brave of you to say so." I wanted to tell her *we all were, we were all so angry. And it was so unfair that Rose, that any of us, had to experience Holmes—maybe for the rest of our lives.*

June 1–16, 2015

Before testifying, I cleared my calendar for the week in order to train as though for an athletic event, knowing proper care of the outside meant restorative calm on the inside. I rescheduled my patients, shut off my cell phone, put emails on auto-response, and told Jane, somewhat ironically, given the gag order, that I was going "incommunicado." I cut out carbs and alcohol—calories that made me fog-headed and sluggish—adopting instead a dancer's high-protein diet of eggs, nuts, and tuna. I scheduled deep-tissue massages, bought ice packs for my knees and ankles in anticipation of swelling, and—after first quieting my mind with a yoga-like calm—headed into my home gym with its wall-to-wall mirrors and "danced" on my treadmill, adjusting the speed, faster, slower, planking, my legs suspended behind me "running" in midair, drenched in sweat, fully engaged as if in a kind of war dance. In that space, my world made sense again; I felt alive, powerful, present, lighter. I didn't want to stop, didn't want to leave; here, good triumphed over evil, spells were reversed, and all duality vanished.

When the day finally arrived, I chose my familiar brown ensemble, a simple skirt paired with a soft ivory blouse and loose scarf; it was "safe"—no broken zippers, loose threads, or constricting waistbands. No chance for a wardrobe malfunction. Brown communicated reliable, sincere, practical—*listen, hear, trust*. I practiced walking to the witness stand, the way I had during the mock trials: slow, even steps. *Eyes forward, tunnel vision.*

When I sat down, my Kevlar vest constricted like a straitjacket. Suddenly SIS and IOG went out of my head. All I thought about was the vest, how uncomfortable it felt, how my silk blouse stuck to it like skin, how I could be shot. I took it off and propped it in my bathroom sink, where it sat stiffly, looking like a torso. My cats watched me as the large clock on the wall ticked too loudly. *Inhale, exhale, ready? You've got this! Get up there and tell them everything you did! It's time.*

Five weeks into Holmes' trial, I was the last of the psychiatrists to testify, but the first to speak about Holmes' behavior in the weeks leading up to his massacre. The prosecution called me last, building the suspense, the big reveal in a confounding mystery, hoping my testimony would at last explain *why* my patient had resorted to murder. *Was he insane,* as his weary defense team insisted, *or were his acts just insanely evil?*

As I entered the courtroom, I felt the jury's intense stare: Did they blame me, hate me, somehow transferring their hostility toward Holmes onto me? The prosecution's strategy was to dehumanize Holmes, make him "monsterlike" and easier for the jury to kill. If Holmes appeared to be this cold, unfeeling individual, he'd be a threat, scary, not human, and exactly who the death penalty was for. Ironically, it was Holmes' approach too. "Death" to him wasn't personal—he killed indiscriminately because he didn't see *people*; he saw nameless, faceless, soulless equations.

I slid into the witness chair, removed my glasses, and held them folded in my lap, unable to face Holmes or look into his emotionless predatory stare, afraid he might throw off my concentration.

Prosecutor George Brauchler stood, unfastened a button in his charcoal gray suit. His team of lawyers—Karen Pearson, Rich Orman, Jacob Edson, and Lisa Teesch-Maguire—was arrayed behind him like combat soldiers at the front lines, seated in three rows shielded by computer screens that flashed photographs of carnage and loss. The time had come to let the jurors "get to know Holmes" through the eyes of the prosecution's most famous silent witness, *me*.

Brauchler's questions were fired like bullets. "Did Holmes ever tell you he was depressed?"

"No."

"Suicidal?"

"No."

"Manic?"

"No."

"Did he ever tell you at any of the sessions . . . that he was hearing voices?"

"No."

"That he was seeing things . . . like hallucinations?"

"No."

"That he was seeing shadows?"

"No."

"Flashes?"

"No."

"Head juggling?"

"No."

"Nothing like that?"

"Nothing like that."

"Did he tell you he had concerns with his nose?"

"No."

"Concerns with his eyes?"

"No."

"That he suffered from catatonia?"

"No."

"That he had an odd sense of himself?"

"No."

Brauchler shoved his hands in his pockets, faced the jury, and reloaded. "Did he ever express to you that he had a long-standing hatred of mankind?"

"Not in so many words." He'd had obsessive *thoughts* of killing, but no plan or target.

"When he left that last visit, was he capable of caring for himself?"

"He seemed to be functioning, but I still had significant concerns about his potential dangerousness. I called our BETA team, asked the police to run a background check. I wanted to know if he had a concealed carry permit, criminal history, military experience, especially combat experience, or had had any altercations at the school."

"Did you get any information back that was other than a clean bill of health?"

"No."

"Did you stop there?" His speech was rapid-fire now as he faced me.

"No."

"Tell us what you did."

I detailed the many people I'd contacted, including professors and even his mother, who might explain his odd presentation.

"Why was that important?"

"If Holmes had always been odd, it made it less likely that he was having some sort of psychotic break."

"Did he ever appear to you to lose control? Rage? Wave his arms, do anything out of the ordinary?"

"No," I said, somewhat conflicted over whether I should mention his reaction to my prescription mix-up. On the contrary, he was seemingly disinterested in human relationships, indifferent, apathetic. Yes, his obsessive thoughts of killing, which he said intruded as much as four times a day, were "getting worse," buzzing in his head like a ticking bomb, but they had never been anything more than *thoughts*.

"If you had known he was buying weapons and making plans, would you have done anything differently?"

"Yes." *I would have been able to lock him up, and that's exactly what I would have done.*

June 19, 2015

Ashley Moser, the third victim to testify from a wheelchair, rolled into Division 201 of the Arapahoe County courthouse. Paralyzed from the waist down, she clutched a tissue in her hand and described how seven bullets irrevocably changed her life. After four months in the hospital, "she had to learn to use a spoon again, make a sandwich, sit upright, dress herself." She would never walk again. Surgery to save her life caused her to miscarry. As she testified, prosecutors flashed a picture of her smiling daughter, Veronica, on the three flat-screens.

The defense strenuously objected to the display, insisting the kindergarten photo of the little girl with the sparkly sandals and tiny stud earrings was "irrelevant" to the charges Holmes faced, saying the "prosecution only wants the photo shown so that the child's mother will start crying." Veronica's relatives, who all wore a gold circle of glitter on their hands in memoriam, sobbed, and several jurors wiped away tears as Ashley struggled to explain what she missed most about her daughter. "Everything," she said. "Her smile, her laugh, the way she was my little silly billy. Once, I was a mother. Now, I don't know who I am anymore."

Gayle had reserved our usual table at the Capital Grille to celebrate the end of my part in the trial. Our waiter brought us a plate of assorted seafood, tiers of grilled shrimp, fried oysters, buttery mussels, lobster tails, seared halibut filets, and flutes of champagne. "I don't know how you survived this"—Gayle raised a glass—"but I'm incredibly grateful Holmes was *your* patient, because if he'd been *mine*, I'm pretty sure I'd be destroyed."

Toby popped an oyster into her mouth. "If it were me, I'd check myself into a resort and disappear into a mud wrap." Everyone laughed.

Relief and exhaustion overwhelmed me equally, but we ordered another bottle and I tried to enjoy my friends' faces glowing in the candlelight. I swallowed the champagne, feeling a little like Tom Hanks in the movie *Cast Away*; his character spent the entire film desperately trying to get off the deserted island and return home, only to learn that everything had changed and he couldn't get his old life back. There was a part of me that had irrevocably changed, and I knew, when I left the restaurant that night and returned home, I would be too empty inside to fill the rooms. It was going to take a while to heal, to align again with the rhythm of the world.

CHAPTER 20

"WHAT IF HE'D STOPPED?"

July 14, 2015

People look so different once you
don't care about them anymore.
—The Joker, *The Dark Knight* (2008)

HOLMES

"When Mr. Holmes stepped into that theater on July 20, 2012, he had lost touch with reality, consumed by a psychotic process that obscured his ability to think about things the way we do . . . This delusional process cannot be separated from him, it's part of him, part of the way he perceives reality and thinks and makes decisions. Mental illness caused this to happen, nothing else." Veteran defense attorney Daniel King addressed the jury in closing arguments. The *Denver Post* had described him as the "most unpopular man in Colorado, if not America." The lawyer who'd once famously defended notorious killer Sir Mario Owens, one of Colorado's last three death row inmates, later humbly admitted he'd "made mistakes" defending him, that he'd been "overwhelmed." He'd delayed

Holmes' trial for nearly three years by challenging the constitution-
ality of Colorado's insanity laws. Holmes' case, he summed up for
the *Los Angeles Times*, was "a referendum on the death penalty." The
question was not whether the death penalty was appropriate in this
case but whether it made any sense.

During his impassioned closing argument, King invoked Al-
dous Huxley's *Brave New World*, urging jurors to consider that "facts
do not cease to exist because they are ignored," presumably referencing Holmes' insanity. He tried to dehumanize the prosecutor,
calling him "this guy," while showing great respect for his client,
"Mr." Holmes, "who was so clearly insane." The defense stressed the
evaluating doctors' consensus about Holmes being "psychotic." Yet
"this guy"—King wagged a finger reproachfully at Brauchler—"wants
to convince you there's nothing wrong with Holmes—he's just a 'de-
ceitful' patient who wants to be treated but not stopped."

King shook his head, pausing for dramatic effect. "Why in the
world would a person see a psychiatrist, tell them he was thinking
about killing a lot of people, if he wasn't psychotic? People get sick.
We, in this country, seem to be in denial about mental illness. Now
is the time, this is the place and you are the people who can change
that perception."

He implored the jury, "We have to understand Mr. Holmes' brain
on July 20, 2012." The attorney swallowed a glass of water and continued. "Here, in the fortress of the law, there's no room for mistake.
He gets one chance, one jury, one decision. You've got to be sure.
There's no second-guessing. Hesitation *is* the reasonable doubt."

He took a breath, letting his words linger like vapor. He tugged
on his red beard, returned to the podium. "Psychotic symptoms,"
he said, "delusions, hallucinations, disorganized thinking, speech,
behavior and negative traits are illnesses, that's why they're in the
DSM, that's why diagnosis is important. How mental illness affected Mr. Holmes' behavior and ability to think and understand
reality matters. Psychosis cannot be divorced from the person. Schizo-

phrenia is a disease. Schizoaffective and schizotypal disorder are all part of the same family, like matching paint, all different shades of red. Because of Holmes' illness, he now faces the death penalty or life in prison." King shuffled a few papers at the podium, even though he spoke without referring to notes. "Mr. Holmes was genetically loaded for psychotic mental illness. Recall Holmes' family history: both of his grandfathers were hospitalized multiple times for these disorders, with onset in their early twenties; Holmes' aunt, his father's fraternal twin, was diagnosed with schizoaffective disorder, we know she suffered from delusions, and was completely disabled from this mental illness, hospitalized several times." King went on to describe how the disease was "progressive," how the aunt, like Holmes, was treated with antipsychotic medications.

The disease, King elucidated, could begin "weeks, months, even years prior to the first psychotic break, which is why Holmes appeared 'normal' as a child; socially interactive, participated in sports, had friends, but in the sixth grade started to feel different, like his brain was broken." The changes were subtle, King stressed; he "wasn't eating paint chips" or confusing his clothes with a "basset hound." He just grew increasingly silent.

With closing arguments finished, the judge read sixty-two pages of jury instructions before leaving the panel to deliberate. Just twelve hours later, on July 16, 2015, nearly three years to the date since the massacre, jurors found Holmes guilty as charged. As the clerk read the verdict forms aloud, Holmes remained stoic, completely unmoved by the fact that he'd been convicted of 165 criminal acts, among them first-degree murder. Survivors in the courtroom were not so silent; they shuddered with relief, "happy at last that this animal, this monster, would never again see the light of day."

Three separate sentencing phases followed; the first asked the same jurors to consider aggravating factors—whether Holmes' murders were "especially cruel or heinous," whether he "ambushed" his victims and "intentionally" killed six-year-old Veronica Moser, "shot her four times, armed with three weapons, a handgun, a rifle, and a shotgun, enough firepower and ammo to kill everybody." Senior Deputy District Attorney Rich Orman's opening statement was, according to the *Los Angeles Times*, "brief, brutal and riveting." One by one he repeated the names of the dead, flashed their photos on the screen behind him, and reminded the jurors, "the defendant killed, and you convicted him of killing . . . all twelve . . . in the course of a single criminal episode."

After only three hours of deliberation, the jurors unanimously found that the People had proven four of the five aggravators (remaining split on the intentional killing of a child); their verdicts qualified Holmes for the death penalty. And, as if punctuating Holmes' fate, that same day another gunman opened fire in another movie theater, in another city, in another state, before taking his own life.

FENTON

"This experience, Holmes, can change a person, make you bury your feelings, cover up, isolate, even minimize." Steve and I were eating lunch at a campus cafeteria; once again he assumed he knew what I was feeling. He picked at his Cobb salad, pushing the crumbled bacon bits to the side of the bowl, and said, "I'd understand if you quit."

"I appreciate that." I smiled weakly, but quitting had never crossed my mind. I'd chosen psychiatry because I believed I could help people, treat people—even people like Holmes. Steve squeezed my hand. "I'll understand if associating with me becomes too painful."

I wasn't sure what he meant, so I asked, "Because you helped me on the Holmes case?"

"I don't want to be a constant reminder of all that you've lost." He put down his fork and studied me for a little too long, maybe trying to read my face for signs that I was falling apart. Then he unwrapped a chocolate chip cookie. "I know I shouldn't," he said, pulling a face, "but I did have a salad."

"I'm fine. Really." I hated lying to him. But frankly neither of us was willing to be real, to delve below the surface and explore that disquieting darkness where we had both lived for so long. That kind of grief could be a deeply disorienting space.

"No one is fine after Holmes." This was the first hint of an admission that Steve, too, had suffered. Perhaps he felt a kind of survivor's guilt—guilt for being grateful he hadn't been outed, hadn't taken over the case, had been spared? It reminded me of the story behind the song "American Pie," with its haunting refrain "the day the music died," a reference to the plane crash that killed music legends Buddy Holly, Ritchie Valens, and the Big Bopper. Future country music star Waylon Jennings was a member of Holly's band but gave up his seat to the Big Bopper; he said many times that for years he felt guilty for surviving.

"Do you remember what I said to you when you resigned as head of Student Mental Health?"

I was incredulous. "I *don't* have PTSD."

He wiped the crumbs from his beard. "I think you might." Was he projecting? Did *he* have symptoms? And I realized in that moment how much I resented him labeling me. No matter how well-meaning, or how sincere he was, this was one area he didn't get to be the expert in; he didn't *know*, couldn't know, what I felt in the wake of Holmes. I could barely get a handle on it myself. This was new territory; there were no instructions, no medications, no diagnoses, to help me recover from him. The notion of recovery was itself a fallacy. Grieving people needed to be *heard*, not fixed.

"I just recognize the signs of sorrow." He leaned forward, the crowded lunchroom nearly drowning out his words: "Has anyone besides me reached out to you, to ask how you're doing?"

Oh, yes. I had lots of friends, people who loved me and cared about me and desperately wanted me to be okay, to be myself again—that strong, resilient physician who'd once jumped out of airplanes.

I, too, wanted to be that person, to wake with the sun in my eyes instead of the glare from my night lamp, or drive straight to campus without zigzagging down alleys, wearing sunglasses and a ball cap, worried I'd picked up a tail. I didn't want to flinch when the phone rang or a deliveryman knocked on my door. I didn't want to worry about being shot or my cats being poisoned. I wanted my life back.

But Steve surprised me. "I'm not just talking about friends. What about other psychiatrists of mass shooters? Have any of them reached out to you?"

I shook my head. I hadn't really considered that before. I suddenly felt even more alone. *Why* hadn't *any of them reached out?*

"We don't even know who they are—but they know who *you* are, know that it must be horrible to be a target, to know that, despite everything you did, it wasn't enough to save him or stop him. And if *you* couldn't, maybe none of us psychiatrists can ever prevent another Holmes."

July 27, 2015

HOLMES

"I thought he was a good kid. I didn't realize his loudest cry for help was his silence." Arlene Holmes dissolved into tears on the witness stand, angry at Jimmy's psychiatrist for failing to warn her about her son's homicidal fantasies. "She didn't tell me, she didn't tell me, she didn't tell me."

"We don't kill people for being sick," said Holmes' attorney Rebekka Higgs during the second phase of Holmes' sentencing.

What followed was a kind of "life review"—brief flashes of history from eighteen witnesses whose recollections of Holmes contrasted starkly with the "disturbing puzzle" he later became. Friends and family described a happy though socially awkward child. His sister tearfully assured jurors Holmes "never wanted to be the center of attention, he kept his feelings to himself so he wouldn't burden others, he was a good brother who loved her very much." Holmes' father recounted his many attempts to connect with his son in the weeks leading up to the massacre, while Holmes "prepped for his mission" and stockpiled his arsenal. "Just calling to see how you're doing, we love you, hope everything's going fine. Thinking of you. Hey Jimmy, we miss you, haven't heard from you, stay in touch." Stiffly, Robert Holmes narrated the many photos of his "smiling Jimmy" at Christmas, Disneyland, the beach, camping, snorkeling, fishing, horseback riding. Former teachers lauded him as an "exceptional leader," a highly intelligent, fairly "normal kid" with a "quirky sense of humor."

"It wasn't as if he was slipping knives underneath the sheets and giggling," one said in a reference to Ted Bundy's early warning signs. Instead, Holmes had the hallmarks of a "normal childhood" and by all rights should have had a "normal adulthood."

"What happened to Holmes," his attorney summed up, "is the very reason he deserves life."

July 30, 2015

"What if he'd stopped killing at three?" George Brauchler displayed the first of Holmes' victims—parents Gordon Cowden, Rebecca Wingo, and Jonathan Blunk. Wails from 911 calls quickly replaced their smiling faces. During this second phase, jurors were faced with the formidable task of "weighing" the aggravating factors against the mitigation and asked to consider whether "anything outweighed what happened."

"Would mercy?" The prosecutor shook his head. "And it's not mercy for the victims' families or those Holmes' murdered, but for *Holmes*. Sympathy? It's okay to feel sympathy for the parents of a mass murderer, but the sympathy in this phase is for *him*." Holmes didn't flinch when the prosecutor pointed dramatically in his direction.

"Nobody's born a mass murderer, that happens later. Kids change. How someone is at 6 or 7 is not how they are at 16, 17, 24. People change with or without anything else going on. Holmes is unchanged, virtually from age 11, nobody sees any difference in this guy. What if he'd chosen to stop murdering at four, at Alex Sullivan, 27, celebrating his birthday? Would the videos and family photos of Holmes, his family's eloquent statements, their passion for Holmes, would all those things have outweighed Sully's life?" Brauchler's voice hitched with emotion.

"The defense wants you to blame the drugs, the drugs that no expert tells you had any impact on this crime, blame Dr. Fenton and her supervisor even though no expert testified that either one made a single mistake, blame them for making a decision based on the information Holmes withheld from them. Blame his mental illness, but it's not a shield; he had the ability to make a million decisions and act completely rationally in every aspect of his life. 'Nobody in his right mind could plan this massacre' and we should take comfort in that. But not having the same brain does not protect a person from the ramifications of those decisions."

"He's *wrong!*" an impassioned spectator yelled, climbing over several rows of seats in the crowded courtroom before being subdued by security and dragged into the hall. "Mental illness is everything!" she cried. "Don't kill him. Don't kill him."

The prosecutor, seemingly rattled, waited for her shrieks to subside before continuing. "The diagnosis isn't important, it's whether that illness impacted his function and capacity. The reason Holmes had a psychosis is because he had a delusion. The reason he had a delusion is because he wanted to improve his self-worth by killing others and it's because he had that belief that some have labeled him 'psychotic' and it's because he had that belief, he qualified for all the other spectrum disorder potential diagnoses. But did that *belief* overwhelm his ability to make decisions?" He faced the jury, hands shoved in his pockets. "Holmes had passed every single test, but he couldn't tell the same story twice about what drove him to kill. His *belief system* was his motive. But for him wanting to kill people he would not have killed people.

"Had Holmes not come to Colorado he wouldn't have killed, had he not broken up with his girlfriend he wouldn't have killed. Where can we find what drove this guy to kill? The G-chats are Holmes 'unplugged'; that's him talking intimately, one on one to the woman he loved. And how about the notebook, it was written in anticipation of something, and it wasn't Dr. Fenton using it to help others.

"He writes, *will you visit me in prison?* There's only one way to get there, his anticipation wasn't that it would be kept secret by Dr. Fenton, he knew it would go somewhere else. The notebook was his way of describing himself going into this horror, he talked about human capital, he *knew* it was wrong, that taking a life would prevent a person from having purpose. *'I don't believe there's absolute good or evil.'* His words. He had the ability to choose. *'My outlook on destroying life is Plan B.'* He didn't mention any of this to Fenton or Roath and with Dr. Woodcock he became confused and said 'killing' was his Plan C. He had the ability to make choices. He was able to make decisions. No one has told you he *had* to kill." Brauchler paused for emphasis before continuing. "What if he'd stopped with [the fifth victim,] John Thomas Larimer, a Navy guy whose friends attempted to drag him to safety."

The prosecutor brilliantly contrasted Holmes' senseless murders with his very *sensible* activities; he filed his taxes in Colorado and California and claimed himself as a dependent. He wrote in his notebook that he was *"deliberately trying to deflect incriminating questions."* Three days after chatting with Gargi about human capital, he talked to his dad about funding his 401(k). Later, he applied for in-state tuition, wrote voluminous emails, and applied for unemployment benefits.

Ordinary, practical, responsible, *life*-affirming actions.

"Where was the impairment? Where was the suggestion that this guy had left the tracks and had no ability to make decisions? July 8th he still had the ability to mislead Hillary Allen, 11 days later he planted bombs in his apartment. He was anticipating the law intervening in his massacre, that's why he bought the Road Stars the day before his prelims and put them on his seat in case he needed to escape from the police."

"This guy"—Brauchler refused to name Holmes—"took Vicodin" to avoid the pain of being shot, he weighed his options, "there was no way to kill and not get caught," and so he needed to kill many people, he had nothing to lose, knew there would be "cruel twists of fate." "This guy knew," he said, wagging a finger in Holmes' direction, "what he was doing was wrong, knew what he was doing was illegal.

"And then there's that interesting thing he wrote, 'research firearms laws and mental illness.' Why would he need to do that? Is that significant impairment of his capacity? That's the opposite. That motive, that delusion, that psychosis or whatever he had, was 'selfish.' It was all about him from start to stop." Brauchler's words tore through the jury. "What if he'd stopped killing at six, Jesse Childress, our other service member. The one who bought all the tickets for his friends. That's halfway. This guy said in his notebook the 'real me,' the 'thinking me,' does things not because I'm programmed to but because I *choose* to. What if he'd chosen to stop killing at seven, at Alex Teves, who'd just received his master's degree in social work before he was shot mercilessly in the head?

"Holmes wrote in his notebook, 'with love gone, my motivation was directed toward'—wait for it"—Brauchler paused for dramatic effect, held up his index finger—"'human capital.'" He shook his head sadly. "Increasing his self-worth? No. His motivation was hatred.

"His closest friend, Ben Garcia, tells us this guy was 'angry at the world'"; we know from his notebook, "if he revealed to Fenton and her supervisor his plan, not only would his normal life be gone but his ideal enactment on hatred would be foiled. 'Love gone, motivation directed to hate, embrace the hatred, my longstanding hatred of mankind. Love and Hate, Hatred unchecked.'

"Dr. Reid asked him what the shootings had to do with hating people, and Holmes said, *after* he's charged with murder and is facing the death penalty, 'people make me anxious and because they make me anxious, I hate them.' He told Dr. Woodcock, four days after he was arrested for this massacre, 'I hate everybody.'"

In fact, "he dedicated his life to killing others after he met with his therapist in his early teens. 'Life shouldn't exist, hatred.' That's what he wrote in his notebook. If he was consumed by his delusion to increase his self-worth, why did he care that 'most fools would misinterpret' why he did this?"

Brauchler flashed a portrait of Holmes' eighth victim, Matthew McQuinn, and reminded jurors that Holmes planned to send selfies to the *New York Times*, wanting to be remembered for the massacre he'd planned for three months.

"What if he'd stopped at Micayla Medek, who tragically sat in Holmes' 'kill box,' struck over and over with steel-penetrator rounds, trapped, ambushed by a killer who patiently waited, watched as his victims took their seats before beginning his especially cruel and unnecessarily tortuous murder.

"What if he'd stopped killing at Jessica Ghawi?" The screen flashed a photo of a strikingly beautiful woman with auburn hair and soulful eyes. The self-described "Redheaded Texan spitfire" was an intern at the Fan 104.3. "Would anything outweigh eleven dead? Think about the cold-bloodedness. This guy standing there surrounded by people he knows he is going to murder as they take their seats. Using a shotgun, he pins them in with tear gas, robs them of the ability to flee, to see. He killed his victims in a crowded movie theater in the darkness, surrounded by screams, anguish, loved ones." He closed his eyes, asked the jury to follow suit, to "picture it all." His voice grew quiet, the packed courtroom hushed, and the jurors closed their eyes, heads bowed as if in prayer. "At the moment of their deaths, his victims not only feared for their own lives but for the lives of their friends, their families. Every decision this guy made was purposeful and rational towards an outrageously evil goal. With 700 rounds he brought enough firepower to kill everyone twice."

For several minutes, the screen behind Brauchler flashed with the faces of the seventy wounded, mostly grievously, and the dead. "I can't linger on them for more than a second," he said. "There are so many." Struggling to maintain his composure, he continued. "He didn't stop killing at eleven dead, there was one more, our six-year-old." His voice quavered. "Can *anything* outweigh that?"

August 5, 2015

Thirteen family members described the traumatic impact of the massacre on their lives. Each reminded the jury that it "sometimes took the very worst of humanity to showcase the very best." As survivors recounted their loved ones' final acts of heroism and sacrifice, some learned for the first time how their loved ones had died. Losing a loved one so violently and suddenly left most shell-shocked and shattered, suffering from PTSD, anxiety, and depression, unable to resume work, reduced to disability benefits, medications, and outpatient therapy. Through sobs, they described how their once close-knit families were now destroyed: Alex Teves' baby brother adored him so much, he'd announced he wanted to be a superhero for Halloween, that he wanted to be *Alex*. Another brother, born with special needs, remembered Alex as the "hero" who had "saved his life" and taught him he "could be better than he ever imagined."

Loved ones celebrated the lives of those Holmes had murdered; they described trips to Hawaii, wedding plans, "bucket lists," things that made up a life. Sobbing, one witness said, "No parent should ever have to endure the death of a child. It's unnatural. It goes against the very order of things."

Another tearfully recalled how it had taken fifteen hours to find out her son had been murdered. In the days and years that followed, she experienced "flashbacks, thought screams were coming from her silent phone." She "relived that night over and over" and described "four memorial services. 1500 mourners filled the church, strangers and friends whose lives had been touched by Alex, all wore jeans and white T-shirts and looked like a sea of angels."

When asked how his death had impacted her life, she paled, her hands trembling. "Nothing is the same. I will never be okay, never be the same person again. There's a hole, a void. I didn't know a heart could actually break." When asked what she missed most about her son, she looked stricken. "I'm petrified I'm going to forget what his laugh sounds like."

One by one parents testified how the senseless murder of their child was a special kind of torment. "The pain is physical"; in a flash their "infectious spirit" is just gone. Sully's father described how he had called his son's cell phone "every half hour, from 3:15 until 6:30 AM," hoping against hope it wasn't ringing in the movie theater like a death knell.

"What kind of a father was Gordon Cowden?" the prosecutor asked his daughter, who was barely able to deflect the emotion from her own voice.

"Funny, charming, kind . . . He used to sing us the 'happy helpers' song,' to make chores fun." And when they argued, and she'd walk off to be alone, he always followed her, staying in the shadows but "making sure she was safe, and never really alone."

Jesse Childress' mom spoke fondly of her Air Force son, who "loved the Broncos so much he once ate ramen for a month so he could afford season tickets." A photo flashed on the screen, Childress' impish grin as he stood at the edge of a cliff. "He lived his life . . . like a superhero." When she learned he'd been murdered, she "went into 'mom' mode, taking care of everyone," even though her son was gone. At one of the many celebrations of life that followed, a Broncos player, #92, gave his jersey in honor of Childress.

"My husband wears it," she said in an effort to explain how grief affected them differently. He "wears Jesse's clothes, his Air Force pants and jackets, we remember him by going to a Broncos game."

Ashley Moser again wheeled into the courtroom; jurors, some openly crying, were clearly overwhelmed with emotion as she described how her child's murder "completely shattered her," the love of her life just gone in an instant. She echoed the sentiments of slain victim Jessica Ghawi, who'd survived another mass shooting at a Toronto shopping mall just one month before Holmes took her life. At that time, Ghawi recalled having an "odd . . . empty, almost sickening feeling that wouldn't go away . . . a feeling that led her to go outside in the rain and unknowingly out of harm's way . . . A weird feeling saved her from being in the middle of a deadly shooting. I thought, who would go into a mall full of thousands of innocent people and open fire? Is this really the world we live in?" Eerily, she'd reflected later, "I was shown how fragile life was. I saw the terror on bystanders' faces. I saw the victims of a senseless crime. I saw lives change. I was reminded that we don't know when or where our time on Earth will end. When or where we will breathe our last breath."

"Justice for Holmes is death," Brauchler said as he addressed the jury for the last time. He reminded them that they had endured fifteen weeks of testimony, 2,695 pieces of evidence, 306 witnesses, including 34 mitigation and 13 prosecution, and had now had a glimpse of the twelve lives Holmes took. "It is difficult to imagine what words, what arguments could justify a life sentence for this guy. Today is about justice. This building that we're in is not the Arapahoe County 'eye for an eye' center, it is the justice center. He picked his victims, picked the time, place and manner of their deaths and some he dismissed as his 'cruel twists of fate.'"

"No more death," said Holmes' attorney Tamara Brady in an impassioned final plea. "The measure of our soul is in how we treat people who are sick and damaged"—she pointed to Holmes—"mercy is not something that is earned, or deserved, it's something that is bestowed by the person who gives it. Justice without mercy is raw vengeance." Many victims and family members left the courtroom during her speech; their wails echoed in the hallways. Brady's voice trembled as she concluded. "The death of a seriously mentally ill man is not justice."

One juror agreed, and that was all it took.

Six hours later, the panel returned its fourth and final verdict, for life. They did so after reviewing a gruesome forty-five-minute crime scene video (never released to the public) that graphically depicted all twelve of Holmes' slain victims.

And amid reports of *another* movie theater attack, this time involving a hatchet-wielding assailant in Tennessee, Judge Samour read the "Final Sentence and Verdict Forms."

We the jury do not have a unanimous verdict and final sentencing verdict on these counts and we the jury understand as a result the court will impose a sentence of life imprisonment without the possibility of parole.

Holmes, who had remained unflinching throughout the testimony and the earlier verdicts, this time quietly took his lawyer's hand, whispering softly, "Thank you."

CHAPTER 21

THE RIPPLE EFFECT

How many of your friends have I killed?
—The Joker, *The Dark Knight* (2008)

August 24–26, 2015

HOLMES

At the sentencing hearing two weeks later, the judge heard statements from family members, survivors, and others affected by Holmes' crimes. "I'm angry," a survivor said through prosecutor Rich Orman. "For some reason his life was spared. He still has visitation from his family and friends. I don't have the right to see my loved one again. Because of him I now have to live some kind of pseudo norm. Killing 12, injuring 70 more, and somehow that wasn't enough for death?"

"So much evil," said Brauchler, reading a statement from Jessica Ghawi's brother. "I've never recovered. Life stopped that day. Something inside me snapped. When I heard the news, I fell to my knees. Wails of sorrow and depression followed as days turned into months, months turned into years."

Commander Mike Dailey, one of the first responders, stood at the podium, his voice shaking as he recalled the "chaos" and "carnage" of July 20, comparing it to combat and "the trauma of war."

"The images are still haunting and have taken their toll on us all. Members of our department suffer from depression, marital, mental and physical health problems. We all receive counseling for an event that is forever seared into our memories. I can't drive by the theater without hearing the fire alarms or smelling the tear gas. My wife, also a first responder, twice drove some of the victims to the hospital. Later I washed the victims' blood out of her gear pack, her jacket, her hat . . . There's no way to describe the devastating effect this crime has had on the Aurora Police Department. Had the crime been carried out the way Holmes' intended . . . my team of officers and I would have been killed in that explosion. Holmes is nothing more than a monster, to be banished. I hope every day is painful for him, that prison is not kind, that he feels every minute he is hated."

"Surviving the senseless death of a loved one is unbearable. No amount of justice will make up for that loss. My life has been forever changed." Alex Sullivan's sister echoed the words of others who came to the podium, equally outraged, wanting to "erase Holmes' name from history," "obliterate him entirely, the way he had eviscerated" them, with indescribable loss, the kind of void Jonathan Blunk's mother compared to "missing half her heart." Though tormented by the constant reminders of what her son would never be, "a teacher, father, brother, student, son," she was forced to accept, like so many others, that "her son would never be anything again."

Those who survived the gunshots spoke of how their injuries had forever changed them, left them in constant pain, unable to perform their ordinary responsibilities, "sobbing in the quiet of their cars on drives home," shaking their heads, wondering *Why?* Fireworks at Independence Day celebrations evoked panic and fear. Many never returned to the movies.

Judge Samour urged the survivors to have "perspective." He acknowledged that the "life" verdict might feel to some of them like rejection. "Some victims insist, 'He got what he wanted.' But what

Holmes wanted was to be excused for his conduct, to avoid being held responsible. What he wanted was to be sent to a hospital."

Many outraged survivors condemned Holmes' trial as a "waste of time and money," arguing he should have just pled guilty and spared them all the trauma. But Samour stressed that even if Holmes had bargained for his life, "a plea wasn't what he wanted"; it was what "he was willing to accept."

Perspective. Glass half-full or half-empty? The judge recalled each of the dead by name, reminding the survivors why the trial was not in vain. "Would we have learned who these extraordinary people were, their 'sparks,' 'angelic personalities,' 'passion for super-heroes,' all the details that made up a life? Would we have truly understood the impact of evil? Holmes will not appeal; had Holmes received death, his case would have been pending in the appellate courts for years, if not decades. At least the victims will be spared the worry of reversal or retrial. Even if Holmes had pleaded, it's possible there would have been post-conviction proceedings."

In his speech to the survivors, the judge omitted the sobering truth that most who are sentenced to death are never executed. In fact, a third of the sentences are overturned on appeal or commuted. Some, after averaging nearly twenty years on "the row," die from natural causes. Others are saved from attempted suicides or drug over-doses only to be "cured enough" to be executed. And since the "death population" is typically older, they tax the health care system and are more likely to suffer from serious mental health disorders, including psychosis and PTSD, that require medical attention and costly management. One death penalty lawyer explained, "The inmates suffer from 'death row phenomenon,' living in isolation, depressed and suicidal, with restricted visitation, and no access to education or prison programs."

Beyond the cost of a lethal injection (more than $16,500), the average death row inmate depletes the state of more than a million dollars.

"But since when do we put money ahead of justice?" Judge Samour reasoned. "Is life in prison a less severe sentence than death? Holmes is going to die there and though the place of death has been determined the time of death remains uncertain. Prison is no four-star hotel. Prison is prison is prison."

And cell life promised to be its own special torture, described by some inmates like "stepping back in time, a few hundred years." Holmes would be relegated to a six-by-nine-foot cage. Subjected to the foul energy of prison, he would face a life of rules in a windowless, dark hole littered with wet toilet paper and trash. Holmes was housed in "protective custody" in solitary confinement, initially in a maximum-security prison somewhere in Colorado. Even so, he was "inadvertently" assaulted by a fellow inmate, who "got in six or seven blows" before being subdued and segregated. Later, Holmes' assailant apologized on national television for failing to send Holmes to "Satan's Lake of Fire."

In an effort to avoid that outcome, prison authorities randomly shuffled Holmes from facility to facility for his own "safety" so that he could "live"—eat, sleep, and defecate inside a concrete box, dying of boredom in a world without people.

"There are no words" for what the victims endured, for their grief, their "suffocating guilt, horror, and the terror to which Holmes subjected their loved ones," the judge acknowledged. "Before this trial, I had never seen a police officer or a first responder break down on the witness stand, but in this case, they didn't just get choked up, they cried. That's a reflection of what they saw, heard, smelled, and felt in that crime scene. These are folks used to seeing blood, suffering, and yet years later when they testified, they cried. It is gut-wrenching and heart-breaking to read the victim impact statements and to hear them in court. The pain was palpable. Nobody should ever have to go through what these victims have had to endure. The nature of the crimes, the anguish experienced by the victims, was caused by some of the most horrific, unthinkable, unspeakable, shocking, cowardly acts and by someone who, after deliberating about it, intended to kill as many innocent people as he possibly could.

"There is no punishment in this world that could equal even a fraction of the suffering as a result of the defendant's horrific crimes. But we can't do 'eye for an eye' because then we would be no different than Holmes. We're different from the criminal who is on trial. The jury rejected the defense of insanity 165 times." Samour paused, let that sink in, before concluding that a significant component of Holmes' crimes was related to "mental depravity" or "passion growing out of hatred, revenge or evil spirits."

And so, the judge sentenced Holmes to twelve consecutive life sentences without the possibility for parole on the charges of murder, and an additional 3,318 years for the remaining acts. It was his intention "that Holmes never set foot in free society again," adding, in direct response to the lone dissenting juror who spared his life, that Holmes "deserved no sympathy."

Defendant James Eagen Holmes stood expressionless in his red jail jumpsuit as he received the longest sentence in US history, his wrists shackled to a chain around his waist. Applause erupted in the courtroom as the judge commanded the sheriffs to "get him out of my sight."

FENTON

For years I'd skimmed flat stones across my koi pond, the circular ripples causing brief surface changes that quickly smoothed over as gravity pulled the stones deeper, their heaviness, like the memories of Holmes, resting on the bottom, permanently obscured, but always there, always part of the pond, part of me. Together with the survivors and the loved ones of the slain, I was part of the ripple effect of Holmes' crimes.

Even the jurors, anguished by their service, found the whole ordeal emotionally wrenching. I read they experienced a kind of post-jury crash, an emotional letdown after "playing God" with strangers in an atmosphere of forced intimacy—"We couldn't talk to anybody about the case . . . not our husbands, wives. It was very hard." Several reported that their relationships suffered, that depression lingered like "emotional indigestion." In the aftermath of the trial, they experienced feelings of grief and helplessness; they were "severely, emotionally drained," plagued by grisly images of the murders, "the screams replaying over and over." For some it was excruciating to have to accept that "society could have done nothing to prevent Holmes."

Some jurors who spoke to the Associated Press after the trial expressed a fear of retaliation from survivors or the defendant's family. Many reported insomnia, recurring nightmares, stomach pains, nervousness, shaking, heart palpitations, depression, anorexia, hives. One cut her hair, worried she might be recognized or accosted by victims unhappy with the verdict. "There's a lot of people who blame us," she said, "and that's a hard burden to bear. . . . The impact on us has been tremendous. We're looking for a little bit of peace, too." Others sought counseling for the horrific flashbacks. Though they "weren't actually in that theater, they listened to and felt the experiences of everyone who was, from every angle . . . they felt their sorrow and when they left the courtroom, they took it all with them."

For weeks, they sat a few feet from a poster-size photo of a child's bullet-ravaged body, heard survivors' horrific accounts, listened to 911 screams, absorbed the sobs of first responders, and endured the anguish of victims. Some coped by forming a support group; they texted, phoned, met for quiet dinners. Some who dared to venture to the movies again "just stared at the floor and cried." One became addicted to sleeping pills, unable to shake the image of Ashley Moser, who, when the verdict was read, slumped against the wheelchair of a similarly paralyzed victim and cried. This juror said, "It would be such a relief to know that the survivors don't hate us."

Research by the nationally recognized Capital Jury Project found the lingering psychological and physiological effects of jury service in capital cases to be overwhelmingly negative. Most regretted their decisions. Those who voted for death were angry when the verdict was life. "The horror of the crime stays with me," one said. "I feel a just punishment wasn't given." Alternatively, jurors who wanted a life sentence but went along with those who favored death were racked with guilt, frustrated that they had succumbed to peer pressure. Some, on the drive home, became "fearful they were being watched or followed," worried about reprisal from the victims' families, condemnation by their community, harsh judgment by friends and coworkers. Most never wanted to serve on another panel. "It was an experience I will never forget, and never do again. I'll check into a mental ward first," said one who was interviewed.

The lawyers, too, were deeply affected. After the trial ended, Brauchler, a father of four and district attorney for the largest jurisdiction in the state, laughed when asked what he would do with his now "free" time. "What the hell is a hobby?"

After the lengthy trial and the three years leading up to it, all Brauchler wanted was to "reconnect with his family" and reignite their tradition of "seeing every superhero movie the weekend it came out." Brauchler was now a kind of celebrity, featured in *People* magazine, and the Republican Party's top pick to launch a career in politics.

Though Holmes' public defenders did not comment directly about their involvement in the case, they offered generalizations to reporters who interviewed them, saying their "clients weren't wicked"; they were "damaged, deprived or in distress. Their crimes were the products of awful lives," poor judgment, youth, or brutal abuse. "There is always a story," they insisted. "All of us just want to understand. We have to believe there is something worth salvaging, otherwise we'd all opt to warehouse them in cells or exterminate them like rats." Because they were charged with defending the "worst of the worst," Holmes included, their job, they insisted, was not to tell the truth, or justify the crimes, or even explain their clients' pathology. In the end, their job was simple: to convince a jury that "none of us wants to be defined by the very worst thing we ever did."

"*Our* lives were," said first responders who still experienced the "darkness." Holmes left a residue, an impenetrable force field. One officer testified he was now nauseated by the smell of butter; another described recurring nightmares of the piles of bloody clothing and shoes as if the theater were a kind of mass grave. They were agitated and angry; like many combat vets, they isolated themselves to avoid triggering the memories. Even the ring of a cell phone brought them back to that terrible night, to the desperate pleas for help.

"No one was prepared for Holmes," one officer said. "Evil just came out of nowhere, like a poisonous gas. I used to think I could make the world a safer place. Now, I know I can't. I can't always protect."

Arlene had tried, too, and now lived in a vacuum of grief— forbidden to openly mourn, condemned for having spawned a monster and unleashing into the world a universal hatred. Had she known, had she been able to stop Holmes, she "would have crawled on all fours to get to him."

"You must be disappointed Holmes didn't get the death penalty," said Steve. We were at one of the many "Thank God it's over" faculty parties celebrating the end of my ordeal, *as if there really ever could be an end to this*. He speared a cube of cheddar, then inclined his plate toward me in offering.

I shook my head. "I am a little incredulous and, yes, I'll admit, disappointed," I said, acutely aware of how strange it sounded for Holmes' psychiatrist to wish for his death. He was that rare malignancy, that silent killer, no one could have predicted. The verdict left me strangely empty, as if evil had prevailed, and suddenly there was no justice—just villains, just Holmes, destined to become exactly what he'd always wanted to be—a "case study." After three years of remembering Holmes, I now only wanted to forget him. It was like I'd completed a marathon, crossed the finish line, and "horror fatigue" had set in; I was dizzy, bone weary; my whole body, once held together with tension, just snapped. There was no "cooldown" no "recovery," no returning to "normal." Life, post-Holmes, just ached.

A fan kicked in, the noise startling me. Colleagues milled around me, offering me tiny food. They all wanted to celebrate, while I only wanted to hide, to be alone in my grief. I felt apart from it all, present but not really there. And, truthfully, I wondered if that sensation would ever really dissipate if my colleagues looked at me differently, like they would a survivor of a terrible crash who'd emerged seemingly unscathed but internally still bleeding.

"He'll never be free." Steve swallowed more cheese.

Neither will I. I thought of the car that had slowed beside me that morning. The driver zipped down his window, his eyes slightly shielded by a baseball cap. "Hey," he'd yelled over the din of traffic, but I'd ignored him, eyes firmly forward as if I had Zen-like focus, even though my heart was fluttering. *Had he recognized me? Did he have a gun? Maybe he was angry at the verdict.*

"Watch your blind spot."

I relaxed a little, realizing I'd cut him off and that he hadn't singled me out as *that* psychiatrist, the one who somehow had no right to mourn her own lost life. It wasn't as if I could just move on, let the ripples subside and the pond's surface smooth over, and pretend all the oxygen hadn't just been sucked out of the world.

I practiced being still, quieting my racing thoughts; I meditated. I liked the idea of meditation, the seduction of silence: *Breathe, om, breathe.* But my "oms" felt forced, and when I closed my eyes it was like being buried alive—trapped between worlds, unable to leave, left to experience the rest of my life undead. I practiced silence in intervals, five minutes at a time. And when that did nothing, I thought maybe doing nothing was still doing something. And maybe I didn't need to fix that today, tomorrow. Maybe I just needed to be. Be in my pain, be this right now.

"Have you thought of protection?" someone asked as if she were talking about software. I was pretty sure she'd never had to think about bodily harm. To her, it was an academic question; she couldn't even say the word "gun." Gun. Weapon. Firearm. Heat. Piece. Rod. Revolver. Arm cannon. Pistol. Rifle. Shotgun . . . Tons of names and types, all meant to do one thing: kill. I didn't want her to say the word, didn't want to have to explain the reasons why I would never own one, engage in an intellectual debate over the risks or my rights. Yes, I'd thought about it . . . a lot. But it wasn't *me*. The threat of bodily harm would probably always be real; people would always want me dead, but at least, for now, I'd decided to hang up my bulletproof vest. I didn't want to exist without living. I just wanted to be left alone—and not chronically *lonely*, an unfortunate fallout from being the only psychiatrist in the history of psychiatrists to be so publicly exposed.

"Have you thought about leaving?" a colleague piped in, standing too close, invading my space. *Only every day.* Every day I thought about disappearing, starting over, having a redo, instead of this ache. My colleague explained how she telecommuted from the suburbs, "surrounding myself with goats, horses and exotic parrots." I loved the idea of farm animals. Denver had become too crowded, my house wedged too close to my neighbors', my garden too complicated. What if I could work elsewhere, live on acres of land, order chickens from Amazon and be a "pioneer psychiatrist"? After a while, no one would check in on me anymore (as if grieving and sadness had an expiration date) and the flurry of concern, casseroles, and heightened security that were once so much a part of my life would stop, replaced by a slow exhale.

"Don't leave without saying goodbye," said Steve, nudging me with his elbow. *I might.* I preferred to slip away undetected, spare myself the pain of endings. To just leave without apology or explanation, live out my days in an undisclosed location where no one knew who I was, where I'd come from, what I'd done, was so enticing I could hardly wait to plan my exit.

"Just so you know, you got it right." Steve smiled. "You got it all right."

P.S. I *did* exit, but I didn't return to any kind of "normal." Instead, I started over, finding peace in the vast wilderness in a tiny cabin I built; my closest neighbor lives in an Airstream travel trailer miles away near a town with one diner, a gas station, and a grocery store. Ironically, after years of forced silence, I now crave anonymity, still somewhat incredulous at how substantially my life has changed. I still see patients (virtually) and am safe in my holographic world, separated by screens and headphones, grateful for the human connection.

ACKNOWLEDGMENTS

This book would not have been possible without the tremendous courage of Lynne Fenton, MD, whose story is not only extraordinary but also inspiring. Special thanks to my literary agent, Jill Marr, and to my editor, Tracy Bernstein. Many thanks to Steffen Andrews for his hospitality and connections, and deep gratitude to all who took the time to speak with me and treat me to a delicious dinner at the Capital Grille.

NOTES

Most of the direct quotes; emails; G-Chats; descriptions of Holmes' behavior inside and outside the classroom, oral presentations, manner of dress, social interactions, interior of his apartment, Internet research and websites, letters from family, "conversations" with professors, friends, and psychiatrists, private thoughts, historical data, university applications, mental health history, and academic performance come from more than seventy-five thousand pages of discovery. Included were hundreds of audio and video files, police reports, photographs, witness and defendant interviews, and multiple psychiatric reports from both the defense and prosecution. Additionally, I reviewed four months' worth of trial testimony, Holmes' notebook (which included his drawings and writings), and twenty-two hours of video-recorded interviews of Holmes' conversations with his court-appointed psychiatrist, Dr. William Reid, summaries of which were contained in Reid's book *A Dark Night in Aurora: Inside James Holmes and the Colorado Mass Shootings*.

All of these are referred to collectively in the notes as The Materials.

The Proceedings reference specific days of trial testimony.

Finally, I conducted hundreds of hours of interviews with Dr. Lynne Fenton and several of her colleagues.

PART I
CHAPTER 1: HERE WE GO
FENTON

Jeff Kass, *Columbine: A True Crime Story: A Victim, the Killers and the Nation's Search for Answers*, 2nd ed. (Denver: Bower House, 2014).

Natasha Tracy, "Treatment for Psychopaths: Can the Psychopath Be Cured?," HealthyPlace, May 31, 2019, https://www.healthy place.com/personality-disorders/psychopath/treatment-for -psychopaths-can-the-psychopath-be-cured?.

Mary Ellen O'Toole, Supervisory Special Agent, Federal Bureau of Investigation, *The School Shooter: A Threat Assessment Perspective* (Quantico, VA: National Center for the Analysis of Violent Crime [NCAVC], FBI Academy, 1999).

Neil Osterweil, "Virginia Tech Missed 'Clear Warnings' of Shooter's Mental Instability," MedPage Today, August 30, 2007, https:// www.medpagetoday.com/psychiatry/anxietystress/6546.

Details of the Columbine massacre are from Schoolshooters.info /sites/default/files/FullReport.pdf.

Dr. Peter Langman, "The Truth at Columbine," https://school shooters.info/sites/default/files/search_for_truth_at_colum bine_2.2.pdf.

Eric believed all humans should be exterminated:

> *I think we are all a waste of natural resources and should be killed off, and since humans have the ability to choose . . . and I'm human . . . I think I will choose to kill and damage as much as nature allows me to.*
>
> *If you recall your history the Nazis came up with a "final solution" to the Jewish problem. Kill them all. Well, in case you haven't figured it out yet, I say "KILL MANKIND" no one should survive.*

People assumed Eric and Dylan were part of the Trench Coat Mafia (TCM). This assumption is wrong: when talking about Eric and Dylan, some students confused them with other people who wore trench coats or were considered misfits. . . . Despite early reports to the contrary, the attack was not targeted toward jocks, Christians, minorities, or any particular individual or group. The attack Eric and Dylan planned would have killed a massive number of people—there were no specific targets. Even Eric and Dylan's friends would have been likely victims. Dylan videotaped Eric saying, 'Morris, Nate—if you guys live I want you to have whatever you want from my room.' Chris Morris and Nate Dykeman were two of his best friends. When Eric said, 'if you guys live,' he demonstrated his willingness to kill everyone, including his own friends.

Several students who knew Klebold and Harris as classmates or even as friends have trouble with the notion that they were really outcasts at all.

Sue Klebold, "My Son Was a Columbine Shooter: This Is My Story," filmed November 2016 in Palm Springs, CA, TED video, 15:33, https://www.tedmed.com/talks/show?id=627332; Sue Klebold, *A Mother's Reckoning: Living in the Aftermath of Tragedy* (New York: Crown, 2016).

"The Adventure of Spanky, by Spanky I." (Seung Cho), https://schoolshooters.info/sites/default/files/Cho_Fiction_Poetry.pdf.

"Mass Shootings at Virginia Tech," April 16, 2007, Report of the Review Panel, presented to Govenor Kaine, Commonwealth of Virginia, https://schoolshooters.info/sites/default/files/Full Report.pdf.

Lucinda Roy, *No Right to Remain Silent: What We've Learned from the Tragedy at Virginia Tech*, reprint ed. (New York: Crown, 2010).

Seung-Hui Cho, *Mr. Brownstone*, a play, act 1, pp. 3, 5.

John Brownlee, "Richard McBeef: Virginia Tech Killer's One-Act Play," *Wired*, April 19, 2007, https://www.wired.com/2007/04/richard-mcbeef-/. Schoolshooters.info/sites/default/files/Cho_fiction_Poetry.pdf.

Robin Bernstein, "Utopian Movements: Nikki Giovanni and the Convocation Following the Virginia Tech Massacre," *African American Review* 45, no. 3 (2012): 341–53.

Matthew Bowers, "Virginia Tech Professor Nikki Giovanni Reflects on Tragedy," *Virginia-Pilot*, April 6, 2008.

"'The notion that a concerned teacher who tries to get someone to counseling and that there are no other options if the student refuses to go—that seems much too limited' . . . psychologist Robert A. Fein told MSNBC . . . 'I understand that students in college are not high school kids . . . but schools should be able to do better than that . . . There's no cookie-cutter solution and there probably are lots of 'right ways,' but the notion of having a team that can gather and examine information and determine 'we may have a problem here' and then work to figure out what to do, or ask others, or keep working on it, still makes sense to me.'" Bill Dedman, "Cho's Words, Actions Fit School Shooting Pattern," NBC News, April 18, 2007, https://www.nbcnews.com/id/wbna18175525.

"Poet Nikki Giovanni Not Surprised 'Mean' Former Student Was Shooter," *Essence*, December 16, 2009, updated October 29, 2020, https://www.essence.com/news/poet-nikki-giovanni-not-surprised-mean-f/.

"Nikki Giovanni Had Virginia Tech Killer Removed from English Class," Writers Write, April 18, 2007, https://www.writerswrite.com/nikki-giovanni-had-virginia-tech-418071.

Roy, *No Right to Remain Silent*.

Jake Tapper and Avery Miller, "Teacher Warned Authorities About Va. Tech Shooter," ABC News, April 18, 2007, https://abcnews.go.com/WNT/VATech/story?id=3050437&page=1.

Manny Fernandez and Marc Santora, "Gunman Showed Signs of Anger," *New York Times*, April 18, 2007, https://www.nytimes.com/2007/04/18/us/18gunman.html.

Marc Santora and Christine Hauser, "Anger of Killer Was on Exhibit in His Writings," *New York Times*, April 20, 2007, https://www.nytimes.com/2007/04/20/us/20english.html.

Neil Osterweil, "Virginia Tech Missed Clear Warnings."

HOLMES

The Materials, including Holmes' recorded interviews with William Reid.

FENTON

Lynne Fenton, interviews with Kerrie Droban; Fenton notes and emails.

Toby, interviews with Kerrie Droban regarding "The Butcher."

CHAPTER 2: THE AMERICAN PSYCHO

HOLMES

The Materials, including G-Chats, emails, photographs, Holmes' notebook, and his recorded interviews with William Reid.

For Holmes' "Slurpee presentation," see U-T Newsbreakers, "A Science Presentation by James Holmes in 2006," video, 4:06, July 24, 2012, https://www.youtube.com/watch?v=L5oVUqFF_mU.

People's Exhibit #12 (full transcript of exchanges between Ben Garcia and Holmes).

People's Exhibit #1243 (Holmes, email to Gargi Datta offering to tell her the world's greatest knock-knock joke).

The Proceedings, Days 7, 29, 33 (Holmes' professors testify, Gargi Datta's testimony, Dr. Lynne Fenton testifies).

People's Exhibit #649 (complete transcript of all email/G-Chat exchanges between Gargi Datta and Holmes).

CHAPTER 3: THE PROBLEM WITH BIOLOGY

FENTON

Lynne Fenton, interviews with Kerrie Droban.

Tarasoff v. Regents of the University of California, 17 Cal. 3d 425, 551 P.2d 334, 131 Cal. Rptr. 14 (Cal. 1976).

Robert Hare, PhD, Without Conscience: The Disturbing World of the Psychopaths Among Us (New York: Guilford Press, 1999).

CHAPTER 4: HUMAN CAPITAL

HOLMES

The Materials; Holmes' recorded interviews with William Reid; Holmes' G-Chats with Gargi Datta; "People's Exhibit #649 (transcribed G-Chats).

The Proceedings, Day 29 (Gargi Datta testifies).

Wynne Parry, "How to Spot Psychopaths: Speech Patterns Give Them Away," Live Science, October 20, 2011 (relying on Jeffrey Hancock's research), https://www.livescience.com/16585-psychopaths-speech-language.html.

FENTON

Lynne Fenton, interviews with Kerrie Droban; review of Fenton's medical notes.

CHAPTER 5: AN INCONVENIENCE

FENTON

Lynne Fenton, interviews with Kerrie Droban; review of Fenton's medical notes and emails.

Gayle, interviews with Kerrie Droban; Toby, interviews with Kerrie Droban.

HOLMES

The Materials, including Holmes' recorded interviews with William Reid (advising he "didn't want Hillary to be the girlfriend of a murderer").

People's Exhibits #370 (purchase of paper, firearms, targets, and other shooting equipment); #1001 (online order invoice for gas mask); #35 (invoice for purchases at the Science Company, including electrodes and chemicals found in the apartment booby traps); #651 (purchase of two teargas grenades from Keepshooting); #1211c (subscriber information for classicjimbo@gmail.com); and #1046 (text exchanges between Holmes and Hillary).

Match.com profile (created April 19, 2012; published July 11, 2012).

People's Exhibit #1094 (Holmes' membership agreement with 24 Hour Fitness).

The Proceedings, Day 35 (Hillary testifies).

FENTON

Lynne Fenton, interviews with Kerrie Droban.

Shannon Symonds, "Death Race and Video Game Violence," Strong National Museum of Play, May 15, 2012, https://www.museu mofplay.org/2012/05/15/death-race-and-video-game-violence/.

Mark Hodge, "What Happened to James Bulger, How Was He Murdered by Killers Jon Venables and Robert Thompson and What Did Mum Denise Fergus Say?," *Scottish Sun*, March 19 2019, https://www.thescottishsun.co.uk/news/1877911/what-hap pened-to-james-bulger-when-was-he-murdered-by-jon-ven ables-and-robert-thompson/.

Iain Hollingshead, "Whatever Happened to the 'Video Nasties' Row?," *Guardian*, October 14, 2005, https://www.theguardian.com/film /2005/oct/15/comment.features.

Terry Kirby, "Video Link to Bulger Murder Disputed," *Independent*, November 26, 1993, https://www.independent.co.uk/news/video -link-to-bulger-murder-disputed-1506766.html.

Colin Blackstock, "Killing 'Incited by Video Game,'" *Guardian*, July 28, 2004, https://www.theguardian.com/uk/2004/jul/29/ukcrime .colinblackstock.

"Born Evil: What Drove James Bulger's Underage Killers?," Crime Investigation, n.d., https://www.crimeandinvestigation.co.uk /article/born-evil-what-drove-james-bulgers-underage-killers.

"The Murder of James Bulger: When Do We Stop Giving Chances?," Crime Investigation, n.d., https://www.crimeandinvestigation .co.uk/article/the-murder-of-james-bulger-when-do-we-stop -giving-chances.

Jeff Kass, *Columbine: A True Crime Story: A Victim, the Killers and the Nation's Search for Answers*, 2nd ed. (Denver: Bower House, 2014).

The American Psychological Association found a link between violent video games and increased aggression. Mike Snider, "Study Confirms Link Between Violent Video Games and Physical Aggression," *USA Today*, October 1, 2018, updated August 8, 2019,

https://www.usatoday.com/story/tech/news/2018/10/01/violent
-video-games-tie-physical-aggression-confirmed-study/1486
188002/.

In 2015, the APA's official position, expressed in a resolution, was that the link between violent video-game exposure and aggressive behavior was "one of the most studied and established" but that "aggressiveness" included "insults, threats, hitting, pushing, hair pulling, biting and other forms of verbal and physical aggression." The association was emphatic that there was "insufficient research on whether violent video games cause lethal violence, though the games are associated with a decrease in empathy and other socially desirable behavior."

The APA's division for media psychology and technology was much more dismissive of any causal link. In a policy statement on June 22, 2017, it found "scant evidence" of any causal connection between playing violent video games and actually committing violent activities and "little evidence" that playing such games "produces violent criminal behavior."

Rider McDowell, *Image*, January 26, 1992.

Robert Hare, PhD, *Without Conscience: The Disturbing World of the Psychopaths Among Us* (New York: Guilford Press, 1999).

Brown v. Entertainment Merchants Association 564 US 786 (2011).

Elisabeth Kübler-Ross, *On Death and Dying* (New York: Macmillan, 1969).

CHAPTER 6: TEACHABLE MOMENTS
HOLMES
The Materials.

People's Exhibits #364 (bulletproof body armor; neck, arm, and groin protectors); #308 (advanced combat helmet); and #1002 (laser, Glock magazine, handgun holster).

The Proceedings, Days 6, 7, 10 (Holmes' professors testify).

Jennifer Greer, "The Chicago Tylenol Murders: Strange, Sad, and Still Unsolved," *Medium*, October 11, 2020.

Howard Markel, "How the Tylenol Murders of 1982 Changed the Way We Consume Medication," *PBS NewsHour,* September 29, 2014, https://www.pbs.org/newshour/health/tylenol-murders-1982.

"Chicago Tylenol Murders," Crime Museum, n.d., https://www.crimemuseum.org/crime-library/cold-cases/chicago-tylenol-murders/.

"The Unabomber," Famous Cases & Criminals, History, FBI, n.d., https://www.fbi.gov/history/famous-cases/unabomber; "Why It Took 17 Years to Catch the Unabomber," History, October 25, 2018, https://www.history.com/news/unabomber-letter-bombs-investigation-arrest.

FENTON

Michael Stone and Gary Brucato, *The New Evil: Understanding the Emergence of Modern Violent Crime* (Amherst, NY: Prometheus Books, 2019).

The MacArthur Violence Risk Assessment Study (MVRAS), which evaluated 1,136 recently discharged psychiatric patients over a year, found the prevalence of violent behaviors among those with major mental disorders who did not abuse substances to be indistinguishable from a general population comparison group drawn from the same neighborhoods. Patients with schizophrenia showed the lowest occurrence of violence (14.8 percent) relative to those with bipolar disorder (22 percent) or major depressive disorder (28.5 percent).

Jeff Kass, *Columbine: A True Crime Story: A Victim, the Killers and the Nation's Search for Answers,* 2nd ed. (Denver: Bower House, 2014).

Dr. Ramani Suryakantham Durvasula, "Narcissism vs. Narcissistic Personality Disorder: How to Spot the Difference," MedCircle, video, 21:56, n.d., https://www.youtube.com/watch?v=IEfS-_a21kk&t=68s.

Peter Langman, *Why Kids Kill: Inside the Minds of School Shooters* (New York: Macmillan, 2009).

https://schoolshooters.info/sites/default/files/jcso_official_columbine_report_0.pdf.

Sue Klebold, *A Mother's Reckoning: Living in the Aftermath of Tragedy* (New York: Crown, 2016).

Kirk Johnson, "Kid Who Tried to Befriend Red Lake Shooter Got Hit H Said Gunman Outside the Door 'Was Aiming at Me'," SFGate, March 25, 2005, https://www.sfgate.com/news/article/Kid-who-tried-to-befriend-Red-Lake-shooter-got-2720505.php.

"School Shooter 'Admired Hitler,'" *Age*, March 23, 2005 , https://www.theage.com.au/world/school-shooter-admired-hitler-20050323-gdzuct.html.

"Red Lake Shooting Survivor Says He Tried to Reach Out to Gunman," Sign on San Diego, March 24, 2005.

"The Killer at Thurston High," *Frontline*, January 2000, episode 2, https://www.pbs.org/wgbh/pages/frontline/shows/kinkel/.

FENTON/STEVE

Lynne Fenton, interviews with Kerrie Droban.

The Proceedings, Days 21–26, 29, 30, 33, 34 (Holmes' recorded interviews with William Reid, Gargi Datta testifies, Dr. Fenton and "Steve" testify).

The case of Armin Meiwes is referenced in Michael Stone and Gary Brucato, *The New Evil: Understanding the Emergence of Modern Violent Crime* (Amherst, NY: Prometheus Books, 2019), pp. 40–43.

The reference to *Übermensch* is from Friedrich Nietzsche, *Thus Spoke Zarathustra* (1883).

The Materials, Holmes' recorded interviews with William Reid.

References to George Hennard come from Mara Bovsun, "Luby's Massacre in Texas Has Eerie Link to Robin Williams' Movie 'The Fisher King,'" *New York Daily News*, September 20, 2014, https://www.nydailynews.com/entertainment/gossip/confidential/texas-massacre-eerie-link-movie-fisher-king-article-1.1946961; and Ron Franscell, *Delivered from Evil: True Stories of Ordinary People Who Faced Monstrous Mass Killers and Survived* (Beverly, MA: Fair Winds, 2011).

Reference to Barry Loukaitis comes from Stone and Brucato, *The New Evil*, p. 44.

Robert Hare, PhD, *Without Conscience: The Disturbing World of the Psychopaths Among Us* (New York: Guilford Press, 1999) (reference to "smell insecurity [and loneliness] the way a pig smells truffles," describing notorious killer, William Bradford); Jeremy Arias, "Susan Reinert, Teacher and Kids Killed by Ex-Principal Jay Smith: Notorious Murders," Penn Live/Patriot-News, May 28, 2013, https://www.pennlive.com/midstate/2013/05/notorious_murder_susan_reinert.html.

Dr. Peter Langman's article, schoolshooters.info/sites/default/files/Williams_contradictions_1.2.pdf, discusses the many sources of contradictory information related to Andy Williams.

Holmes' admission that he was bullied at the pill factory, "whether I pass or fail," and questions posed about how others might regard him come from The Materials and Holmes' recorded interviews with William Reid.

The session exchanges between Steve and Holmes come from Lynne Fenton, interviews with Kerrie Droban, Fenton's chart note.

Excerpts from Holmes' writings "the mind rapists" come from Holmes' notebook. The question posed by William Reid comes from Holmes' recorded interviews with him and from Reid's own observations.

The Materials; Holmes' recorded interviews with William Reid. In police interviews Holmes sounded "normal."

Dr. William Reid, *A Dark Night in Aurora: Inside James Holmes and the Colorado Mass Shootings* (New York: Skyhorse, 2018) (Holmes' employment at MeriCal, Inc., and reference to "the Giggler").

CHAPTER 7: GRAVITY
HOLMES

Information about *The Big Bang Theory* and Holmes' identification with Leonard Hofstadter comes from Holmes' recorded interviews with William Reid.

Holmes' fascination with *The Dark Knight* comes from Stephen Singular and Joyce Singular, *The Spiral Notebook: The Aurora Theater*

Shooter and the Epidemic of Mass Violence Committed by American Youth (Berkeley, CA: Counterpoint Press, 2015), p. 69, and Simone Wilson, "MTV's Diggity Dave Says James Holmes Called Him Before Dark Knight Massacre; Did His Sick Batman Spinoff Inspire Aurora Shooting?," *LA Weekly*, August 1, 2012, https://www.laweekly.com/mtvs-diggity-dave-says-james -holmes-called-him-before-dark-knight-massacre-did-his-sick -batman-spinoff-inspire-aurora-shooting/.

References to Batman in the Materials, police reports, and photos of a Batman mask found in Holmes' apartment. Crime scene photos showed the state of Holmes' apartment. Later, in his interview with William Reid, when asked whether he ever identified with the Joker or thought of himself as the Joker, Holmes replied, "I don't think so . . . but I can see why people would call me the Joker given my dyed hair and the setting, the movie being the Batman movie."

Exchanges with "Diggity Dave" are referenced in Wilson, "MTV's Diggity Dave."

Holmes journaled his thoughts in a computation spiral notebook he titled "Of Life," People's Exhibit #341; there are no dates, and the first twenty-five pages are missing, leaving thirty pages of handwritten writings and hand-drawn illustrations. Holmes' thoughts about human capital and his "simple theory" also come from his recorded interviews with William Reid.

The Proceedings, Days 21–26 (Holmes' recorded interviews with William Reid).

The Proceedings, Day 6 (Holmes' exchange with his professor Sukumar Vijayaraghavan).

Subsequent firearms purchases come from the Materials and People's Exhibits #1002, #308, #1102.

The Proceedings, Day 35 (Hillary testifies); People's Exhibit #1046 (text exchanges between Holmes and Hillary).

FENTON

Exchanges between Lynne Fenton and Arlene Holmes come from Lynne Fenton, interviews with Kerrie Droban.

Arlene Holmes, *When the Focus Shifts: The Prayer Book of Arlene Holmes* (Bloomington, IN: AuthorHouse, 2015).

The Proceedings, Days 6, 7, 10 (Holmes' professors testify).

People's Exhibit #1078 (Holmes' application for unemployment).

The Materials, Holmes' credentials, admissions essays, and applications.

CHAPTER 8: TARGET PRACTICE

FENTON

The information comes from Lynne Fenton, interviews with Kerrie Droban.

HOLMES

Information concerning Holmes' firearms purchases comes from the Materials and witness testimony from *The Proceedings*, Days 11, 31.

The Proceedings, Days 21–26 (Holmes' recorded interviews with William Reid).

People's Exhibit #539 (Lead Valley Range membership application).

The Materials, police reports, and receipts regarding Holmes' arsenal.

The Proceedings, Day 5 (testimony from Lead Valley rangemaster).

Excerpts from Holmes' notebook.

"Devilishly evil" black possession lenses, *The Proceedings*, Days 21–26 (Holmes' recorded interviews with William Reid).

FENTON

Lynne Fenton, interviews with Kerrie Droban.

HOLMES

Excerpts from Holmes' notebook.

The Proceedings, Days 21–26 (Holmes' recorded interviews with William Reid).

The Proceedings, Days 11, 13, 20, 31 (testimony regarding weapons purchased).

The Materials, police reports, witness statements from rangemasters at Byers Canyon, emails from "Goober" to Holmes, FedEx receipts evidencing bulk purchases of ammunition, websites visited, and X-rated dating sites.

The Proceedings, Day 19 (Match.com).

The Proceedings, Day 35 (testimony from Hillary).

The Proceedings, Day 5 (Byers Canyon Rifle Range).

CHAPTER 9: TICK TOCK
FENTON

Case studies come from James Knoll and Joan Gerbasi, "Psychiatric Malpractice Case Analysis: Striving for Objectivity," *Journal of the American Academy of Psychiatry and the Law* 34, no. 2 (2006): 215–23; William Glaberson, "Killer Blames His Therapist, and Jury Agrees," *New York Times*, October 10, 1998, https://www.nytimes.com/1998/10/10/us/killer-blames-his-therapist-and-jury-agrees.html.

HOLMES

"Why, Why, Why," excerpts taken from Holmes' notebook.

People's Exhibit #1046 (text exchanges between Holmes and Hillary).

The Proceedings, Days 21–26 (Holmes' recorded interviews with William Reid).

The Materials, police reports, crime scene photos.

The Proceedings, Days 11, 13, 20, 31 (testimony regarding firearms purchases).

People's Exhibit #1023(b) (transcript of Holmes' interview conducted by FBI; Aurora Police Department concerning his booby-trapped apartment).

The reenactment of the massacre comes from the Materials, a compilation of survivor and first responder accounts, 911 calls, and Holmes' recorded interviews with William Reid.

The Proceedings, Days 1–4 (survivor and first responder accounts).

PART II

CHAPTER 10: MADNESS AT MIDNIGHT

Information contained in this chapter comes from Lynne Fenton, interviews with Kerrie Droban.

The Proceedings, Days 1–4 (survivor and first responder accounts).

CHAPTER 11: JUST SAYING

FENTON

Lynne Fenton, interviews with Kerrie Droban; Jane (Fenton's attorney), interviews with Kerrie Droban.

Tarasoff v. Regents of the University of California; the legal case was brought by the Tarasoff family after their daughter, Tatiana Tarasoff, was murdered by Prosenjit Poddar, who had received psychological services in the university counseling center.

HOLMES

Louise Boyle, "'I Am Attracted to Him . . . I Think He Is Cute': The Court Groupie So in Love with Dark Knight 'Shooter' She Carries His Picture in Her Wallet and Dyes Her Hair Red (and, Incredibly, She's Not Alone)," *Daily Mail*, January 10, 2013, https://www.dailymail.co.uk/news/article-2260580/Aurora -massacre-Woman-tells-love-Dark-Knight-suspect-James-Holmes .html.

The Proceedings, Day 29 (Gargi Datta testifies).

The Materials, police reports, court pleadings.

Brett LoGiurato, "A Court Case That No One's Talking About Could Have Huge Implications for Every Journalist in America," Yahoo! News, November 12, 2013, https://www.yahoo.com /news/court-case-no-ones-talking-133000125.html.

CHAPTER 12: "GOTCHA!"

Information in this chapter comes from Lynne Fenton, interviews with Kerrie Droban, and Fenton's notes and records containing emails received.

The Proceedings, Day 4 (first responder testimony).

The Materials, police reports of a suspicious package in the mail room, emails to Lynne Fenton, and pleadings "outing" Fenton. *The Proceedings*, Day 18, 19 (experts testify regarding James Holmes' notebook).

CHAPTER 13: "WOULD YOU RECOGNIZE ME?"

Information in this chapter comes from Lynne Fenton, interviews with Kerrie Droban; Jane (Fenton's attorney), interviews with Kerrie Droban; and Steffen Andrews, interviews with Kerrie Droban.

CHAPTER 14: SAFE

FENTON

Information in this chapter comes from Lynne Fenton, interviews with Kerrie Droban.

CHAPTER 15: SLOW AND STEADY

FENTON

Information in this chapter comes from Lynne Fenton, interviews with Kerrie Droban; and Jane (Fenton's attorney), interviews with Kerrie Droban.

HOLMES

The Materials, video recordings, jail notes, psychologist reports, Holmes' notebook, photos of letters Holmes received.

Hannah Parry, "From Valentine's Day Cards to Pilgrimages to the Movie Theater Where He Gunned Down 12: 'Holmies' Show Their Support for Mass Murderer in Chilling Online Fanbase," *Daily Mail*, March 14, 2016, https://www.dailymail.co.uk/news/article-3491804/From-love-letters-pilgrimages-movie-theater-James-Holmes-gunned-12-Holmies-support-mass-murderer-chilling-online-fanbase.html.

Katherine Ramsland, PhD, "Women Who Love Serial Killers," *Psychology Today*, April 20, 2012, https://www.psychologytoday

.com/us/blog/shadow-boxing/201204/women-who-love-serial
-killers.

Katherine Ramsland, PhD, "Killer Pen Pals: Getting Close to a Murderer Can Have Unforeseen Consequences," *Psychology Today*,
July 9, 2018, https://www.psychologytoday.com/us/blog/shadow
-boxing/201807/killer-pen-pals.

Diane Dimond, "The 'Prison Groupie' Syndrome," *Northern Virginia
Daily*, November 19, 2019, https://www.nvdaily.com/nvdaily/di
ane-dimond-the-prison-groupie-syndrome/article_320e0526
-bb99-54a0-bba4-53040920022e.html..

Ogi Ogas and Sai Gaddam, *A Billion Wicked Thoughts: What the Internet Tells Us About Sexual Relationships* (New York: Plume, 2011).

Wesley Yang, "Sex, Lies and Data Mining," *New York Times*, July 29, 2011,
https://www.nytimes.com/2011/07/31/books/review/a-billion
-wicked-thoughts-by-ogi-ogas-and-sai-gaddam-book-review
.html.

FENTON

Information in this section comes from Lynne Fenton, interviews
with Kerrie Droban; and Jane (Fenton's attorney), interviews
with Kerrie Droban.

CHAPTER 16: TUNNEL VISION

Information in this chapter comes from Lynne Fenton, interviews
with Kerrie Droban.

Matthew Lysiak, *Newtown: An American Tragedy* (New York: Gallery
Books, 2013).

People's Exhibit #1093(b) (University of Colorado Hospital phone
records).

CHAPTER 17: POSSESSED JAMES

HOLMES

Information in this chapter comes from The Materials (psychiatrist
reports).

The Proceedings, Days 27, 38, 43–45 (defense experts Dr. Woodcock
and Dr. Gur testify).

Samina Hassan, "Billy Milligan—A Man with 24 Personalities in
His Head," Planet Today, September 21, 2019, https://www.the
planettoday.com/billy-milligan-man-with-24-personalities/.

Joni Johnston, PsyD, "Multiple Personality or Malingering," *Psychology Today*, December 11, 2017, https://www.psychologytoday.com
/us/blog/the-human-equation/201712/multiple-personality
-or-malingering.

FENTON

Lynne Fenton, interviews with Kerrie Droban.

PART III

CHAPTER 18: WHY?

FENTON

Lynne Fenton, interviews with Kerrie Droban.

Sadie Gurman, "Arapahoe High School Gunman Planned to Attack Multiple Classrooms," *Denver Post*, December 12, 2013,
https://www.denverpost.com/2013/12/17/arapahoe-high
-school-gunman-planned-to-attack-multiple-classrooms/.

"Colorado High School Shooter Kept 'Diary of a Madman' about
Bullying," *Guardian*, October 11, 2014, https://www.theguard
ian.com/world/2014/oct/11/colorado-school-shooter-diary
-bullying-arapahoe-high-karl-pierson.

The Proceedings, Day 38.

HOLMES

Michael Stone and Gary Brucato, *The New Evil: Understanding the
Emergency of Modern Violent Crime* (Amherst, NY: Prometheus
Books, 2019).

"'Joe the Plumber' Pens 'Harsh' Open Letter to Isla Vista Relatives,"
NBC News, May 27, 2014, https://www.nbcnews.com/storyline
/isla-vista-rampage/joe-plumber-pens-harsh-open-letter-isla
-vista-relatives-n115561.

Jack Healy and Ian Lovett, "Oregon Killer Described as Man of Few Words," *New York Times*, October 3, 2015, https://www.nytimes.com/2015/10/03/us/chris-harper-mercer-umpqua-community-college-shooting.html.

Ben Jacobs and Nicki Woolf, "Chris Harper Mercer: Details Emerge of Oregon College Killer," *Guardian*, October 2, 2015, https://www.theguardian.com/us-news/2015/oct/02/chris-harper-mercer-first-details-emerge-of-oregon-college-killer.

The Proceedings, Days 21–26 (Holmes' recorded interviews with William Reid).

The Materials (William Reid's report).

"MONSTER/MASTER" HOLMES

The Materials (pleadings and juror questionnaires).

Carol McKinley, "James Holmes Trial Marked by Emotional Moments, Key Evidence," ABC News, January 14, 2015, https://abcnews.go.com/US/10-notable-aspects-james-holmes-trial/story?id=32388217..

The Proceedings, Day 1 (opening statements).

"George Brauchler," Colorado Law, University of Colorado, Boulder, https://www.colorado.edu/law/george-brauchler.

CHAPTER 19: THE WALKING WOUNDED

HOLMES

The Proceedings, Days 1–4, 6–8, 18, 28, 30–33 (opening statements, survivor and first responder testimony, the notebook, Dr. Woodcock, Gargi Datta, Dr. Fenton testimony).

FENTON

Information in this section comes from Lynne Fenton, interviews with Kerrie Droban.

The Proceedings, Days 32, 35 (Dr. Fenton and Hillary testify).

CHAPTER 20: "WHAT IF HE'D STOPPED?"

HOLMES

Vicky Collins and Jon Schuppe, "'Dark Knight' Shooting Trial's Final Arguments Hinge on James Holmes' Sanity," NBC News, July 14, 2015 updated July 14, 2015, https://www.nbcnews.com/news/us-news/holmes-n392056.

"Dan King, James Holmes' Lawyer, 5 Fast Facts You Need to Know," Heavy, April 27, 2015, https://heavy.com/news/2015/04/dan-daniel-king-james-holmes-lawyer-public-defender-aurora-theater-shooting/.

The Proceedings, Day 67 (sentencing for James Holmes)

FENTON

Information in this section comes from Lynne Fenton, interviews with Kerrie Droban.

HOLMES

The Proceedings, Days 59, 63, 67 (closing arguments [penalty phase sentencing], for James Holmes).

Susan Bozorgi, "Public Defender Tamara Brady Saves Another Life," Women Criminal Defense Attorneys, August 12, 2015, https://www.womencriminaldefenseattorneys.com/blog/public-defender-tamara-brady-saves-a-life.

CHAPTER 21: THE RIPPLE EFFECT

HOLMES

The Proceedings, Day 67 (sentencing, James Holmes).

Lynne Fenton, interviews with Kerrie Droban.

Associated Press, "'That's How You Know It Was Justice': Judge Defends Colorado Theater Shooter's Trial," 7 San Diego, August 24, 2015 updated August 24, 2015, https://www.nbcsandiego.com/news/local/colorado-shooting-victims-of-james-holmes-describe-drowning-in-pain/51315/.

Lynne Fenton, interviews with Kerrie Droban.

Michael Roberts, "James Holmes Moved Out of Colorado Due to 'Satan's Lake of Fire' Attack," Westword, March 4, 2016, https://www.westword.com/news/james-holmes-moved-out-of-colorado-due-to-satans-lake-of-fire-attack-7669498.

Michael Antonio, "Stress and the Capital Jury: How Male and Female Jurors React to Serving on a Murder Trial," *Justice System Journal* 29, no. 3 (2008).

M. E. Antonio, "'I Didn't Know It'd Be So Hard': Jurors' Emotional Reactions to Serving on a Capital Trial," *Judicature* 89, no. 5 (2006): 282–88.

L. H. Bienen, "Helping Jurors Out: Post-Verdict Debriefing for Jurors in Emotionally Disturbing Trials," *Indiana Law Journal* 68 (1993): 13.

W. J. Bowers, "The Capital Jury Project: Rationale, Design, and Preview of Early Findings," *Indiana Law Journal* 70, no. 4 (Fall 1995): 1043.

S. Costanzo and M. Costanzo, "Life or Death Decisions: An Analysis of Capital Jury Decision Making Under the Special Issues Sentencing Framework," *Law and Human Behavior* 18, no. 2 (1994): 151.

R. M. Cusack, "Stress and Stress Symptoms in Capital Murder Jurors: Is Jury Duty Hazardous to Jurors' Mental Health?" (PhD diss., St. Mary's University [Texas], 1999).